The Houghton Mifflin
Guide to Reading Textbooks

Houghton Mifflin Company   Boston   New York

Publisher: Patricia A. Coryell
Senior Sponsoring Editor: Lisa Kimball
Development Editor: Kellie Cardone
Editorial Assistant: Peter Mooney
Editorial Assistant: Lisa M. Goodman
Senior Manufacturing Coordinator: Marie Barnes
Marketing Manager: Annamarie Rice

Acknowledgments

Roy M. Berko et al., *Communicating: A Social and Career Focus,* Ninth Edition. Copyright © 2004 by Houghton Mifflin Company. Reprinted with permission.

Douglas Bernstein et al., *Psychology,* Sixth Edition. Copyright © 2003 by Houghton Mifflin Company. Reprinted with permission.

Standly Chernicoff et al., *Geology,* Third Edition. Copyright © 2002 by Houghton Mifflin Company. Reprinted with permission.

Ricky W. Griffin, *Management,* Seventh Edition. Copyright © 2002 by Houghton Mifflin Company. Reprinted with permission.

John McKay et al., *A History of Western Society,* Seventh Edition. Copyright © 2003 by Houghton Mifflin Company. Reprinted with permission.

Mary Beth Norton et al., *A People and a Nation,* Sixth Edition. Copyright © 2001 by Houghton Mifflin Company. Reprinted with permission.

Marvin Perry et al., *The Humanities in the Western Tradition: Ideas and Aesthetics,* Volume 2. Copyright © 2003 by Houghton Mifflin Company. Reprinted with permission.

William Pride et al., *Business,* Seventh Edition. Copyright © 2002 by Houghton Mifflin Company. Reprinted with permission.

James Shipman et al., *An Introduction to Physical Science,* Tenth Edition. Copyright © 2003 by Houghton Mifflin Company. Reprinted with permission.

John Taylor, *Economics,* Fourth Edition. Copyright © 2004 by Houghton Mifflin Company. Reprinted with permission.

James Wilson et al., *American Government: The Essentials,* Ninth Edition. Copyright © 2004 by Houghton Mifflin Company. Reprinted with permission.

Steven Zumdahl et al., *Chemistry,* Sixth Edition. Copyright © 2003 by Houghton Mifflin Company. Reprinted with permission.

Printed in the U.S.A.

ISBN: 0-618-45527-2

23456789-CRS-08 07 06 05

Contents

Part 1

Features of College Textbooks

The purpose of all college textbooks is informative; that is, their goal is to help you increase your knowledge of a subject. Therefore, textbooks usually present a great deal of information about a subject in a relatively limited amount of space. The amount and density of information in a textbook can seem intimidating, but since textbook authors and publishers want students to understand and to remember this information, they incorporate a number of features to assist you as you read and master the material. Becoming aware of these features and learning how to use them to your advantage is the first step to reading textbooks effectively.

In this section, you will learn to recognize and use the following features, which are all common in college textbooks:

- Learning goals or chapter objectives

- Key terms and definitions

- Chapter outlines

- Organization and headings

- Visual aids

- Chapter summary

- Review questions, discussion questions, and exercises

- Study guides

Learning Goals or Chapter Objectives

Many textbooks include lists of *learning goals*, statements about what you should know or be able to do after reading a chapter. These learning goals, which are also called *chapter objectives* or *learning objectives*, help you focus on the most important ideas and information in each chapter. They ask you to demonstrate your knowledge of the subject matter by performing different actions. These actions include:

■ explain	■ contrast
■ describe	■ summarize
■ define	■ solve
■ identify	■ name
■ list	■ compute
■ compare	■ write

The learning goals may appear in the form of a list at the beginning of a chapter. They might also appear in the margins throughout the chapter. Finally, they might be incorporated into the text itself, as in the following example from a physical science textbook:

planet Jupiter. What is the potential danger to both planet Earth and you from celestial impacts of asteroids or comets?

15.6 The Origin of the Solar System

LEARNING GOAL

▼ Describe the theory for the origin of the solar system that is most widely accepted by astronomers.

Any theory that purports to explain the origin and development of the solar system must account for the system as it presently exists. The preceding sections in this chapter have given a general description of the system in its present state, which, according to our best measurements, has lasted for about 4.56 billion years.

Presently, most astronomers believe that the formation of the solar system began with a large, swirling volume of cold gases and dust—a rotating **primordial nebula,** * positioned in space among the stars of the Milky Way Galaxy, that contracted under the influence of its own gravity. Through the process of condensation, the nebula evolved into the system we observe today. This explanation is known as the **condensation theory,** and it is supported by the fact that today we observe such nebulae throughout the universe. What initiated the process of forming the nebula from interstellar matter is unknown.

Astronomers think the interstellar dust played a major role in the condensation process by allowing condensation to take place before the gas had a chance to disperse. The collection of particles was slow at first but became faster and faster as the central mass increased in size. As the particles moved inward, the rotation of the mass had to increase to conserve angular momentum. Because of the rapid turning, the cloud began to flatten and spread out in the equatorial plane (see ● Fig. 15.31).

This motion set up shearing forces, which, coupled with variations in density, produced the formation of other masses that moved around the large central portion, the "protosun," sweeping up more material and forming the protoplanets. Over a vast expanse of time, these evolved into the planets of our present solar system.

*This flattened, rotating disk of gas and dust around the protosun, from which the planets were formed, is sometimes called a *solar nebula.*

RELEVANCE QUESTION: Day after day you live in the only known solar system in the universe that harbors life. Do you think that other "protosuns" and "protoplanets" may have developed in the universe?

15.7 Other Planetary Systems

LEARNING GOAL

▼ Describe the latest information concerning other planetary systems.

Are there other planetary systems in the universe? As mentioned in the preceding section, our solar system is believed to have originated from a rotating primordial nebula that was disk-shaped during the early stages of its formation.   Figure 15.32 shows a star called Beta Pictoris that is about 50 light-years (ly) from the Earth. * This star, with its apparently dust-laden disk, is one clue we have that other planetary systems may exist.

Detecting extrasolar planets is no easy task. One method used to detect a star with a companion planet is to observe a star's motion. A star with a large planet has a small wobble superimposed on its motion as a result of gravitational effects. The change in motion is very small and difficult to detect. It is best detected by the Doppler shifts that change the pattern of the star's spectrum. As the star approaches the observer, the wavelengths are compressed. As the star moves away from the observer, the wavelengths are lengthened (see Section 6.5).

The astronomer must detect the changes generated by the Doppler shifts, which emerge from motions at speeds of only a few meters per second. To detect a star's wobble caused by a planet the size of Jupiter requires a measurement of about three meters per second. Because gravitational forces produce the wobble, the size of the wobble gives the planet's mass, and the wobble's cycle time is used to determine the orbital period. Using the period and Kepler's third law, we can determine the planet's average distance from the star.

Pulsars are very dense, rapidly rotating stars with precise periods. The rotation rate is observable because the pulsar emits pulses of radio waves that sweep past the Earth like the beam of a rotating searchlight. (See Section 18.5.) When the beam

*A light-year (ly) is the distance that light travels in 1 year, which is 6 trillion miles.

You should get into the habit of using learning goals to check your understanding of what you read and to make sure that you have retained critical information. Try to perform the action stated in each goal, either in writing or by talking aloud to yourself or to a study partner. For example, the learning goal in the excerpt about the origins of the solar system is: Describe the theory for the origin of the solar system that is most widely accepted by astronomers. You might say to yourself:

> Most astronomers believe that the solar system began when a large rotating mass of gas and dust began to contract and condense. As particles moved toward the center and increased the size of the mass, it rotated faster and began to flatten and spread out. Eventually, the center formed a "protosun" and the material around it began to evolve into planets.

Try to put the information in your own words to make sure that you understand it. If you find that you cannot perform the action stated in a learning goal, go back and reread the sections of the chapter that correspond to this particular goal.

Exercise 1 Using Learning Goals

Look carefully at the excerpt from a business textbook on pages 5–6. Then, answer the questions by circling the letter beside the correct answer.

1. In this particular textbook, the learning goal is called a
   a. learning goal.
   b. learning objective.
   c. chapter objective.
   d. chapter goal.

2. In this textbook, learning goals are located
   a. in a list at the beginning of the chapter.
   b. in the margins of the chapter.
   c. both at the beginning of the chapter and in the margins.
   d. in the text of the chapter.

3. How many objectives are there for this particular chapter?
   a. One
   b. Two
   c. Ten
   d. Fifteen

4. Which of the following is NOT one of the things you should be able to do upon mastering the information in the chapter?
   a. Define the term *product mix*
   b. Explain the importance of packaging
   c. Discuss the life cycle of a product
   d. Compare and contrast different pricing methods

creating and pricing products that satisfy customers

14

LEARNING OBJECTIVES

1 Explain what a product is and how products are classified.

2 Discuss the product life cycle and how it leads to new-product development.

3 Define *product line* and *product mix*, and distinguish between the two.

4 Identify the methods available for changing a product mix.

5 Explain the uses and importance of branding, packaging, and labeling.

6 Describe the economic basis of pricing and the means by which sellers can control prices and buyers' perceptions of prices.

7 Identify the major pricing objectives used by businesses.

8 Examine the three major pricing methods that firms employ.

9 Explain the different strategies available to companies for setting prices.

10 Describe three major types of pricing associated with business products.

their first product, a football, was received so well, they moved quickly to introduce new designs of basketballs, volley balls, soccer balls, and baseballs.

381

383

A **product** is everything one receives in an exchange, including all tangible and intangible attributes and expected benefits. A Classic Sport football for example, includes not only the ball itself but also instructions, an inflation needle, and a warranty. A car includes a warranty, owner's manual, and perhaps free emergency road service for a year. Some of the intangibles that may go with an automobile include the status associated with ownership and the memories generated from past rides. Developing and managing products effectively is crucial to an organization's ability to maintain successful marketing mixes.

A product may be a good, service, or idea. A *good* is a real, physical thing that we can touch, such as a Classic Sport football. A *service* is the result of applying human or mechanical effort to a person or thing. Basically, a service is a change we pay others to make for us. A real estate agent's services result in a change in the ownership of real property. A barber's services result in a change in your appearance. An *idea* may take the form of philosophies, lessons, concepts, or advice. Often, ideas are included with a good or service. Thus, we might buy a book (a good) that provides ideas on how to lose weight. Or we might join Weight Watchers for ideas on how to lose weight and for help (services) in doing so.

Our definition of the term *product* is based on the concept of an exchange. In a purchase, the product is exchanged for money—an amount of money equal to the *price* of the product. When the product is a good, the price may include such services as delivery, installation, warranties, and training. A good *with* such services is not the same product as the good *without* such services. In other words, sellers set a price for a particular "package" of goods, services, and ideas. When the makeup of that package changes, the price should change as well.

We look first in this chapter at products. We examine product classifications and describe the four stages, or life cycle, through which every product moves. Next we illustrate how firms manage products effectively by modifying or deleting existing products and by developing new products. We also discuss branding, packaging, and labeling of products. Then our focus shifts to pricing. We explain competitive factors that influence sellers' pricing decisions and also explore buyers' perceptions of prices. After considering organizational objectives that can be accomplished through pricing, we outline several methods for setting prices. Finally, we describe pricing strategies by which sellers can reach target markets successfully.

product everything one receives in an exchange, including all tangible and intangible attributes and expected benefits; it may be a good, service, or idea

Classification of Products

LEARNING OBJECTIVE

1 Explain what a product is and how products are classified.

Different classes of products are directed at particular target markets. A product's classification largely determines what kinds of distribution, promotion, and pricing are appropriate in marketing the product.

Products can be grouped into two general categories: consumer and business (also called *business-to-business* or *industrial products*). A product purchased to satisfy personal and family needs is a **consumer product**. A product bought for resale, for making other products, or for use in a firm's operations is a **business product**. The buyer's use of the product determines the classification of an item. Note that a single item can be both a consumer and a business product. A broom is a consumer product if you use it in your home. However, the same broom is a business product if you use it in the maintenance of your business. After a product is classified as a consumer or business product, it can be further categorized as a particular type of consumer or business product.

consumer product a product purchased to satisfy personal and family needs

business product a product bought for resale, for making other products, or for use in a firm's operations

Key Terms and Definitions

Textbooks often highlight *key terms*, or words that you should know, so that they stand out. Many textbooks emphasize key terms—which are also referred to as *key words, vocabulary,* or *important terms*—with boldface or colored type. Some textbooks go one step further by listing all key terms at either the beginning or end of a chapter. Some textbooks provide brief definitions of key terms, too. In the excerpt from a business textbook on pages 8–9, key terms are not only highlighted within the text itself, but they are also defined in the margins.

Use key terms to check your understanding of what you read. Create a list of these terms, and make sure you can define or explain each one. You may even want to create flashcards with a key term on one side and the definition on the other; use these flashcards for study and review. Always go back and reread sections that include the terms you do not yet understand.

Exercise 2 *Using Key Terms*

On page 10 is a list of key terms from a chapter entitled "Interpersonal Skills" in a textbook about communication. Circle the key terms in this list that are defined in the chapter excerpt that follows it. Then, on your own paper, write a brief definition of each of the terms you circled.

Psychological Pricing Strategies

Psychological pricing strategies encourage purchases based on emotional responses rather than on economically rational responses. These strategies are used primarily for consumer products rather than business products.

Odd-Number Pricing   Many retailers believe that consumers respond more positively to odd-number prices like $4.99 than to whole-dollar prices like $5. **Odd-number pricing** is the strategy of setting prices using odd numbers that are slightly below whole dollar amounts. Nine and five are the most popular ending figures for odd-number prices.

> **odd-number pricing** the strategy of setting prices using odd numbers that are slightly below whole dollar amounts

Sellers who use this strategy believe that odd-number prices increase sales. The strategy is not limited to low-priced items. Auto manufacturers may set the price of a car at $11,999 rather than $12,000. Odd-number pricing has been the subject of various psychological studies, but the results have been inconclusive.

Multiple-Unit Pricing   Many retailers (and especially supermarkets) practice **multiple-unit pricing**, setting a single price for two or more units, such as two cans for 99 cents rather than 50 cents per can. Especially for frequently purchased products, this strategy can increase sales. Customers who see the single price, and who expect eventually to use more than one unit of the product, regularly purchase multiple units to save money.

> **multiple-unit pricing** the strategy of setting a single price for two or more units

Reference Pricing   **Reference pricing** means pricing a product at a moderate level and positioning it next to a more expensive model or brand in the hope that the customer will use the higher price as a reference price (i.e., a comparison price). Because of the comparison, the customer is expected to view the moderate price favorably. When you go to Sears to buy a VCR, a moderately priced VCR may appear especially attractive because it offers most of the important attributes of the more expensive alternatives on display and at a lower price.

> **reference pricing** pricing a product at a moderate level and positioning it next to a more expensive model or brand

Bundle Pricing   **Bundle pricing** is the packaging together of two or more products, usually of a complementary nature, to be sold for a single price. To be attractive to customers, the single price is usually considerably less than the sum of the prices of the individual products. Being able to buy the bundled combination of products in a single transaction may be of value to the customer as well. Bundle pricing is commonly used for banking and travel services, computers, and automobiles with option packages. Bundle pricing can help to increase customer satisfaction. Bundling slow-moving products with ones with higher turnover, an organization can stimulate sales and increase its revenues. Selling products as a package rather than individually may also result in cost savings.

> **bundle pricing** packaging together two or more complementary products and selling them for a single price

Everyday Low Prices (EDLP)   To reduce or eliminate the use of frequent short-term price reductions, some organizations use an approach referred to as **everyday low prices (EDLP)**. When EDLP is used, a marketer sets a low price for its products on a consistent basis rather than setting higher prices and frequently discounting

> **everyday low prices (EDLP)** setting a low price for products on a consistent basis

Everyday low prices. Wal-Mart employs the everyday low price strategy, as indicated by the sign above this display.

them. Everyday low prices, though not deeply discounted, are set far enough below competitors' prices to make customers feel confident they are receiving a fair price. EDLP is employed by retailers like Wal-Mart and by manufacturers like Procter & Gamble. A company that uses EDLP benefits from reduced promotional costs, reduced losses from frequent mark-downs, and more stability in its sales. A major problem with this approach is that customers have mixed responses to it. In some instances, customers simply don't believe that everyday low prices are what they say they are, but are instead a marketing gimmick.

customary pricing pricing on the basis of tradition

Customary Pricing   In **customary pricing**, certain goods are priced primarily on the basis of tradition. Examples of customary, or traditional, prices would be those set for candy bars and chewing gum.

Key Terms

conversation
small talk
analytical thinking
holistic thinking
directions
requesting
asking
conflict
conflict-active societies
conflict-avoidance societies
anger
fight-or-flight mechanism
fair fighting
conflict avoidance
conflict accommodation
conflict smoothing over
conflict compromise
conflict competition
conflict integration

apologizing
assertive communication
assertiveness
nonassertive behavior
aggressive behavior
direct aggression
passive aggression
simple assertion
empathic assertion
follow-up assertion
DESC scripting
negotiation
win-lose negotiation
lose-lose negotiation
win-win negotiation
arbitration
litigation
mediation
criticism

Assertive Communication

Have you ever found yourself saying, "I didn't want to come here, but she made me," or "I ordered this steak well done, and it's rare. Oh well, I guess I'll eat it anyway"? If so, the communication skill you probably were missing in either of these cases was the ability to be assertive.

Assertive Behavior Defined   **Assertive communication** takes place when a person stands up for and tries to achieve personal right without damaging others. It begins by acknowledging that you have a right to choose and control your life. A person who is assertive takes action instead of just thinking about it. Rather than saying, "Why didn't I tell her?" or "If the waiter was here now, I'd say . . . ," the assertive person takes action at the appropriate time.

The root of many communication problems is the lack of assertion. You know you are being taken advantage of and are upset because others are getting their needs met and you aren't. You may know how you feel but are afraid to state your needs because you're afraid somebody won't like you, you'll get in trouble, or you don't know exactly how to go about making your needs clear.

Assertion, Nonassertion, and Aggression   As illustrated in Table 7.1, the goal of assertive behavior is to communicate your needs through honest and direct communication.[30] **Assertiveness** does not mean taking advantage of others; it means taking charge of yourself and your world.

In contrast, the goal of **nonassertive behavior** is to avoid conflict. Nonassertive statements include "Think of others first," "Be modest," and "Let's keep the peace." The consequence of nonassertive behavior is that you do not get what you want. Because of this, anger may build, and you may be alienated from yourself and others.

The goal of **aggressive behavior** is to dominate, to get your own way. If you are aggressive, you are likely to make such statements as "Win at all costs," "Give them what they gave you," and "They only understand if they're yelled at." Aggressive behavior may well get you what you want, but it can also lead to alienation, thereby putting emotional distance between you and others that can lead to loneliness and frustration. **Direct aggression** is the outward expression of dominating or humiliating communication—for example: "That's the way it's going to be, and if you don't like it, that's tough. I'm bigger, and I'm stronger. You lose!" **Passive aggression** attacks or embarrasses in a manipulative way. This can be done by pretending that there is nothing wrong but, at the same time, derailing any attempt to solve a problem that isn't to your liking in a way that doesn't appear to be aggressive. Devices for passive aggression include using sarcasm that sounds like teasing, withholding something from the other person (some service, compliance with a request, or courtesy), or being sweet and polite but in fact controlling what is being done. Passive aggression is a common cultural pattern in places where direct aggression is considered bad manners, such as England, China, and Japan. In the United States, the direct aggressive sign would read, "No Dogs Allowed. This Means You and Your Mutt, Butt-Head!" In Britain it would say, "We Regret That in the Interest of Hygiene, Dogs Are Not Allowed on These Premises."

Chapter Outlines

Some textbooks will provide you with outlines of each chapter's content. Usually, these outlines list at least the major headings, or section titles, in the chapter. Sometimes, they include sub-headings as well. Most of the time, a chapter outline will appear at the very beginning of the chapter, for it provides a preview of the chapter's parts and information. The chapter outline on the following page, which includes both major headings and sub-headings, is from a chapter entitled "Congress" in an American government textbook.

You can use a chapter outline in different ways. At the very least, study the outline prior to reading a chapter to familiarize yourself with the chapter's main ideas and organization. You might also photocopy the outline and keep it beside you for reference as you read. Refer to it often to understand how specific sections and details fit into the larger framework of ideas. You can also use a chapter outline as a study tool. It will probably contain only the skeleton of main ideas in the chapter. As you read, though, you can flesh it out by adding key words or other information to help you remember the content of each section. For example, if you were going to jot down important ideas under the first item in the outline, "Congress Versus Parliament," you could add the following information, which is in this section of the chapter:

Congress Versus Parliament
    Congress: U.S. and many Latin American nations
    Parliament: Great Britain and most Western European nations
    Two important differences:
        How one becomes a member
            Parliament: national parties select candidates who will support their agendas
            Congress: candidates selected by voters in primary elections
        What one does as a member
            Parliament: only decision is whether or not to support the government
            Congress: members free to express their views and vote as they wish

Adding to the overall chapter outline in this way will not only help you to better understand what you read, but it will also provide you with a more concise summary of the chapter's information that you can study from.

Both in the minds of the Federalists (see Chapter 2) and in terms of its present-day constitutional powers and prerogatives, Congress was and remains the "first branch" of American national government. As we shall explain, it has the ultimate power of the purse, can pass a law even if the president vetoes it, and can alter, profoundly at times, how existing laws are administered through its oversight of executive agencies. Congress can likewise expand or contract the appellate jurisdiction of the U.S. Supreme Court. It may use these powers only rarely, but it has them, and myriad others, in reserve.

However, Congress is now considered by many to be the system's broken branch, badly in need of fixing. It has probably been the object of more mass public mistrust and more elite reform proposals than either the presidency or the federal judiciary combined. This is true even though most incumbent members of Congress who seek reelection win it, and even though Congress as a whole has pretty consistently expanded the programs and adopted the reforms that most citizens favor.

281

Exercise 3 *Using a Chapter Outline*

Look over the following outline of the chapter "Motivation and Emotion" from a psychology textbook. Then, answer the questions by circling the letter of the correct response:

1. How many different theories of motivation will be covered in this chapter?
    a. One
    b. Two
    c. Four
    d. Eight

2. True or False: The disorder known as schizophrenia is discussed in this chapter.
    a. True
    b. False

3. True or False: This chapter will cover eating disorders.
    a. True
    b. False

4. How many sections of the chapter are devoted to the topic of emotion?
    a. One
    b. Three
    c. Five
    d. Eight

11

Motivation and Emotion

380

Organization and Headings

Because college textbooks contain a great deal of information, textbook authors take great pains to organize the information. They are careful to present the information in a logical order and to divide it into sections that will help students understand and learn it more easily.

In particular, textbooks almost always include *headings*, which are the titles of smaller sections within chapters. These headings serve two purposes. First, they divide related information into smaller, more easily digestible segments. Second, a system of headings and sub-headings shows how all of the sections within a chapter are related to one another. Headings that name sections of equal information will be in the same position, size, style, and color, while sub-headings of information will be either smaller, in a different color, or positioned differently. Look, for example, at the excerpt from a geology textbook on pages 17–18.

The excerpt, which is one section of a chapter entitled "Sedimentation and Sedimentary Rocks," demonstrates three levels of headings. The larger size typeface of the heading "Classifying Sedimentary Rocks" indicates that it's one of the major section headings in the chapter. This section is then divided into two sub-sections, which are identified with the sub-headings "Detrital Sedimentary Rocks" and "Chemical Sedimentary Rocks," because there are two main types of sedimentary rocks. Notice how these two sub-headings are smaller than the main heading to indicate their status as sub-sections. The first sub-section is further divided into three more sub-sections: "Mudstones," "Sandstones," and "Conglomerates and Breccias," each of which covers a particular type of detrital sedimentary rock. These three headings are not only smaller in size, but they are also positioned within the paragraphs themselves instead of on lines of their own. Their size and positioning indicates that they are sub-headings of the first sub-heading. All of these headings help readers understand how different kinds of rock are related to one another.

182   **Part I**   Forming the Earth

Classifying Sedimentary Rocks

We generally classify sedimentary rocks as either detrital or chemical, depending on their source material. Each of these broad categories, however, includes a wide variety of rock types, each reflecting the diverse transport, deposition, and lithification processes that formed it.

Detrital Sedimentary Rocks

Classification of detrital sedimentary rocks depends on their particle sizes, rather than the composition of these particles (Table 6-1). Shales and mudstones are the finest-grained; sandstones have grains of intermediate size; and conglomerates and breccias contain the largest grains. Note that all detrital rocks are *clastic* because they consist of solid particles cemented together.

Conglomerates and breccias contain pebble-sized rock fragments, collectively called *gravel*. The other detrital sedimentary rocks consist mainly of smaller grains of the abundant rock-forming silicate minerals, such as quartz, feldspar, and the clay minerals. The sand- and silt-sized grains contain mostly quartz. Because it is relatively hard and chemically stable (and therefore resistant to chemical weathering), quartz is more likely than other common minerals to survive the journey from source rock to deposition site. Clay minerals, which naturally form fine, flat particles, dominate the fine-sized grains. They are also chemically stable at the Earth's surface, so they can survive the rigors of the Earth's weathering environment. Feldspar minerals, which are less stable at the surface, appear only in sediment subject to minimal chemical weathering, such as in cold, dry regions, or in sediment buried rapidly enough to reduce chemical weathering.

Mudstones More than half of all sedimentary rocks are **mudstones,** the detrital sedimentary rocks containing the smallest particles (less than 0.004 millimeter in diameter). Such fine particles only settle out of relatively still waters (more energetic waters keep them suspended). Thus most mudstones originate in lakes and lagoons, in deep ocean basins, and on river floodplains after floodwaters recede. The extremely fine particles in mudstones consist largely of clay minerals and micas. They are so small that their mineral composition is best analyzed by X-ray diffraction (discussed in Chapter 2). When these flat or tabular particles become buried beneath hundreds of meters of sediment, compaction arranges them into parallel layers resembling a deck of cards, a characteristic called *fissility* (Fig. 6-12). **Shale** is a fissile mudstone noted for its ability to split easily into very thin parallel surfaces.

A geologist will often nibble on bits of fine-grained sedimentary rock to distinguish clay-rich mudstones from the slightly coarser quartz-rich siltstones. The particles of the clay minerals feel smooth, whereas the abrasive quartz grains of siltstones feel noticeably gritty.

Shales vary considerably in color, depending on their mineral composition. Red shale contains iron oxides that precipitated from water containing both dissolved iron and abundant oxygen. In contrast, green shale includes iron minerals that precipitated in an oxygen-poor environment. Black shale forms in water with insufficient oxygen to decompose all of the organic matter in its sediment, leaving a black, carbon-rich residue. Such conditions might occur in the still waters of a swamp, lagoon, or deep-marine environment, where little circulation of oxygen-rich surface water takes place.

Shales have numerous practical uses. They are a source of the clays used for making bricks and ceramics, such as pottery, fine china, and tile. Mixing shale at various stages with sand, gypsum (hydrous calcium sulfate), and calcium carbonate produces Portland cement, a staple of the construction industry. Oil shale (fine-grained rocks that contain abundant tar) may some day provide a key source of energy.

Sandstones **Sandstones** are detrital sedimentary rocks whose grains range from 1/16 millimeter to 2 millimeters in diameter. Sandstones account for approximately 25% of all sedimentary rocks. Silica or carbonate cement generally surrounds the mineral grains in sandstones. Three major types of sandstones exist, each with its own distinctive composition and appearance.

Sandstones are given special names depending on the source of their sand grains. A sandstone composed predominantly of quartz grains (90%), with very little surrounding *matrix* (the finer material between the larger grains), is a *quartz arenite* (from the Latin *arena*, or "sand"). Quartz arenites generally have a light color, varying from white to red depending on the cementing agent (Fig. 6-13a). Their grains are rounded and well sorted, suggesting that they were transported over a long distance.

Arkoses (named for a Greek word that denotes a rock created by consolidation of debris) are distinctive pink-to-red sandstones containing more than 25% feldspar (Fig. 6-13b). The grains, which are typically derived from feldspar-rich granitic source rocks, are generally poorly sorted and angular. This pattern suggests that the grains underwent short-distance transport, minimal chemical weathering under relatively dry climatic conditions, and rapid deposition and burial.

Graywackes (derived from the German *wacken,* or "waste"), are dark, gray-to-green sandstones that contain a mixture of quartz and feldspar grains, abundant dark rock fragments (commonly of volcanic origin), and a fine-grained clay-and-mica matrix (Fig. 6-13c). The poor sorting, angular grains, and presence of such easily weathered minerals as feldspar suggest that the sediments settled rapidly after short-distance transport.

Sandstone's durability has made it a popular building stone. You can see it in the Gothic-style buildings found on many college campuses (Fig. 6-14). Sandstones also hold much of the world's crude oil, natural gas, and drinkable groundwater, thanks to the pore space between their sand grains, which is easily saturated with migrating fluids.

Conglomerates and Breccias Conglomerates and **breccias** (BRETCH-ahs), the coarsest of detrital sedimentary rocks, contain grains larger than 2 millimeters in diameter. Conglomerates are characterized by rounded grains; breccias include angular grains (Fig. 6-15). Both contain fine matrix material, which is typically cemented by silica, calcium carbonate, or iron oxides. The size of conglomerate and breccia grains makes it relatively easy to identify their parent rocks. Likewise, the shape of the grains provides clues to their transport path: The rounded particles in conglomerates suggest lengthy transport by vigorous currents. The angular grains in breccias suggest short-distance transport, such as when shattered rock debris accumulates at the base of a cliff.

Chemical Sedimentary Rocks

Detrital sedimentary rocks are made of fragments of preexisting grains that have been bound together by compaction or cementation. In contrast, chemical sedimentary rocks typically consist of interlocking mineral crystals that form in the rock as it is deposited. There are two kinds of chemical sediments: **inorganic,** which precipitate directly from water; and **biogenic,** which are produced by animals and plants.

Inorganic Chemical Sedimentary Rocks Inorganic chemical sedimentary rocks form when the dissolved products of chemical weathering precipitate from solution. Typically precipitation occurs when the water in which they are dissolved evaporates or undergoes a significant temperature change. Four common types of inorganic chemical sedimentary rocks form by varying processes: *inorganic limestones* and *cherts* precipitate directly from both seawater and freshwater; *evaporites* precipitate when ion-rich water (freshwater or seawater) evaporates; *dolostone* is a rock whose origin remains the subject of much debate.

Exercise 4 Using Headings to Understand Organization

Look over the following excerpt from a chapter entitled "Creating and Pricing Products That Satisfy Customers," which is from a business textbook. Then, answer the questions by circling the letter of the correct response.

1. Which two headings are equal to one another?
   a. Psychological Pricing Strategies and Odd-Number Pricing
   b. Psychological Pricing Strategies and Product-Line Pricing
   c. Customary Pricing and Product-Line Pricing
   d. Product-Line Pricing and Premium Pricing

2. Which of the following is a type of psychological pricing strategy?
   a. Everyday low prices (EDLP)
   b. Product-line pricing
   c. Premium pricing
   d. Price lining

3. Which of the following is a type of product-line pricing?
   a. Psychological pricing strategies
   b. Reference pricing
   c. Bundle pricing
   d. Premium pricing

4. Multiple-unit pricing and captive pricing are both types of
   a. psychological pricing strategies.
   b. odd-number pricing.
   c. product-line pricing.
   d. pricing strategies.

Psychological Pricing Strategies

Psychological pricing strategies encourage purchases based on emotional responses rather than on economically rational responses. These strategies are used primarily for consumer products rather than business products.

Odd-Number Pricing   Many retailers believe that consumers respond more positively to odd-number prices like $4.99 than to whole-dollar prices like $5. **Odd-number pricing** is the strategy of setting prices using odd numbers that are slightly below whole dollar amounts. Nine and five are the most popular ending figures for odd-number prices.

> **odd-number pricing** the strategy of setting prices using odd numbers that are slightly below whole dollar amounts

Sellers who use this strategy believe that odd-number prices increase sales. The strategy is not limited to low-priced items. Auto manufacturers may set the price of a car at $11,999 rather than $12,000. Odd-number pricing has been the subject of various psychological studies, but the results have been inconclusive.

Multiple-Unit Pricing   Many retailers (and especially supermarkets) practice **multiple-unit pricing**, setting a single price for two or more units, such as two cans for 99 cents rather than 50 cents per can. Especially for frequently purchased products, this strategy can increase sales. Customers who see the single price, and who expect eventually to use more than one unit of the product, regularly purchase multiple units to save money.

> **multiple-unit pricing** the strategy of setting a single price for two or more units

Reference Pricing   **Reference pricing** means pricing a product at a moderate level and positioning it next to a more expensive model or brand in the hope that the customer will use the higher price as a reference price (i.e., a comparison price). Because of the comparison, the customer is expected to view the moderate price favorably. When you go to Sears to buy a VCR, a moderately priced VCR may appear especially attractive because it offers most of the important attributes of the more expensive alternatives on display and at a lower price.

> **reference pricing** pricing a product at a moderate level and positioning it next to a more expensive model or brand

Bundle Pricing   **Bundle pricing** is the packaging together of two or more products, usually of a complementary nature, to be sold for a single price. To be attractive to customers, the single price is usually considerably less than the sum of the prices of the individual products. Being able to buy the bundled combination of products in a single transaction may be of value to the customer as well. Bundle pricing is commonly used for banking and travel services, computers, and automobiles with option packages. Bundle pricing can help to increase customer satisfaction. Bundling slow-moving products with ones with higher turnover, an organization can stimulate sales and increase its revenues. Selling products as a package rather than individually may also result in cost savings.

> **bundle pricing** packaging together two or more complementary products and selling them for a single price

Everyday Low Prices (EDLP)   To reduce or eliminate the use of frequent short-term price reductions, some organizations use an approach referred to as **everyday low prices (EDLP)**. When EDLP is used, a marketer sets a low price for its products on a consistent basis rather than setting higher prices and frequently discounting them. Everyday low prices, though not deeply discounted, are set far enough below competitors' prices to make customers feel confident they are receiving a fair price. EDLP is employed by retailers like Wal-Mart and by manufacturers like Procter & Gamble. A company that uses EDLP benefits from reduced promotional costs, reduced losses from frequent mark-downs, and more stability in its sales. A major problem with this approach is that customers have mixed responses to it. In some instances, customers simply don't believe that everyday low prices are what they say they are, but are instead a marketing gimmick.

> **everyday low prices (EDLP)** setting a low price for products on a consistent basis

Customary Pricing   In **customary pricing**, certain goods are priced primarily on the basis of tradition. Examples of customary, or traditional, prices would be those set for candy bars and chewing gum.

> **customary pricing** pricing on the basis of tradition

Product-Line Pricing

Rather than considering products on an item-by-item basis when determining pricing strategies, some marketers employ product-line pricing. *Product-line pricing* means establishing and adjusting the prices of multiple products within a product line. Product-line pricing can provide marketers with flexibility in price setting. For example, marketers can set prices so that one product is quite profitable while another increases market share by virtue of having a lower price than competing products.

When marketers employ product-line pricing, they have several strategies from which to choose. These include captive pricing, premium pricing, and price lining.

captive pricing pricing the basic product in a product line low, but pricing related items at a higher level

Captive Pricing
When **captive pricing** is used, the basic product in a product line is priced low, but the price on the items required to operate or enhance it can be at a higher level. For example, a manufacturer of cameras and film may price a camera at a low level to attract customers, but price the film at a relatively high price because customers must continue to purchase film in order to use their cameras.

premium pricing pricing the highest-quality or most versatile products higher than other models in the product line

Premium Pricing
Premium pricing occurs when the highest-quality product or the most versatile version of similar products in a product line is given the highest price. Other products in the line are priced to appeal to price-sensitive shoppers or to those who seek product-specific features. Marketers that use premium pricing often realize a significant portion of their profits from premium-priced products. Examples of product categories in which premium pricing is common are small kitchen appliances, beer, ice cream, and television cable service.

price lining setting a limited number of prices for selected groups or lines of merchandise

Price Lining
Price lining is the strategy of selling goods only at certain predetermined prices that reflect definite price breaks. For example, a shop may sell men's ties only at $22 and $37. This strategy is widely used in clothing and accessory stores. It eliminates minor price differences from the buying decision—both for customers and for managers who buy merchandise to sell in these stores.

Visual Aids

Visual aids are visual representations of information. They include photographs, tables or charts, graphs, drawings, diagrams, cartoons, and maps. It's important to note that visual aids do not *substitute* for text; instead, they reinforce, emphasize, and summarize information presented in text form, and they also effectively illustrate relationships in that information. The following diagram from a physical science textbook, for example, reinforces the textual explanation of what happens during a total solar eclipse.

If you did not spend some time studying the diagram, you might not completely understand what happens during an eclipse.

When a textbook includes visual aids, don't ignore them. Use them as another tool for helping you understand the content. To get the most out of visual aids in a textbook, read them in conjunction with the textual explanation. If the author refers you to a visual aid, first read the text, and then locate the visual aid to see how that information is presented in visual form. Read the visual aid's title and caption, which will often indicate the point of the information contained in that visual. Make sure you understand how the visual aid conveys that point.

Exercise 5 *Using Visual Aids*

Read the excerpt from a psychology textbook on page 23 and study the visual aid that accompanies it (figure 7.13). On a separate piece of paper, and in your own words, explain the purpose of the visual aid.

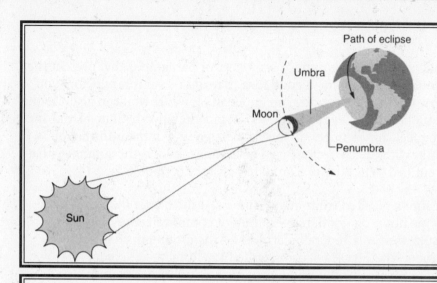

FIGURE 17.15 A Total Solar Eclipse

This diagram shows the positions of the Sun, Moon, and Earth during a total solar eclipse. The umbra and penumbra are, respectively, the dark and semidark shadows cast by the Moon on the surface of the Earth.

Retrieving Memories   **245**

Memory, Perception, and Eyewitness Testimony

There are few situations in which accurate retrieval of memories is more important—and constructive memory is more dangerous—than when an eyewitness testifies in court about a crime. Eyewitnesses provide the most compelling evidence in many trials, but they can sometimes be mistaken (Kassin et al., 2001; Loftus & Ketcham, 1991). In 1984, for example, a North Carolina college student, Jennifer Thompson, confidently identified Ronald Cotton as the man who had raped her at knifepoint. Mainly on the basis of Thompson's testimony, Cotton was convicted of rape and sentenced to life in prison. He was released eleven years later, when DNA evidence revealed that he was innocent (and it identified another man as the rapist). The eyewitness-victim's certainty had convinced a jury, but her memory had been faulty (O'Neill, 2000). Let's consider the accuracy of eyewitness memory and how it can be distorted (Loftus, 1993).

Like the rest of us, eyewitnesses can remember only what they perceive, and they can perceive only what they attend to (Backman & Nilsson, 1991). As described in the perception chapter, perception is influenced by a combination of the stimulus features we find "out there" in the world and what we already know, expect, or want—that is, by both bottom-up and top-down processing.

Witnesses are asked to report exactly what they saw or heard; but no matter how hard they try to be accurate, there are limits to how faithful their reports can be (Kassin, Rigby, & Castillo, 1991). As mentioned earlier, semantic encoding into long-term memory may result in the loss of certain details. Further, new information, including questions posed by police or lawyers, can alter a witness's memory (Loftus, 1979). For example, when witnesses were asked, "How fast was the blue car going when it *smashed into* the truck?" they were likely to recall a higher speed than when they were asked, "How fast was the blue car going when it *hit* the truck?" (Loftus & Palmer, 1974; see Figure 7.13). There is also evidence that an object mentioned after the fact is often mistakenly remembered as having been

figure 7.13

The Impact of Leading Questions on Eyewitness Memory

After seeing a filmed traffic accident, people were asked, "About how fast were the cars going when they (smashed, hit, or contacted) each other?" As shown here, the witnesses' responses were influenced by the verb used in the question; *smashed* was associated with the highest average speed estimates. A week later, people who heard the question that used *smashed* remembered the accident as being more violent than did people in the other two groups (Loftus & Palmer, 1974).

Question	Verb	Estimated mph
About how fast were the cars going when they _____ each other?	smashed into	40.8
	hit	34.0
	contacted	30.8

Original information   **External information**   **The "memory"**

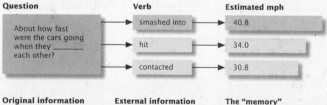

About how fast were the cars going when they SMASHED INTO each other?

there in the first place (Dodson & Reisberg, 1991). So if a lawyer says that a screwdriver was lying on the ground (when it was not), witnesses often recall with great certainty having seen it (Ryan & Geiselman, 1991). Some theorists have speculated that mentioning a new object makes the original memory more difficult to retrieve (Tversky & Tuchin, 1989). However, there is now considerable evidence that when new objects are mentioned, they are integrated into the old memory representation and subsequently are not distinguished from what was originally seen (Loftus, 1992).

Chapter Summary

Many textbook chapters conclude with a brief summary, sentences or paragraphs that present the main ideas of the chapter in a condensed form. It's a good idea to read this summary before you read a chapter to get a concise overview of the chapter's main ideas. However, you can also use the summary as a study tool. Copy the summary by rewriting it or typing it, but substitute blanks for most of the key terms. When you feel confident about your understanding of the information in the chapter, try to fill in the blanks with the correct terms. For example, here is the summary that appears at the end of a chapter entitled "The Rise of Rome" in a history textbook:

> The rise of Rome to greatness resulted from many factors. At the outset the geographical position of Rome put it on good, natural lines of communication within Italy. The Italian peninsula itself was generally fertile, and the mountains did not prevent political unification. The Etruscans transformed the Roman settlements into a city. Once free of the Etruscans, the Romans used their political organization, their prosperity, and their population to conquer their neighbors. Yet instead of enslaving them, the Romans extended citizenship to the conquered. Having united Italy under them, the Romans became a major power that looked to the broader Mediterranean world. In a succession of wars with Carthage, in Spain, and in the Hellenistic East, Rome won an empire. These conquests not only prompted the Romans to invent a system to administer the empire but also brought them into the mainstream of Hellenistic civilization. The wealth derived from the empire meant that life for many Romans became richer. But there was also a dark side to these developments. Personal ambition, as well as defects in the Roman system of government, led some ambitious leaders to seize unprecedented power. Others resisted, throwing the republic into a series of civil wars. Finally, Caesar and his grandnephew Octavian restored order, but in the process the Roman republic had become a monarchy. (McKay et al., *A History of Western Society,* 7th ed., Boston: Houghton Mifflin, 2003, p. 146.)

Below is the same summary with key terms replaced with blanks:

> The rise of Rome to greatness resulted from many factors. At the outset the _____ position of Rome put it on good, natural lines of _____ within Italy. The Italian peninsula itself was generally _____, and the mountains did not prevent _____ unification. The Etruscans transformed the Roman settlements into a _____. Once free of the Etruscans, the Romans used their _____, their _____, and their _____ to conquer their neighbors. Yet instead of enslaving them, the Romans extended _____ to the conquered. Having united Italy under them, the Romans became a major power that looked to the broader _____ world. In a succession of wars with _____, in Spain, and in the _____, Rome won an empire. These conquests not only prompted the Romans to invent a system to _____ the empire but also brought them into the mainstream of _____. The _____ derived from the empire meant that life for many Romans became richer. But there was also a dark side to these developments. _____, as well as _____ in the Roman system of government, led some ambitious leaders to seize unprecedented _____. Others resisted, throwing the republic into a series of _____. Finally, _____ and his grandnephew _____ restored order, but in the process the Roman republic had become a _____.

As you substitute blanks for key terms, take care that you do not remove too much key information. Take out only one or two words or phrases in a sentence and leave enough context to be able to figure out the missing information.

Exercise 6 Using a Chapter Summary

In the following chapter summary from a communication textbook, circle all of the words and phrases that you would substitute for blanks to create a fill-in-the-blank study tool.

Listening is as important to communication as speaking. Listening involves hearing, paying attention, comprehending, and interpreting a message. The major types of listening are *discriminative listening, comprehensive listening, critical listening, empathetic listening,* and *appreciative listening. Constructive listening* suggests the additional vital role of the listener in the creation of meaning.

Effective listeners are less vulnerable to unethical advertising or dishonest political communication. Improved listening skills will help your performance as a student and may mean the difference between success and failure at work. Effective listening also benefits interpersonal relationships. An audience that listens effectively can help improve public speaking skills. A supportive audience can help relieve some of the communication apprehension that speakers experience and boost a speaker's self-esteem.

Listening problems may arise from external sources, such as a noisy environment. They may also be a function of the use of language that the audience does not understand or of a speaker whose presentation skills are distracting. However, most serious listening problems arise from factors within the listener, such as personal reactions to words, worries, attitudes, or bad listening habits. Personal reactions to trigger words may set off strong emotions that block effective listening. Biases can interfere with listening. Bad habits, such as pretending we are listening when we are not or listening only for facts, can also interfere with listening.

Effective listening skills can be developed. The first step is to identify your listening problems. Strive for objectivity, withholding value judgments until you are certain you understand the message.

Critical listening skills help you analyze and evaluate messages more effectively. Critical listeners question what they hear, require support for assertions and claims, and evaluate the credentials of sources. Critical listeners differentiate among facts, inferences, and opinions. They become wary when language seems overly vague or incomprehensible, when inflammatory speech takes the place of cool reason, or when a message promises too much. When what they hear does not fit with what they know, critical listeners consider the message very carefully and ask questions.

Listeners have ethical responsibilities. Ethical listeners do not prejudge a speech, but remain open to ideas and receptive to different perspectives. They test what they hear and are sensitive to the impact of ideas on others. (Osborn and Motley, *Improving Communication,* Boston: Houghton Mifflin, 1999, pp. 83–84.)

Review Questions, Discussion Questions, and Exercises

Many textbooks will include questions and exercises that will help you review and check your understanding of the information. These questions and exercises most often appear at the end of chapters, but sometimes they are in the margins or integrated into the text of the chapter itself. *Review questions*, which are also known as *study questions*, can be in the form of multiple-choice questions or short-answer questions. These questions test your memory of the most important concepts or information in the chapter. Even if your instructor does not require you to submit answers to these questions, you should make sure that you can answer them in order to check your understanding of the material. Go back and reread the sections of the chapter that correspond to the questions you cannot yet answer.

Discussion questions, which are also known as *critical thinking questions* and *questions for analysis*, usually ask you to apply the information in the chapter. Unlike review questions, which require simple recall of the chapter's facts and ideas, discussion questions ask you to think about how you can use the information. For example, they may ask you to tie the concepts presented in the chapter to your own experiences, or think about hypothetical situations, or examine case studies. To answer these questions, you must possess a thorough understanding of what you have read, so if your instructor does not address these questions in class, try to discuss them with a classmate or study group. At the very least, consider your own answers to help you understand the chapter content.

Some textbooks will also provide *exercises* that will help you verify your understanding of the material. These exercises may be in the form of problems to solve or activities to complete. Again, even if your instructor does not assign these exercises, complete them and check your answers to make sure you have understood the material.

The excerpt from a management textbook on pages 27–28 illustrates review questions, discussion questions (which are called "Questions for Analysis" and "Questions for Application"), and an exercise that asks students to search for information on the Internet.

28 **PART ONE** *An Introduction to Management*

Discussion Questions

Questions for Review

1. What are the four basic activities that comprise the management process? How are they related to one another?
2. Identify different kinds of managers by both level and area in the organization.
3. Briefly describe the ten managerial roles identified by Mintzberg. Give an example of each.
4. Identify the different important skills that help managers succeed. Give an example of each.

Questions for Analysis

5. The text notes that management is both a science and an art. Is one of these more important than the other? Under what circumstances might one characteristic be more important than the other?
6. Recall a recent group project or task in which you have participated. Explain how each of the four basic management functions was performed.
7. Some people argue that CEOs in the United States are paid too much. Find out the pay

for a CEO and discuss whether you think he or she is overpaid.

Questions for Application

8. Interview a manager from a local organization. Learn about how he or she performs each of the functions of management, the roles he or she plays, and the skills necessary to do the job.
9. Locate a recent business management publication like *Fortune*, *Business Week*, or *Forbes*. Read an article in the magazine that profiles a specific manager or executive. Identify as many examples in the article as you can that illustrate management functions, roles, and/or skills.
10. Watch a television program that involves an organization of some type. Good choices include *N.Y.P.D. Blue*, *The West Wing*, *Spin City*, or *E.R.* Identify as many management functions, skills, and roles as you can.

BUILDING EFFECTIVE *technical* SKILLS

Exercise Overview

Technical skills refer to the manager's abilities to accomplish or understand work done in an organization. More and more managers today are realizing that having the technical ability to use the Internet is an important part of communication, decision making, and other facets of their work. This exercise helps you see the link between the Internet and management.

Exercise Background

The so-called information highway, or the Internet, is an interconnected network of information and information-based resources accessed by computers, computer systems, and other devices. While electronic mail was perhaps the first widespread application of the Internet, increasingly popular applications are based on home pages and search engines.

A home page is a file (or set of files) created by an individual, business, or other entity. It contains whatever information its creator chooses to include. For example, a company might create a home page for itself that includes its logo, its address and telephone number, information about its products and services, and so forth. An individual seeking employment might create a home page that includes a résumé and a statement of career interests. Home pages are indexed by key words chosen by their creators.

A search engine is a system through which an Internet user can search for home pages according to their indexed key words. Suppose an individual is interested in knowing more about art collecting. Key words that might logically be linked to home pages related to this interest include *art*, *artists*, *galleries*, and *framing*. A search engine will take these key words and provide a listing of all home pages that are indexed to them. The user can then browse each page to see what information it contains. Popular search engines include Yahoo, Google, and Webcrawler.

Exercise Task

1. Review the content of this chapter and identify three or four general management-related terms (i.e., *management, organization, business*).
2. Using whichever search engine you prefer, conduct a search for these terms.
3. Now select a more specific management topic and search for two or three specific terms (if you cannot think of any terms, scan the margin notes in this book).
4. Finally, select three or four companies and search for their home pages.
5. Comment on the relative ease and value of each of these searches from the standpoint of a practicing manager.

Exercise 7 Using Review Questions, Discussion Questions, and Exercises

Look over the excerpt from a physical science textbook on pages 29–33, and then answer the
questions below by circling the letter of the correct response.

1. What type(s) of review questions are included in this excerpt?
   a. Multiple-choice questions
   b. Short-answer questions
   c. Both a and b
   d. None of the above

2. What does this textbook call the discussion questions?
   a. Review Questions
   b. Applying Your Knowledge
   c. Exercises
   d. On the Web

3. True or False: Answers to all of the review questions are provided.
   a. True
   b. False

4. What type(s) of exercises are included in this chapter?
   a. Problems to solve
   b. Activities
   c. Both a and b
   d. None of the above

5. True or False: Answers to the exercises are provided.
   a. True
   b. False

Review Questions **433**

Review Questions

16.1 Cartesian Coordinates

1. A coordinate system must have
   (a) an indicated origin.
   (b) two dimensions.
   (c) a unit length expressed.
   (d) both (a) and (c).

2. Which of the following is true? A Cartesian coordinate system
   (a) is a two-dimensional system.
   (b) normally designates the horizontal line the x-axis.
   (c) normally designates the vertical line the y-axis.
   (d) all of the above.

3. What common thing is laid out in a Cartesian coordinate system?

4. Give three examples of a one-dimensional reference system.

5. Draw a three-dimensional reference system.

6. What, on a sphere, is analogous to a two-dimensional Cartesian coordinate system?

7. State a reference point; then use a three-dimensional reference system to give the position of your textbook in the room where you are located.

434   Chapter 16   PLACE AND TIME

16.2 Latitude and Longitude

8. Which of the following is true? Latitude
   (a) is a linear measurement.
   (b) can have greater numerical values than longitude.
   (c) is measured in an east-west direction.
   (d) can have negative values.
   (e) none of the above.

9. Which of the following is true? Longitude
   (a) can have a maximum value of 180°.
   (b) is an angular measurement.
   (c) has east or west values.
   (d) is measured along parallels.
   (e) all of the above.

10. Meridians
    (a) run east and west.
    (b) are associated with longitude.
    (c) are great circles.
    (d) all of the above.

11. Which of the following is false?
    (a) Parallels become smaller as the distance from the equator becomes greater.
    (b) Parallels are all small circles.
    (c) Most parallels are small circles
    (d) All of the above are false.

12. What are the minimum and maximum values for latitude and for longitude?

13. What is the Greenwich, or prime, meridian?

14. What is the name of a line of equal longitude?

15. What is the latitude of the North Pole?

16. What is a Mercator projection map?

17. Are meridians great circles? Explain.

18. Are any parallels great circles? Explain.

16.3 Time

19. The 24-h apparent solar day
    (a) begins at midnight.
    (b) involves two successive crossings of the same meridian.
    (c) is not exactly 82,400 seconds every solar day.
    (d) all of the above.

20. The Sun is overhead on a person's meridian at a local time of
    (a) 12 A.M.   (c) 12 noon.
    (b) 12 P.M.   (d) all of these.

21. The solar day is approximately
    (a) 1 minute longer than the sidereal day.
    (b) 2 minutes longer than the sidereal day.
    (c) 3 minutes longer than the sidereal day.
    (d) 4 minutes longer than the sidereal day.

22. During the month of January, the number of daylight hours at Washington, D.C., is _____ at Orlando, Florida.
    (a) more than   (b) less than   (c) the same as

23. Give the longitude of the central meridian for each of the time zones in the conterminous United States.

24. What do A.M. and P.M. mean?

25. Is it correct to state the time as 12 A.M.? Explain your answer.

26. What are some advantages of Daylight Saving Time?

27. What is the direction of rotation (clockwise or counterclockwise) of the shadow cast by a sundial located at (a) 30°N and (b) 30°S?

28. How is 12 midnight local time defined?

29. Define one solar day.

30. Define one sidereal day.

31. How does the day of the year change when one crosses the IDL traveling westward?

32. What periodic motion is used as a reference for our year?

33. Describe the apparent north-south motion of the overhead Sun throughout the year. What causes this?

16.4 The Seasons

34. Select the correct answer. The seasons
    (a) are a function of the inclination of the Earth's axis.
    (b) are a function of the Earth's revolving around the Sun.
    (c) would be hotter or colder if the solstices were at 25°.
    (d) all of the above.

35. An observer at 20°N
    (a) always looks south to see the Sun.
    (b) observes the Sun directly overhead twice a year.
    (c) is near the Tropic of Capricorn.
    (d) none of the above.

36. From September 23 to March 20, in what direction must an observer in the Northern Hemisphere look to see sunrise?
    (a) east   (b) northeast   (c) southeast

37. Suppose the Earth's axis did *not* maintain its constant 23.5° tilt but instead changed so that the axis was always tilted toward the Sun in the Northern Hemisphere. What effect would this have on the seasons in (a) the Northern Hemisphere and (b) the Southern Hemisphere?

38. Distinguish between a tropical year and a sidereal year.

39. Give the times (dates) during the year when a place on the equator receives (a) the maximum daily amount of solar radiation and (b) the minimum daily amount.

40. Distinguish between altitude and zenith angle. At what angle is the zenith relative to the horizon?

41. What is the altitude of Polaris (the North Star) for an observer at the equator (0° latitude)? At the North Pole (90°N)?

42. Where is the noon Sun directly overhead on (a) the beginning of our summer, (b) the beginning of our winter, (c) the beginning of spring, and (d) the beginning of fall?

16.5 Precession of the Earth's Axis

43. Precession of the Earth's axis
    (a) is counterclockwise as viewed from above the North Pole.
    (b) changes the angle between the axis and the vertical.
    (c) has no important effect on the Earth's seasons.
    (d) none of the above.

44. The precession of the Earth's axis is caused by
    (a) the tilt of the axis.
    (b) the Earth's equatorial bulge.
    (c) the apparent north-south movement of the Sun.
    (d) gravitational torque.

45. What effect does the precession of the Earth's axis have with respect to the pole star, or North Star?

46. What evidence is there to support precession of the Earth's axis?

47. How long does it take for the Earth's axis to precess once?

48. Precession of the Earth's axis *does* or *does not* have a noticeable effect on the seasons?

16.6 The Calendar

49. Which of the following is a natural unit of the calendar?
    (a) the day, which is based on the period of rotation of the Earth
    (b) the month, which is based on the period of revolution of the Moon
    (c) the year, which is based on the period of revolution of the Earth around the Sun
    (d) all of the above

50. The Gregorian calendar
    (a) is our present calendar.
    (b) is accurate to 1 day in 6000 years.
    (c) skips a leap year every century year.
    (d) all of the above.

51. What is the origin of the month?

52. Distinguish between the Julian and Gregorian calendars.

53. How often is there a leap year in the Gregorian calendar?

54. How was the zodiac used as a primitive calendar?

55. Which century year will next be a leap year?

Applying Your Knowledge

1. If the Earth rotated in a clockwise direction as observed from above the North Pole, how would the solar day compare with the sidereal day?

2. Is there a place on the Earth's surface where 1° of latitude and 1° of longitude have approximately equal numerical values in nautical miles? Explain.

3. October is the tenth month of the year, but octo means "eight." Explain.

4. (a) Can you travel continuously eastward and circle the Earth? Why or why not? (b) Can you travel continuously southward and circle the Earth? Why or why not?

5. Why do some people born in December celebrate their birthdays in the summer?

Exercises

16.2 Latitude and Longitude

1. What is the minimum angle between place *A* (50°N, 90°W) and place *B* (60°N, 90°E)?

2. What is the minimum angle between place *A* (20°N, 75°W) and place *B* (30°S, 75°W)?

3. What is the number of nautical miles between place *A* and place *B* in Exercise 1?

4. What is the number of nautical miles between place *A* and place *B* in Exercise 2?

436   Chapter 16 PLACE AND TIME

5. Suppose you start at Washington, D.C. (39°N, 77°W), and travel 300 n mi due north, then 300 n mi due west, then 300 n mi due south, and then 300 n mi due east. Where will you arrive with respect to your starting point—at your starting point, or north, south, east, or west of it?

6. Suppose you start at Washington, D.C. (39°N, 77°W), and travel 600 n mi due south, then 600 n mi due west, then 600 n mi due north, and then 600 n mi due east. Where will you arrive with respect to your starting point?

7. What are the latitude and longitude of the point on the Earth that is opposite Washington, D.C. (39°N, 77°W)?

8. What are the latitude and longitude of the point on the Earth that is opposite Tokyo (36°N, 140°E)?

16.3 Time

9. What are the standard time and date at (40°N, 118°W) when the local solar time at (35°N, 80°W) is 6 P.M. on October 8?

10. What are the standard time and date at (40°N, 110°W) when the local solar time at (30°N, 70°W) is 1 A.M. on October 16?

11. When it is 9 P.M. standard time on November 26 in Moscow (56°N, 38°E), what are the standard time and date in Tokyo (36°N, 140°E)?

12. When it is 10 A.M. standard time on February 22 in Los Angeles (34°N, 118°W), what are the standard time and date in Tokyo (36°N, 140°E)?

13. A professional basketball game is to be played in Portland, Oregon. It is televised live in New York beginning at 9 P.M. EST. What time must the game begin in Portland?

14. If the polls close during a presidential election at 7 P.M. EST in New York, what is the standard time in California?

15. Some military personnel stationed at a base in Germany (51°N, 10°E) wanted to watch a figure skating event live in the Salt Lake, Utah, Winter Olympics that was scheduled for 7 P.M. on February 22. At what time and date should they have watched the television to see this?

16. It is 2 P.M. on July 1 in London, England (51.5°N, 0°). What are the time and date in Anchorage, Alaska (62°N, 150°W)?

17. What is the altitude angle of the Sun for someone at Atlanta, Georgia (34°N) on June 21?

18. What is the altitude angle of the Sun for someone at Atlanta, Georgia (34°N) on December 22?

19. What is the latitude of someone in the United States who sees the Sun at an altitude of 71.5° on June 21?

20. What is the latitude of someone in the United States who sees the Sun at an altitude of 65.5° on December 22?

21. Determine the month and day when the Sun is at maximum altitude for an observer at Washington, D.C. (39°N). What is the altitude of the Sun at this time?

22. Determine the month and day when the Sun is at minimum altitude for an observer at Washington, D.C. (39°N). What is the altitude of the Sun at this time?

Answers to Multiple-Choice Review Questions

1. d	9. e	19. d	22. b	36. c	49. d
2. d	10. b	20. c	34. d	43. c	50. a
8. e	11. c	21. d	35. b	44. d	

On the Web

1. Einstein's Legacy

No doubt one of the greatest minds of all time, Albert Einstein left both a scientific and a philosophical legacy, encouraging the use of hard science and mathematics, as well as intuition and imagination. What's so special about relativity? How do the theories of general and specific relativity differ from each other? What problems arose in astronomy and physics between the eighteenth and nineteenth centuries that challenged Newton's concept of the universe and what was Einstein's role in dealing with these problems?

Explore answers to these questions by following the recommended links at **http://www.physicalscience.college/hmco.com/students.**

Study Guides

Many textbooks are accompanied by a *study guide*—a separate book, website, or computer disk that offers additional tools to help you master the material in the text. A study guide usually includes one or more of the following:

- Lists of learning objectives

- Lists of key terms or vocabulary

- Flashcards of key terms and concepts

- Chapter outlines or summaries

- Additional examples

- Additional exercises

- Multimedia tutorials

- Review questions or discussion questions

- Practice tests or interactive quizzes

- Lists of additional readings

- Learning tips

Study guides in electronic form on computer disks or websites are often particularly valuable, for they employ audio and/or visual presentations that can enhance your understanding of the information explained in the text.

Exercise 8 Using a Study Guide

Look over the following index of an online study guide for a psychology textbook. Then, answer the questions that follow by circling the letter of the correct response.

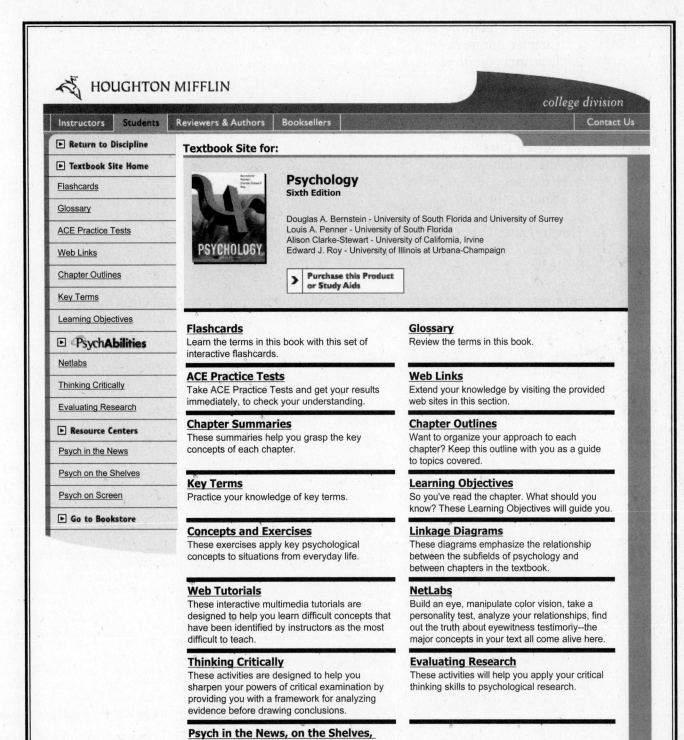

1. Which of the following study tools is NOT included in this online study guide?
    a. Chapter summaries
    b. Learning objectives
    c. Learning tips
    d. Chapter outlines

2. Which of the following type of activity is NOT included in this online study guide?
    a. Review questions
    b. Discussion questions
    c. Exercises
    d. None of the above

3. True or False: This website includes computer-graded practice tests.
    a. True
    b. False

4. How many sections of this website are devoted to learning or remembering key terms?
    a. One
    b. Two
    c. Three
    d. Four

Part 2

Strategies for Reading College Textbooks

Now that you're aware of the various features that are common in college textbooks, you can practice several reading strategies that will help you understand and remember the information in these texts. This section will offer you valuable tips and techniques for improving your reading skills.

Your Physical Reading Environment

Your reading will be more productive if you do it in the right place at the right time. You'll probably be able to concentrate best in a quiet location with few distractions. Reading in a soft, comfortable chair may make you sleepy, so sit upright in a firm chair.

Exercise 9 Describing Your Own Reading Environment

1. Describe the place where you usually read course materials, including textbooks. Does the physical environment of this place interfere with your concentration as you read?

   _____

   _____

2. List two or three specific locations where you believe you could read most effectively.

   _____

   _____

   _____

The best time to read is the time of day or night when you are most mentally alert. If you're a night owl, read at night. If you're a morning person, try to fit in your reading time at the beginning of your day.

Exercise 10 Determining Your Best Reading Time

1. At what time of day are you most mentally alert? Is this the time when you usually try to read?

   _____

   _____

   _____

2. If you don't read during the time of day when you're most mentally alert, how can you alter your schedule to change your reading time?

   _____

   _____

   _____

Dealing with Distractions

Finding a completely distraction-free environment is difficult, so you will need to learn to concentrate in spite of the other things that will compete for your attention. No matter where you read, you'll probably encounter external and internal distractions, but you can develop strategies for dealing with both kinds.

External distractions are the sights, sounds, and other sensations that will tempt you away from your reading. These distractions include ringing phones, people talking or walking nearby, the sound of a stereo, or a friend who stops by to chat. Obviously, the best strategy for handling this type of distraction is prevention. Try to choose a location for reading—such as an individual study carrel in your library—where these kinds of distractions are minimal. Notify your friends and family that you'll be unavailable for conversation and socializing. If you must read in places with more activity, try wearing earplugs and/or sitting with your back to the activity so you're not tempted to watch the comings and goings of others.

Exercise 11 Combating External Distractions

1. What external distractions most often pull your attention away from your reading?

_____

_____

_____

2. Based on the advice given above, what can you do to reduce these distractions?

_____

_____

_____

Internal distractions are often even more challenging for readers. They are the thoughts, worries, plans, daydreams, and other types of mental "noise" inside your own head. They will inhibit you from concentrating on what you are reading and from absorbing the information you need to learn.

You can try to ignore these thoughts, but they will usually continue trying to intrude. How do you temporarily silence them so you can devote your full attention to your reading? Instead of fighting them, try focusing on them completely for a short period of time. For five or ten minutes, allow yourself to sit and think about your job, your finances, your car problems, your boyfriend or girlfriend, the paper you need to write, or whatever is on your mind. Better yet, write these thoughts down. Do a freewriting* exercise to empty your mind onto a piece of paper. If you can't stop thinking about all of the other things you need to do, devote ten minutes to writing a detailed "To Do" list. Giving all of your attention to distracting thoughts will often clear your mind so you can focus on your reading.

*Freewriting involves quickly writing thoughts on paper without censoring them or worrying about spelling or grammar.

Exercise 12 Clearing Your Mind Before Reading

1. On your own paper, freewrite or create lists for five to ten minutes to clear your mind of distracting thoughts.

2. Immediately after completing your freewriting or list, read the excerpt on pages 41–42 entitled, "The Origins of the Revolution," which is from a history textbook.

3. On the blanks provided below, evaluate the effectiveness of the technique you used to clear your mind. Were you able to concentrate better as you read?

_____

_____

_____

context of the times. And in founding a government firmly based on liberal principles, the Americans set an example that had a forceful impact on Europe and sped up political development there.

The Origins of the Revolution

The American Revolution had its immediate origins in a squabble over increased taxes. The British government had fought and decisively won the Seven Years' War (see pages 647–648) on the strength of its professional army and navy. The American colonists had furnished little real aid. The high cost of the war to the British, however, had led to a doubling of the British national debt. Anticipating further expense defending its recently conquered

Toward Revolution in Boston The Boston Tea Party was only one of many angry confrontations between British officials and Boston patriots. On January 27, 1774, an angry crowd seized a British customs collector and then tarred and feathered him. This French engraving of 1784 commemorates the defiant and provocative action. *(The Granger Collection, New York)*

western lands from native American uprisings, the British government in London set about reorganizing the empire with a series of bold, largely unprecedented measures. Breaking with tradition, the British decided to maintain a large army in North America after peace was restored in 1763 and to tax the colonies directly. In 1765 the government pushed through Parliament the Stamp Act, which levied taxes on a long list of commercial and legal documents, diplomas, pamphlets, newspapers, almanacs, dice, and playing cards. A stamp glued to each article indicated the tax had been paid.

This effort to increase taxes as part of a tightening up of the empire seemed perfectly reasonable to the British. Heavier stamp taxes had been collected in Great Britain for two generations, and Americans were being asked only to pay a share of their own defense costs. Moreover, Americans had been paying only very low local taxes. The Stamp Act would have doubled taxes to about 2 shillings per person per year, whereas the British paid the highest taxes in the Western world—26 shillings per person. The colonists protested the Stamp Act vigorously and violently, however, and after their rioting and boycotts against British goods, Parliament reluctantly repealed the new tax.

As the fury over the Stamp Act revealed, much more was involved than taxes. The key questions were political. To what extent could the home government refashion the empire and reassert its power while limiting the authority of colonial legislatures and their elected representatives? Accordingly, who should represent the colonies, and who had the right to make laws for Americans? The British government replied that Americans were represented in Parliament, albeit indirectly (like most British people themselves), and that the absolute supremacy of Parliament throughout the empire could not be questioned. Many Americans felt otherwise. As John Adams put it, "A Parliament of Great Britain can have no more rights to tax the colonies than a Parliament of Paris." Thus imperial reorganization and parliamentary supremacy came to appear as grave threats to Americans' existing liberties and time-honored institutions.

Americans had long exercised a great deal of independence. In British North America, unlike England and Europe, no powerful established church existed, and personal freedom in questions of religion was taken for granted. The colonial assemblies made the important laws, which were seldom overturned by the home government. The right to vote was much more widespread than in England. In many parts of colonial Massachusetts, for example, as many as 95 percent of the adult males could vote.

Moreover, greater political equality was matched by greater social and economic equality. Neither a hereditary nobility nor a hereditary serf population existed, although the slavery of the Americas consigned blacks to a legally oppressed caste. Independent farmers were the largest group in the country and set much of its tone. In short, the colonial experience had slowly formed a people who felt themselves separate and distinct from the home country, and the controversies over taxation intensified those feelings.

In 1773 the dispute over taxes and representation flared up again. The British government had permitted the financially hard-pressed East India Company to ship its tea from China directly to its agents in the colonies rather than through London middlemen who sold to independent merchants in the colonies. Thus the company secured a vital monopoly on the tea trade, and colonial merchants were suddenly excluded from a lucrative business. The colonists were quick to protest.

In Boston men disguised as Indians had a rowdy "tea party" and threw the company's tea into the harbor. This led to extreme measures. The so-called Coercive Acts closed the port of Boston, curtailed local elections and town meetings, and greatly expanded the royal governor's power. County conventions in Massachusetts protested vehemently and urged that the acts be "rejected as the attempts of a wicked administration to enslave America." Other colonial assemblies joined in the denunciations. In September 1774, the First Continental Congress met in Philadelphia, where the more radical members argued successfully against concessions to the Crown. Compromise was also rejected by the British Parliament, and in April 1775 fighting began at Lexington and Concord.

Independence

The fighting spread, and the colonists moved slowly but inevitably toward open rebellion and a declaration of independence. The uncompromising attitude of the British government and its use of German mercenaries went a long way toward dissolving long-standing loyalties to the home country and rivalries among the separate colonies. *Common Sense* (1775), a brilliant attack by the recently arrived English radical Thomas Paine (1737–1809), also mobilized public opinion in favor of independence. A runaway bestseller with sales of 120,000 copies in a few months, Paine's tract ridiculed the idea of a small island ruling a great continent. In his call for freedom and republican government, Paine expressed Americans' growing sense of separateness and moral superiority.

On July 4, 1776, the Second Continental Congress adopted the Declaration of Independence. Written by Thomas Jefferson, the Declaration of Independence boldly listed the tyrannical acts committed by George III (r. 1760–1820) and confidently proclaimed the natural rights of mankind and the sovereignty of the American states. Sometimes called the world's greatest political editorial, the Declaration of Independence in effect universalized the traditional rights of English people and made them the rights of all mankind. It stated that "all men are created equal. . . . They are endowed by their Creator with certain unalienable rights. . . . Among these are life, liberty, and the pursuit of happiness." No other American political document has ever caused such excitement, either at home or abroad.

Many American families remained loyal to Britain; many others divided bitterly. After the Declaration of Independence, the conflict often took the form of a civil war pitting patriot against Loyalist. The Loyalists tended to be wealthy and politically moderate. Many patriots, too, were wealthy—individuals such as John Hancock and George Washington—but willingly allied themselves with farmers and artisans in a broad coalition. This coalition harassed the Loyalists and confiscated their property to help pay for the American war effort. The broad social base of the revolutionaries tended to make the liberal revolution democratic. State governments extended the right to vote to many more men (but not to any women) in the course of the war and re-established themselves as republics.

On the international scene, the French sympathized with the rebels and supplied guns and gunpowder from the beginning. The French wanted revenge for the humiliating defeats of the Seven Years' War. By 1777 French volunteers were arriving in Virginia, and a dashing young nobleman, the marquis de Lafayette (1757–1834), quickly became one of Washington's most trusted generals. In 1778 the French government offered a formal alliance to the American ambassador in Paris, Benjamin Franklin, and in 1779 and 1780 the Spanish and Dutch declared war on Britain. Catherine the Great of Russia helped organize the League of Armed Neutrality in order to protect neutral shipping rights, which Britain refused to recognize.

Thus by 1780 Great Britain was engaged in an imperial war against most of Europe as well as the thirteen colonies. In these circumstances, and in the face of severe reverses in India, in the West Indies, and at Yorktown in Virginia, a new British government decided to cut its losses. American negotiators in Paris were receptive. They feared that France wanted a treaty that would bottle up the new United States east of the Allegheny Mountains and give British holdings west of the Alleghenies to

Time Management

How often should you read? How long should you try reading in one sitting? How many times should you read a chapter? Is it better to read the whole chapter at once or just a section at a time?

There are no right or wrong answers to these questions. The most effective length, amount and frequency of reading time will differ from student to student and class to class. You will have to experiment to discover what works best for you, and you will probably need to make adjustments for each different course you take.

However, be aware of the following general principles of effective time management:

- *Schedule time to read.* Don't just try to fit reading in whenever you can; actually make an appointment to read by blocking out regular times in your calendar. Try to schedule time for multiple readings of the same chapter.

- *Keep up with the reading assignments in a course by following the schedule provided by your instructor.* Following the schedule will give you the basic understanding of the material you'll need to get the most out of class lectures, discussions, and activities.

- *Repeated exposure to information helps increase your retention of the material.* If you hurriedly read large chunks of information all at once just before a test, you probably won't remember much of it. If you digest information slowly and regularly over a longer period of time, you'll remember more.

Exercise 13 *Applying the Time Management Guidelines*

Do you follow the time-management guidelines described above? Which of these principles should you apply to read more productively?

_____

_____

_____

_____

The Reading Process

To get the most from textbooks, practice reading as a *process*. This process has three essential steps:

STEP 1: PREVIEW

STEP 2: READ

STEP 3: REVIEW

Practicing these steps will not only increase your comprehension of the information *as* you read, but they will also improve your retention of that information *after* you read.

Step 1: PREVIEW

During the *preview* step, you prepare your mind to make sense of the new information by creating a mental framework for it. Construct this framework by doing the following:

Get an idea of the chapter's content that you'll be reading. You do this by looking over the chapter's title and subtitle, the list of learning goals or objective, the headings throughout the chapter, the marginal information (such as definitions), the graphics (such as charts or photographs), the chapter summary, and the end-of-chapter questions. All of these features will give you a brief preview of the material you'll be reading.

Understand the overall organization of the content. Having a "big picture" of the information will help you know how the details fit in while you're reading the chapter. Learn about the chapter's organization by examining the book's table of contents. If the book provides a chapter outline, study it before you read. Also, look over the headings throughout the chapter to understand the main ideas and relationships between the sections.

Exercise 14 Previewing a Textbook Chapter

Study the excerpt of a chapter opening page from a management textbook on pages 45–46. Then, answer the questions below by circling the letter of the correct response.

1. On what topic does this chapter focus?
   a. Management
   b. Leadership
   c. Behavior
   d. Influence

2. How many different situational approaches to leadership are covered in this chapter?
   a. One
   b. Two
   c. Three
   d. Four

3. True or False: After reading this chapter, you should be able to distinguish leadership from management.
   a. True
   b. False

4. In what section of the chapter will you find a discussion of power?
   a. The Nature of Leadership
   b. Leadership Behaviors
   c. Related Perspectives on Leadership
   d. Political Behavior in Organizations

CHAPTER

17 Managing Leadership and Influence Processes

OPENING INCIDENT

In many ways Jacques Nasser may be the quintessential business leader for the twenty-first century. He was born in Lebanon but grew up in Australia. He joined Ford's Australian operation more than thirty years ago as a financial analyst. As Nasser worked his way up the company's hierarchy, he subsequently held increasingly important jobs, first in Latin America and then in Europe. He moved to the United States after being promoted to the key position of president of Ford Automotive Operations. Finally, in 1999 he became Ford's CEO.

Almost from the day he arrived in Detroit, Nasser began to shake things up. For decades the firm had been a stable, hierarchical company that efficiently made cars and, in recent years at least, earned solid profits. But Nasser had a new vision for Ford, one that will, in his opinion, take the company to the very forefront of its indus-

try and transform it into a nimble, flexible organization better attuned to the international automobile industry he sees emerging.

And indeed, the forefront of the industry is exactly where Nasser has set his sights, even though he downplays that goal publicly. After all, General Motors has held the crown as the world's largest automobile company for decades. But while GM's global market share has slowly declined to around 16 percent, Ford's has surged to about 13 percent—clearly putting Ford within striking distance. To help him achieve his ambitions, Nasser has also brought in dozens of senior managers from outside the staid Ford ranks.

Nasser has also made several major changes in Ford's organization structure. Most significantly, he decided to group newly acquired Volvo with Jaguar and Aston Martin,

English properties Ford had acquired years earlier, with its own Lincoln division, creating a new unit called the Premier Automotive Group. This new unit is headed by Wolfgang Reitzle, a recruit from BMW, and headquartered in Europe. Nasser also overhauled the structure of Ford's new car design operation and mandated that all senior executives move into the same building to promote interaction and stimulate new ways of thinking.

Nasser's own approach to running Ford is also a bit unique. He is seldom in his office; instead he visits Ford facilities around the world. Indeed, he keeps a calendar marked with national holidays from around the world to coordinate his travel schedule better. For example, he recently took advantage of the

> *"You've got to earn [a promotion]. The days of entitlement at Ford Motor Co. are gone forever."*
> —*Jacques Nasser, CEO of Ford Motor Company*

518

LEARNING OBJECTIVES

After studying this chapter, you should be able to:

- Describe the nature of leadership and distinguish leadership from management.

  Discuss and evaluate the trait approach to leadership.

- Discuss and evaluate models of leadership, focusing on behaviors.

- Identify and describe the major situational approaches to leadership.

- Identify and describe three related perspectives on leadership.

- Discuss political behavior in organizations and how it can be managed.

Thanksgiving lull in the United States to visit Australia. Nasser also communicates with Ford employees regularly. For instance, every week he writes a chatty e-mail updating employees on what's going on, sending it to more than 89,000 employee mailboxes around the world. He is also stressing the importance of motivation and hard work. For example, he has tied executive compensation to stock performance for the first time since Ford went public in the 1950s. And a recurring message he takes to all Ford employees—who own about 20 percent of the firm's stock—is how their individual contributions add to shareholder value.

Finally, Nasser also won rave reviews for his handling of the recent crisis involving the recall of thousands of sets of Firestone tires on Ford Explorers. Nasser assumed personal responsibility for helping address the problem and routinely met with representatives from the media, the government, and Firestone to ensure that consumers received new tires as quickly as possible. He also did an excellent job of simultaneously acknowledging Ford's role in solving the problem while protecting the corporate reputation by keeping it framed as an issue with Firestone's tires.[1]

CHAPTER OUTLINE

The Nature of Leadership
The Meaning of Leadership
Leadership Versus Management
Power and Leadership

- The Search for Leadership Traits

- Leadership Behaviors
Michigan Studies
Ohio State Studies
Managerial Grid

- Situational Approaches to Leadership
LPC Theory
Path-Goal Theory
Vroom's Decision Tree Approach
The Leader-Member Exchange Approach

- Related Perspectives on Leadership
Substitutes for Leadership
Charismatic Leadership
Transformational Leadership

- Political Behavior in Organizations
Common Political Behaviors
Managing Political Behavior

519

Think before you read. We digest new information more easily when we can relate it to what we already know. Therefore, before you read, take a little time to consider your prior knowledge about the topic. Also, think about your own personal experiences that relate to the chapter content you previewed. Writing will clarify your existing ideas and beliefs even more, so you may want to record your thoughts in a reading journal.

| **Exercise 15 Thinking Before Reading**

On the blanks provided below, write at least one paragraph about your ideas, beliefs, and experiences related to leadership. What do you already believe to be the characteristics of good leaders? (You might want to continue writing your paragraph on a separate sheet of paper if there isn't enough space here.)

_____

_____

_____

_____

_____

_____

_____

Step 2: READ

The second step of the reading process is to *read*. However, to read for increased comprehension and retention of information, you must do much more than just passively move your eyes over the words on the page. Instead, read actively. *Active reading* means marking the text with pens and/or highlighters.

What should you mark? First, turn all of the headings in the chapter into questions. In the "Managing Leadership Influence Processes" chapter, for example, you could change the first few headings of the chapter outline into these questions:

What is the nature of leadership?

What is the meaning of leadership?

How are leadership and management different?

What is the relationship between power and leadership?

Exercise 16 Turning Headings into Questions

Turn back to the chapter outline for "Managing Leadership and Influence Processes" on page 46 and transform the remaining headings into questions by adding words and question marks.

After you turn a heading into a question, read the section looking for the answer(s) to that question. When you encounter the answers, mark them by highlighting, underlining, or circling them. However, don't make the mistake of highlighting entire paragraphs. That won't help you quickly and easily see the main ideas. The excerpt from the chapter, "Managing Leadership and Influence Processes" on pages 49–50 illustrates how several sections have been actively read:

520 **PART FIVE** | *The Leading Process*

Jacques Nasser has a relatively rare combination of skills that sets him apart from many others: he is both an astute leader and a fine manager, and he recognizes many of the challenges necessary to play both roles. He knows when to make tough decisions, when to lead and encourage his employees, and when to stand back and let them do their jobs. And thus far, Ford is reaping big payoffs from his efforts.

This chapter examines people like Jacques Nasser more carefully by focusing on leadership and its role in management. We characterize the nature of leadership and trace the three major approaches to studying leadership—traits, behaviors, and situations. After examining other perspectives on leadership, we conclude by describing another approach to influencing others—political behavior in organizations.

What is The Nature of Leadership ?

In Chapter 16, we described various models and perspectives on employee motivation. From the manager's standpoint, trying to motivate people is an attempt to influence their behavior. In many ways, leadership too is an attempt to influence the behavior of others. In this section, we first define leadership, then differentiate it from management, and conclude by relating it to power.

The Meaning of Leadership

leadership As a process, the use of noncoercive influence to shape the group's or organization's goals, motivate behavior toward the achievement of those goals, and help define group or organization culture; as a property, the set of characteristics attributed to individuals who are perceived to be leaders

leaders People who can influence the behaviors of others without having to rely on force; those accepted by others as leaders

Leadership is both a process and a property.[2] As a process—focusing on what leaders actually do—leadership is ① the use of noncoercive influence to shape the group's or organization's goals, motivate behavior toward the achievement of those goals, and help define group or organization culture.[3] As a property, leadership is ② the set of characteristics attributed to individuals who are perceived to be leaders. Thus, leaders are people who can influence the behaviors of others without having to rely on force; leaders are people whom others accept as leaders.

How does Leadership ~~Versus~~ *differ from* Management ?

From these definitions, it should be clear that leadership and management are related, but they are not the same. A person can be a manager, a leader, both, or neither.[4] Some of the basic distinctions between the two are summarized in Table 17.1. At the left side of the table are four elements that differentiate leadership from management. The two columns show how each element differs when considered from a management and a leadership point of view. For example, when executing plans, managers focus on monitoring results, comparing them with goals, and correcting deviations. In contrast, the leader focuses on energizing people to overcome bureaucratic hurdles to help reach goals. Thus, when Jacques Nasser

Table 17.1

Distinctions Between Management and Leadership

Management and leadership are related, but distinct, constructs. Managers and leaders differ in how they create an agenda, develop a rationale for achieving the agenda, and execute plans, and in the types of outcomes they achieve.

Activity	Management	Leadership
① Creating an agenda	**Planning and budgeting.** Establishing detailed steps and timetables for achieving needed results; allocating the resources necessary to make those needed results happen.	**Establishing direction.** Developing a vision of the future, often the distant future, and strategies for producing the changes needed to achieve that vision.
② Developing a human network for achieving the agenda	**Organizing and staffing.** Establishing some structure for accomplishing plan requirements, staffing that structure with individuals, delegating responsibility and authority for carrying out the plan, providing policies and procedures to help guide people, and creating methods or systems to monitor implementation.	**Aligning people.** Communicating the direction by words and deeds to everyone whose cooperation may be needed to influence the creation of teams and coalitions that understand the vision and strategies and accept their validity.
③ Executing plans	**Controlling and problem solving.** Monitoring results versus planning in some detail, identifying deviations, and then planning and organizing to solve these problems.	**Motivating and inspiring.** Energizing people to overcome major political, bureaucratic, and resource barriers by satisfying very basic, but often unfulfilled, human needs.
④ Outcomes	Produces a degree of predictability and order and has the potential to produce consistently major results expected by various stakeholders (for example, for customers, always being on time; for stockholders, being on budget).	Produces change, often to a dramatic degree, and has the potential to produce extremely useful change (for example, new products that customers want, new approaches to labor relations that help make a firm more competitive).

4 differences between managers and leaders

Source: Reprinted with permission of The Free Press, a division of Simon & Schuster Inc. from *A Force for Change: How Leadership Differs from Management* by John P. Kotter. Copyright © 1990 by John P. Kotter, Inc.

monitors the performance of his employees, he is playing the role of manager. But when he inspires them to work harder at achieving their goals, he is a leader.

Organizations need both management and leadership if they are to be effective. Leadership is necessary to create change, and management is necessary to achieve orderly results. Management in conjunction with leadership can produce orderly change, and leadership in conjunction with management can keep the organization properly aligned with its environment. *Management Infotech* describes Selina Lo, an individual who is clearly both a manager and a leader.

Power and Leadership

To understand leadership fully, it is necessary to understand power. **Power** is the ability to affect the behavior of others. One can have power without actually using it. For example, a football coach has the power to bench a player who is not performing up to par. The coach seldom has to use this power because players recognize that the power exists and work hard to keep their starting positions. In organizational settings, there are usually five kinds of power: legitimate, reward, coercive, referent, and expert.[5]

power The ability to affect the behavior of others

Exercise 17 *Reading Actively*

In the section entitled "Power and Leadership" on pages 52–54 turn the headings into questions and then highlight or underline the answers to the questions you've created.

You may want to add distinctive marking—such as boxes or another highlight color—to key terms within the chapter. This will make them stand out when you review later.

Finally, read with a dictionary close at hand, and always look up definitions of unfamiliar words. If you skip over words you don't know, you may lose important information or misinterpret the author's meaning. Circle each word that you do not know, look it up in your dictionary, and write its definition in the book's margin.

Exercise 18 *Defining Unfamiliar Words*

Reread the section entitled "Power and Leadership." Circle all of the words that are new to you, look them up, and write their definitions in the margins. If there is more than one definition for a word, use your understanding of the word's context within the sentence to determine the appropriate meaning.

Table 17.1

Distinctions Between Management and Leadership

Management and leadership are related, but distinct, constructs. Managers and leaders differ in how they create an agenda, develop a rationale for achieving the agenda, and execute plans, and in the types of outcomes they achieve.

Activity	Management	Leadership
Creating an agenda	**Planning and budgeting.** Establishing detailed steps and timetables for achieving needed results; allocating the resources necessary to make those needed results happen.	**Establishing direction.** Developing a vision of the future, often the distant future, and strategies for producing the changes needed to achieve that vision.
Developing a human network for achieving the agenda	**Organizing and staffing.** Establishing some structure for accomplishing plan requirements, staffing that structure with individuals, delegating responsibility and authority for carrying out the plan, providing policies and procedures to help guide people, and creating methods or systems to monitor implementation.	**Aligning people.** Communicating the direction by words and deeds to everyone whose cooperation may be needed to influence the creation of teams and coalitions that understand the vision and strategies and accept their validity.
Executing plans	**Controlling and problem solving.** Monitoring results versus planning in some detail, identifying deviations, and then planning and organizing to solve these problems.	**Motivating and inspiring.** Energizing people to overcome major political, bureaucratic, and resource barriers by satisfying very basic, but often unfulfilled, human needs.
Outcomes	Produces a degree of predictability and order and has the potential to produce consistently major results expected by various stakeholders (for example, for customers, always being on time; for stockholders, being on budget).	Produces change, often to a dramatic degree, and has the potential to produce extremely useful change (for example, new products that customers want, new approaches to labor relations that help make a firm more competitive).

Source: Reprinted with permission of The Free Press, a division of Simon & Schuster Inc. from *A Force for Change: How Leadership Differs from Management* by John P. Kotter. Copyright © 1990 by John P. Kotter, Inc.

monitors the performance of his employees, he is playing the role of manager. But when he inspires them to work harder at achieving their goals, he is a leader.

Organizations need both management and leadership if they are to be effective. Leadership is necessary to create change, and management is necessary to achieve orderly results. Management in conjunction with leadership can produce orderly change, and leadership in conjunction with management can keep the organization properly aligned with its environment. *Management Infotech* describes Selina Lo, an individual who is clearly both a manager and a leader.

Power and Leadership

To understand leadership fully, it is necessary to understand power. **Power** is the ability to affect the behavior of others. One can have power without actually using it. For example, a football coach has the power to bench a player who is not performing up to par. The coach seldom has to use this power because players recognize that the power exists and work hard to keep their starting positions. In organizational settings, there are usually five kinds of power: legitimate, reward, coercive, referent, and expert.[5]

power The ability to affect the behavior of others

522 **PART FIVE** | *The Leading Process*

MANAGEMENT INFOTECH

HARD-DRIVING MANAGEMENT IN THE HIGH-TECH ARENA

Managers in high-tech industries have to race the clock as well as the competition, as Selina Y. Lo well knows. Lo is the vice president of product management and marketing for Alteon WebSystems, a young, fast-growing company that makes sophisticated networking systems for web-based businesses such as Ticketmaster Online and Yahoo! Competing against well-established, fleet-footed rivals such as Cisco Systems, Lo uses her considerable power to speed product innovation, spur higher performance, and meet customers' needs.

One reason the CEO of Alteon hired Lo was for her keen sense of cutting-edge technology and her understanding of customer needs, developed during a rising-star background in a series of well-regarded information technology firms. She started with Hewlett-Packard after college, moved to Network Equipment Technologies, and then co-founded Centillion Networks, where she was part of the team that invented an innovative new data-switching device. Small wonder that employees and customers alike respect Lo's judgment and pay close attention when she talks about products and features.

Lo supervises product development for Alteon, a critical function in an industry where a product's life can be measured in months. She spends most of her day in the field, sniffing out customer problems. When she comes back to the office to hammer out design changes with development engineers, her aggressive management style— sometimes pounding the table, sometimes raising her voice—makes it hard for engineers to say no. Although Lo is known as a tough manager, she's also known for her habit of giving away trips and other valuable rewards to recognize performance. After fifteen years in the networking industry, Lo is anything but shy about using her hard-driving approach to overpower the competition and push Alteon to the top of a crowded but lucrative market.

> *I've left a few dead bodies behind me.*
>
> —*Selina Y. Lo, vice president of marketing for Alteon WebSystems**

Reference: Andy Reinhardt, "'I've Left a Few Dead Bodies,'" *Business Week*, January 31, 2000, pp. 69–70 (*quote on p. 69).

---

legitimate power Power granted through the organizational hierarchy; it is the power accorded people occupying particular positions as defined by the organization

Legitimate Power **Legitimate power** is power granted through the organizational hierarchy; it is the power accorded people occupying particular positions as defined by the organization. A manager can assign tasks to a subordinate, and a subordinate who refuses to do them can be reprimanded or even fired. Such outcomes stem from the manager's legitimate power as defined and vested in her or him by the organization. Legitimate power, then, is authority. All managers have legitimate power over their subordinates. The mere possession of legitimate power, however, does not by itself make someone a leader. Some subordinates follow only orders that are strictly within the letter of organizational rules and policies. If asked to do something not in their job description, they refuse or do a poor job. The manager of such employees is exercising authority but not leadership.

reward power The power to give or withhold rewards, such as salary increases, bonuses, promotion recommendations, praise, recognition, and interesting job assignments

Reward Power **Reward power** is the power to give or withhold rewards. Rewards that a manager may control include salary increases, bonuses, promotion recommendations, praise, recognition, and interesting job assignments. In general, the greater the number of rewards a manager controls and the more important the rewards are to subordinates, the greater is the manager's reward power. If the subordinate sees as valuable only the formal organizational rewards provided by the manager, then he or she is not a leader. If the subordinate also wants and appreciates the manager's informal rewards like praise, gratitude, and recognition, however, then the manager is also exercising leadership.

Coercive Power   **Coercive power** is the power to force compliance by means of psychological, emotional, or physical threat. In the past physical coercion in organizations was relatively common. In most organizations today, however, coercion is limited to verbal and written reprimands, disciplinary layoffs, fines, demotion, and termination. Some managers occasionally go so far as to use verbal abuse, humiliation, and psychological coercion in an attempt to manipulate subordinates. (Of course, most people would agree that these managerial behaviors are not appropriate.) James Dutt, former CEO of Beatrice Company, once told a subordinate that if his wife and family got in the way of his working a twenty-four-hour day seven days a week, he should get rid of them.[6] The more punitive the elements under a manager's control and the more important they are to subordinates, the more coercive power the manager possesses. On the other hand, the more a manager uses coercive power, the more likely he is to provoke resentment and hostility and the less likely he is to be seen as a leader.[7]

Referent Power   Compared with legitimate, reward, and coercive power, which are relatively concrete and grounded in objective facets of organizational life, **referent power** is abstract. It is based on identification, imitation, loyalty, or charisma. Followers may react favorably because they identify in some way with a leader, who may be like them in personality, background, or attitudes. In other situations, followers might choose to imitate a leader with referent power by wearing the same kinds of clothes, working the same hours, or espousing the same management philosophy. Referent power may also take the form of charisma, an intangible attribute of the leader that inspires loyalty and enthusiasm. Thus, a manager might have referent power, but it is more likely to be associated with leadership.

Expert Power   **Expert power** is derived from information or expertise. A manager who knows how to interact with an eccentric but important customer, a scientist who is capable of achieving an important technical breakthrough that no other company has dreamed of, and a secretary who knows how to unravel bureaucratic red tape all have expert power over anyone who needs that information. The more important the information and the fewer the people who have access to it, the greater is the degree of expert power possessed by any one individual. In general, people who are both leaders and managers tend to have a lot of expert power.

Expert power is often an important ingredient in the success of many people. Dr. Susan Love, for example, is a world-renowned expert on women's health in general and breast cancer in particular. Her work is widely recognized and cited, giving her the power to influence public opinion, government health policy, and the daily health habits of millions of women.

coercive power The power to force compliance by means of psychological, emotional, or physical threat

referent power The personal power that accrues to someone based on identification, imitation, loyalty, or charisma

expert power The personal power that accrues to someone based on the information or expertise that they possess

Step 3: REVIEW

The third and final step of the reading process is *review*. When you follow reading with review, you'll reinforce your understanding of the information. Your review should include some or all of the following activities:

- Reread as necessary.

- Answer the study questions or complete the exercises at the end of the chapter.

- Write a summary of the chapter.

- Discuss the chapter with your classmates and/or instructor in or outside of class.

- Outline the chapter.

- Reflect on what you have learned. Determine how you can use the information in your career, in your other courses, and in your personal life. Think about the content that surprised you, corrected your misconceptions, or reinforced information you already knew. Consider recording your reflections in a reading journal.

Exercise 19 *Reviewing a Reading Selection*

Reflect on your reading by writing at least one paragraph (on a separate sheet of paper) about what you gained from the section called "Power and Leadership." While reflecting, you might want to consider the following questions: How can you use this information in your career, in your other courses, and/or in your personal life? Did any of the information surprise you? Did the material correct any misconceptions you had? Did it reinforce ideas or information you already knew?

In summary, you may want to think about the entire reading process in terms of the *SQ3R System* created in 1941 by Francis P. Robinson. SQ3R stands for:

SURVEY	Preview the chapter's content and organization.
QUESTION	Turn headings into questions.
READ	Find answers to the questions.
RECITE	Say (silently or aloud) the answers to the questions.
REVIEW	Periodically go back over the questions to make sure you can still answer them.

More Active Reading Techniques

The previous section of this text described the basics of *active reading*: turning headings into questions, highlighting the answers, and looking up definitions of unfamiliar words. Using a few additional techniques will increase your comprehension and retention even further.

Writing notes in the margins is another effective active reading technique. As you read each paragraph, write in the margin the main idea, a brief summary, or key phrases. For instance, to see an example of the notes you might write in a section about giftedness from a psychology textbook entitled "Unusual Cognitive Ability," look to the excerpt on pages 57–58.

Completing the extra step of writing down this information may help you remember it better. Marginal notes will also allow you to quickly see important ideas when you review the material later.

Exercise 20 Writing Marginal Notations

Jot down notes in the margins of the remainder of the section on pages 59–60.

Amabile and her colleagues found that external rewards can deter creativity (e.g., Amabile, Hennessey, & Grossman, 1986). In one study, they asked groups of children or adults to create artistic products such as collages or stories. Some were simply asked to work on the project. Others were told that their project would be judged for its creativity and excellence and that rewards would be given or winners announced. Experts, who had no idea which products were created by which group, judged those from the "reward" group to be significantly less creative. Similar effects have been found in many other studies (Deci, Koestner, & Ryan, 1999, 2001).

Is creativity inherited? To some extent, perhaps it is; but there is evidence that a person's environment—including the social, economic, and political forces in it—can influence creative behavior at least as much as it influences intelligence (Amabile, 2001; Nakamura & Csikszentmihalyi, 2001). For example, the correlation between the creativity scores of identical twins reared apart is lower than that between their IQ scores (Nichols, 1978). Do you have to be smart to be creative? Creativity does appear to require a certain degree of intelligence (Simonton, 1984; Sternberg, 2001), but it may not necessarily appear as an extremely high IQ score (Simonton, 1984). Correlations between scores on IQ tests and on tests of creativity are only modest, between +.10 and +.30 (Barron & Harrington, 1981; Rushton, 1990; Simonton, 1999). This result is not surprising, because creativity as psychologists measure it requires broad, divergent thinking, whereas traditional IQ tests assess **convergent thinking**—the ability to apply logic and knowledge in order to *narrow down* the number of possible solutions to a problem. The pace of research on creativity, and its relationship to intelligence, has picked up lately (Sternberg & Dess, 2001). One result of that research has been to define the combination of intelligence and creativity in the same person as *wisdom* (Sternberg, 2001; Sternberg & O'Hara, 1999).

Unusual Cognitive Ability

Our understanding of cognitive abilities has been advanced by research on people whose cognitive abilities are unusual—people who are gifted, mentally retarded, or have learning disabilities (Robinson, Zigler, & Gallagher, 2000).

Giftedness   People with especially high IQ scores are often referred to as *gifted,* but this does not mean that they share exactly the same pattern of exceptional cognitive abilities. In one study, Robert Sternberg (2000) found that gifted people can display at least seven different combinations of the analytic, creative, and practical skills measured by his Triarchic Abilities Test.

Do all people with unusually high IQs become famous and successful in their chosen fields? One of the best-known studies of the intellectually gifted was conducted by Louis Terman and his colleagues (Oden, 1968; Sears, 1977; Terman & Oden, 1947, 1959). This study began in 1921 with the identification of more than 1,500 children whose IQ scores were very high—most higher than 135 by age 10. Periodic interviews and tests over the next 60 years revealed that few, if any, became truly creative geniuses—such as world-famous inventors, authors, artists, or composers—but only 11 failed to graduate from high school, and more than two-thirds graduated from college. Ninety-seven earned Ph.D.s; 92, law degrees; and 57, medical degrees. In 1955 their median family income was well above the national average (Terman & Oden, 1959). In general, they were physically and mentally healthier than the nongifted people and appear to have led happier, or at least more fortunate, lives (see the Focus on Research Methods section of the chapter on health, stress, and coping).

In short, although high IQ scores tend to predict longer, more successful lives (Whalley & Deary, 2001), an extremely high IQ does not guarantee special

Gifted people have high IQs but different combinations of skills

One study showed that few gifted people become world-famous creative geniuses, but they tended to have successful lives.

convergent thinking The ability to apply logic and knowledge to narrow down the number of possible solutions to a problem or perform some other complex cognitive task.

A high IQ doesn't guarantee special achievements, but studies show that gifted children have not only more basic cognitive abilities but also more motivation to achieve

distinction. Some research suggests that gifted children are not fundamentally different from other children; they just have "more" of the same basic cognitive abilities seen in all children (Dark & Benbow, 1993). Other work suggests that there may be other differences as well, such as an unusually intense motivation to master certain tasks or areas of intellectual endeavor (Lubinski et al., 2001; Winner, 2000).

Mental Retardation   People whose score on an IQ test is less than about 70 *and* who fail to display the skill at daily living, communication, and other tasks expected of those their age have traditionally been described as *mentally retarded* (American Psychiatric Association, 1994). They now are often referred to as *developmentally disabled* or *mentally challenged*. People within this very broad category differ greatly in their cognitive abilities, as well as in their ability to function independently in daily life. Table 10.3 shows a classification that divides the range of low IQ scores into categories that reflect these differences.

Some cases of mental retardation have a clearly identifiable origin. The best-known example is *Down syndrome,* which occurs when an abnormality during conception results in an extra twenty-first chromosome (Hattori et al., 2000). Children with Down syndrome typically have IQ scores in the range of 40 to 55, though some may score higher than that. There are also several inherited causes of mental retardation. The most common of these is *Fragile X* syndrome, caused by a defect on chromosome 23 (known as the *X chromosome*). More rarely, retardation is caused by inheriting *Williams syndrome* (a defect on chromosome 7) or by inheriting a gene for *phenylketonuria,* or *PKU* (which causes the body to create toxins out of milk and other foods). Retardation can also result from environmental causes, such as exposure to German measles (rubella) or alcohol or other toxins before birth; oxygen deprivation during birth; and head injuries, brain tumors, and infectious diseases (such as meningitis or encephalitis) in childhood (U.S. Surgeon General, 1999).

These categories are approximate. Especially at the upper end of the scale, many retarded persons can be taught to handle tasks well beyond what their IQ scores might suggest. Furthermore, IQ is not the only diagnostic criterion for retardation. Many people with IQs lower than 70 can function adequately in their communities and so would not be classified as mentally retarded.

table 10.3
Categories of Mental Retardation

Level of Retardation	IQ Scores	Characteristics
Mild	50–70	A majority of all the mentally retarded. Usually show no physical symptoms of abnormality. Individuals with higher IQs can marry, maintain a family, and work in unskilled jobs. Abstract reasoning is difficult for those with the lower IQs of this category. Capable of some academic learning to a sixth-grade level.
Moderate	35–49	Often lack physical coordination. Can be trained to take care of themselves and to acquire some reading and writing skills. Abilities of a 4- to 7-year-old. Capable of living outside an institution with their families.
Severe	20–34	Only a few can benefit from any schooling. Can communicate vocally after extensive training. Most require constant supervision.
Profound	Below 20	Mental age less than 3. Very limited communication. Require constant supervision. Can learn to walk, utter a few simple phrases, and feed themselves.

The Eagle Has Landed In February 2000, Richard Keebler, twenty-seven, became an Eagle Scout, the highest rank in the Boy Scouts of America. His achievement is notable not only because only 4 percent of all Scouts reach this pinnacle but also because Keebler has Down syndrome. As we come to better understand the potential, and not just the limitations, of mentally retarded people, their opportunities and their role in society will continue to expand.

 LINKAGES (a link to Memory)

metacognition   The knowledge of what strategies to apply, when to apply them, and how to deploy them in new situations.

Familial retardation refers to the 30 to 40 percent of (usually mild) cases in which there is no obvious genetic or environmental cause (American Psychiatric Association, 1994). In these cases, retardation appears to result from a complex, and as yet unknown, interaction between heredity and environment that researchers are continuing to explore (Croen, Grether, & Selvin, 2001).

In what ways are the cognitive skills of mentally retarded people deficient? Actually, they are just as good as others at recognizing simple stimuli, and their rate of forgetting information from short-term memory is no more rapid (Belmont & Butterfield, 1971). But mildly retarded people do differ from other people in three important ways (Campione, Brown, & Ferrara, 1982):

1. They perform certain mental operations more slowly, such as retrieving information from long-term memory. When asked to repeat something they have learned, they are not as quick as a person of normal intelligence.

2. They simply know fewer facts about the world. It is likely that this deficiency is a consequence of the third problem.

3. They are not very good at using particular mental strategies that may be important in learning and problem solving. For example, they do not spontaneously rehearse material that must be held in short-term memory.

What are the reasons for these deficiencies? In some ways, the differences between normal and retarded children resemble the differences between older and younger children discussed in the chapter on human development. Both younger children and retarded children show deficiencies in *metamemory*—the knowledge of how their memory works. More generally, retarded children are deficient in **metacognition:** the knowledge of what strategies to apply, when to apply them, and how to deploy them in new situations so that new specific knowledge can be gained and different problems mastered (Ferretti & Butterfield, 1989).

It is their deficiencies in metacognition that most limit the intellectual performance of mildly retarded people. For example, if retarded children are simply taught a strategy, they are not likely to use it again on their own or to transfer the strategy to a different task. It is important, therefore, to teach retarded children to evaluate the appropriateness of strategies (Wong, 1986) and to monitor the success of their strategies. Finally, like other children, retarded children must be shown that effort, combined with effective strategies, pays off (Borkowski, Weyhing, & Turner, 1986).

Despite such difficulties, the intellectual abilities of mentally retarded people can be improved to some extent. One program emphasizing positive parent-child communications began when the children were as young as thirty months old. It ultimately helped children with Down syndrome to master reading skills at a second-grade level, providing the foundation for further achievement (Rynders & Horrobin, 1980; Turkington, 1987). However, designing effective programs for retarded children is complicated because the way people learn depends not just on cognitive skills but also on social and emotional factors, including *where* they learn. Currently, there is debate about *mainstreaming*, the policy of teaching children with disabilities, including those who are retarded, in regular classrooms with children who do not have disabilities. Is mainstreaming good for retarded children? A number of studies of the cognitive and social skills of students who have been mainstreamed and those who were separated show few significant differences overall, although it appears that students at higher ability levels may gain more from being mainstreamed than their less mentally able peers (Cole et al., 1991).

Learning Disabilities   People who show a significant discrepancy between their measured intelligence and their academic performance may have a *learning disability* (National Information Center for Children and Youth with Disabilities, 2000). Learning disabilities are often seen in people with average or

Summary   **377**

An Inventive Genius When, as in the case of inventor Thomas Edison, students' academic performance falls short of what intelligence tests say they are capable of, a learning disability may be present. However, poor study skills, lack of motivation, and even the need for eyeglasses are among the many factors other than learning disabilities that can create a discrepancy between IQ scores and academic achievement. Accordingly, accurately diagnosing learning disabilities is not an easy task.

above-average IQs. For example, the problems with reading, writing, and math that Leonardo da Vinci and Thomas Edison had as children may have been due to such a disability; the problems certainly did not reflect a lack of cognitive ability!

There are several kinds of learning disabilities (Myers & Hammill, 1990; Wadsworth et al., 2000). People with *dyslexia* find it difficult to understand the meaning of what they read; they may also have difficulty in sounding out and identifying written words. *Dysphasia* is difficulty with understanding spoken words or with recalling the words one needs for effective speech. *Dysgraphia*—problems with writing—appears as an inability to form letters or as the omission or reordering of words and parts of words in one's writing. The least common learning disability, *dyscalculia*, is a difficulty with arithmetic that reflects not poor mathematical ability but rather an impairment in the understanding of quantity and/or in the comprehension of basic arithmetic principles and operations, such as addition and subtraction.

The National Joint Committee on Learning Disabilities (1994) suggests that these disorders are caused by dysfunctions in the brain; however, although brain imaging studies are helping to locate areas of dysfunction (e.g., Pugh et al., 2000; Richards et al., 2000), specific neurological causes have not yet been found. Accordingly, most researchers describe learning disabilities in terms of dysfunctional information processing (Kujala et al., 2001; Shaw et al., 1995). Diagnosis of a learning disability includes several steps. First, it is important to look for significant weaknesses in a person's listening, speaking, reading, writing, reasoning, or arithmetic skills (Brinckerhoff, Shaw, & McGuire, 1993). The person's actual ability is compared with that predicted by the person's IQ score. Tests for brain damage are also given. To help rule out alternative explanations of poor academic performance, the person's hearing, vision, and other sensory systems are tested, and factors such as poverty, family conflicts, and inadequate instruction are reviewed. Finally, alternative diagnoses such as attention deficit disorder (see the chapter on psychological disorders) must be eliminated.

LINKAGES

As noted in the chapter that introduced psychology, all of psychology's subfields are related to one another. Our discussion of test anxiety illustrates just one way in which the topic of this chapter, cognitive abilities, is linked to the subfield of motivation and emotion (which is the focus of the chapter by that name). The Linkages diagram shows ties to two other subfields as well, and there are many more ties throughout the book. Looking for linkages among subfields will help you see how they all fit together and help you better appreciate the big picture that is psychology.

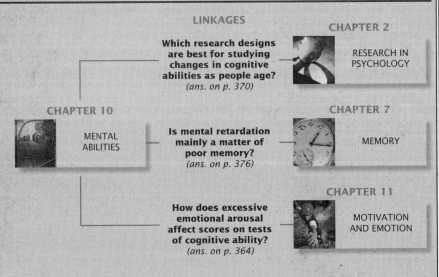

LINKAGES

Which research designs are best for studying changes in cognitive abilities as people age?
(ans. on p. 370)

CHAPTER 2
RESEARCH IN PSYCHOLOGY

CHAPTER 10
MENTAL ABILITIES

Is mental retardation mainly a matter of poor memory?
(ans. on p. 376)

CHAPTER 7
MEMORY

How does excessive emotional arousal affect scores on tests of cognitive ability?
(ans. on p. 364)

CHAPTER 11
MOTIVATION AND EMOTION

Another good active reading technique is *outlining* or *diagramming* the information as you read. An outline is a linear representation of the relationships between topics and ideas. Creating an outline will not only help you understand the relationships of ideas better, but the finished product will also become a valuable study tool. You can write either a formal, Roman numeral outline or an informal pattern you create yourself. For example, a partial formal outline of the "Unusual Cognitive Ability" section might look like this:

I. Unusual Cognitive Ability
- A. Giftedness: high IQs
- B. Mental retardation
    - 1. Levels of retardation
        - a. Mild: IQ 50 to 70
        - b. Moderate: IQ 35 to 49
        - c. Severe: IQ 20 to 34
        - d. Profound: IQ below 20
    - 2. Origins of mental retardation
        - a. Down syndrome
        - b. Inherited causes
        - c. Environmental causes
        - d. Familial retardation

An informal outline of the same section might look like this:

Unusual Cognitive Ability
1. Giftedness – high IQ
2. Mental retardation

Levels: Mild (IQ 50 to 70), Moderate (IQ 35 to 49),
           Severe (IQ 20 to 34), Profound (IQ below 20)

Origins: Down syndrome, inherited causes, environmental causes, familial retardation

Exercise 21 *Outlining Textbook Information*

On a separate sheet of paper, create an informal or formal outline for the rest of the "Unusual Cognitive Ability" section. Continue your outline from the point where the example ends.

Rather than outlining a chapter, you may find diagramming to be a more effective study aid. Like an outline, a diagram illustrates relationships; however, it uses more of a visual than a linear structure. For example, you could diagram the "Unusual Cognitive Ability" section as follows:

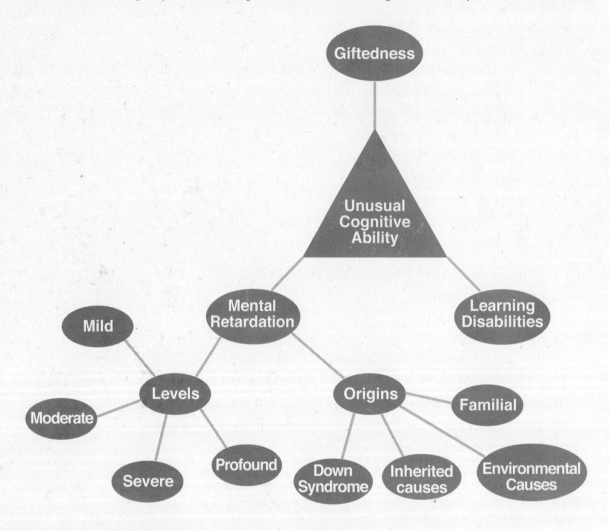

Exercise 22 *Diagramming Textbook Information*

Add to the diagram above by completing the "Learning Disabilities" section. Use a separate sheet of paper if you need more room.

One final active reading technique you might consider using is *tape-recording* your notes or outline and then listening to that recording as part of your review process. Many people find it beneficial to listen to this information as they drive or complete household tasks such as washing dishes. If you try this technique, though, remember that it's not enough to just *hear* the tape; you'll have to *listen* and pay attention to increase your retention.

"Speed" Reading and Efficient Reading

How fast should you be reading? There is no right answer to that question because your reading speed will vary depending on *what* you are reading. Factors such as the complexity of the information, the style of the writing, your prior knowledge of the subject, and your understanding of the vocabulary will all affect how fast you can read. Because of these factors, textbook reading tends to be slower than other types of reading.

Some people who dislike reading textbooks believe they can get the task over with faster by learning to "speed read." It's true that, to some extent, speed and comprehension are related. Unusually slow readers may experience more difficulty in forming an understanding of complex ideas. Also, because it's so tedious, slow reading can inhibit the reader's concentration on the material.

However, if your textbook reading skills need improvement, increasing your speed may or may not be the answer. Reading faster is meaningless if you can't remember the information when you're finished, so it's usually much more productive to focus your efforts on improving your concentration and active reading skills. Practice will also improve your reading efficiency.

If you still believe, though, that reading seems to be an unusually slow process for you, many reading experts have produced books and courses that may help you increase your speed. In general, the experts advise you to:

- **Read groups of words instead of each individual word**. If your eyes pause on each word, your reading will be much slower. Practice taking in phrases of two or three words at a time to increase your speed.

- **Stop vocalizing (moving your lips) as you read.** This habit slows down reading.

- **Avoid regression (rereading)**. Though you should always reread material that you don't understand, you want to avoid having to reread because your attention wandered. Work on developing your concentration skills to avoid having to regress.

If you are successfully practicing active reading techniques, speed may be important only as a consideration for scheduling your time. You may want to determine your pages-per-hour rate to make sure you set aside adequate time to complete your reading assignments. To determine your pages-per-hour rate, simply count the number of pages you were able to read in one hour. Divide the number of pages in a reading assignment by that rate to know how much time to schedule. Remember, though, that your rate will likely change for each different textbook, so you'll want to calculate a specific rate for each book.

Exercise 23 *Considering Reading Speed*

Do you think unusually slow reading may be inhibiting your concentration? Based on the advice in this section, what could you do to increase your reading speed?

_____

_____

_____

Critical Reading

Throughout college, you will need to develop and practice *critical-reading* skills. Reading critically does not mean finding fault with a text; it means evaluating the text and judging its validity and value. Critical readers are open-minded, yet they do not passively accept everything they see in print. Instead, they maintain a healthy skepticism, expecting the author to convince them to believe or accept his or her ideas. In other words, critical readers think for themselves as they read.

Critical reading offers several benefits. Because it requires analysis, synthesis, and evaluation of ideas and information, it improves your thinking skills. It will also help expand your knowledge and help you decide how to apply that knowledge to your own life. Finally, it will help you prepare for class assignments such as essays and research papers.

Reading critically requires the highest level of concentration. It also requires all three steps—preview, read (actively), and review—of the reading process. While you are reading and reviewing a textbook chapter, practice all of the techniques for increasing comprehension and retention. At the same time, think about the following:

- **Evaluate the information and its sources.** Authors and publishers take great care to verify the accuracy of the information they include in textbooks, so you don't necessarily need to question the facts or their sources as you would when you read other types of publications, such as editorials. However, you should evaluate the author's conclusions that are based on the evidence provided in the textbook. Ask yourself these questions and try to get in the habit of recording your thoughts in brief marginal notes as you read:

    Is there enough evidence to support each conclusion?

    Does the evidence lead logically to the state conclusion?

    Could other conclusions arise from the same information?

- **Try to make new connections beyond those provided by the author.** When you can connect new information to what you already know, you increase your understanding and your ability to recall new information. As you read about a subject, think of your own related experiences. Do they match the book's ideas and conclusion? Also, try to recall what you've learned about the subject in other courses, in other readings, or from the media. For example, connect what you learn from your humanities textbook to what you studied in your history and government classes, or think of current events in the news that relate to the information you're reading. Strive to create new "webs" of knowledge within your mind. For example, the following is an excerpt from an American government textbook. Notice how the notes in the margins illustrate critical reading:

Interpreting Political News   **273**

News shows are just giving the public what it wants, but it's a vicious cycle: the more sensational the news gets, the more it has to increase its sensationalism to feed the public's appetite for ever more sensational stories!

negative campaign advertising—that is, of ads that lambaste opponents and attack them on a personal level. Adversarial media coverage has helped make these types of ads more socially acceptable. The reason candidates use attack ads is simple: they work. A good negative ad will change the preferences of some voters. But this change is purchased at a price. Research shows that a negative ad not only changes voter preferences, it reduces voter turnout. Negative advertising may help a candidate win, but only by turning other people against elections.

Sensationalism in the Media

Back in the 1930s newspaper reporters knew that President Franklin Roosevelt had a romantic affair with a woman other than his wife. They did not report it. In the early 1960s many reporters knew that President John Kennedy had many sexual affairs outside his marriage. They did not report this. In 1964 the director of the Federal Bureau of Investigation played for reporters secret tape recordings of the Reverend Martin Luther King, Jr., having sex with women other than his wife. They did not report it.

I've never heard this—author's source?

By the 1980s sex and politics were extensively covered. When presidential candidate Gary Hart was caught in adultery and when President Bill Clinton was accused of adultery by Gennifer Flowers, of asking for sexual favors by Paula Jones, and of having sex with Monica Lewinsky in the Oval Office, these were headline news stories.

What had changed? Not politics: all of the people whom the press protected or reported on were Democrats. The big change was in the economics of journalism and the ideas of reporters.

and in changes in the public, too!

Until the 1970s Americans gathered their political news from one of three networks—ABC, CBS, or NBC. For a long time these networks had only one half-hour news show a day. Today, however, viewers have the same three networks plus three cable news networks, two sports networks, ten weekly newsmagazine shows, countless radio talk shows, and the Internet. Many of the cable networks, such as CNN, carry news 24 hours a day. The result of this intense competition is that each radio or television network has a small share of the audience. Today less than half the public watches the evening network news shows. Dozens of news programs are trying to reach a shrinking audience, with the result that the audience share of each program is small. To attract any

audience at all, each program has a big incentive to rely on sensational news stories—sex, violence, and intrigue. Reinforcing this desire to go with sensationalism is the fact that covering such stories is cheaper than investigating foreign policy or analyzing the tax code. During its first month, the Lewinsky story consumed more than one-third of the on-air time of the news networks—more than the U.S. showdown with Iran, the Winter Olympics, the pope's visit to Cuba, and the El Niño weather pattern combined.

Since the days of Vietnam and Watergate, journalists have become adversaries of the government. They instinctively distrust people in government. But to that attitude change can be added an economic one: in their desperate effort to reclaim market share, journalists are much more likely to rely on unnamed sources than once was the case. When the *Washington Post* broke the Watergate story in the 1970s, it required the reporters to have at least two sources for their stories. Now many reporters break stories that have only one unnamed source, and often not a source at all but a rumor posted on the Internet.

Yes—I learned this in my journalism class

As a result, reporters are more easily manipulated by sources than once was the case. Spokesmen for President Clinton tried to "spin" the news about his affairs, usually by attacking his critics. Gennifer Flowers, Paula Jones, and Monica Lewinsky were portrayed as bimbos, liars, or stalkers. Much of the press used the spin. To see how successful spin can be, compare independent counsel Lawrence Walsh's investigation of aides to President Ronald Reagan over the sale of arms to Iran with independent counsel Kenneth Starr's investigation of the Clinton administration. Walsh's inquiry got full press support, while Starr was regularly attacked by the press.

Americans seem to be more adversarial in general

Since the terrorist attack on the United States on September 11, 2001, there has been scattered evidence to suggest that sensationalism in the media has declined a bit, while public interest in national news and trust of news organizations have increased somewhat. The big stories of the preceding years were the sexual conduct of President Clinton and the connection between California representative Gary Condit and a missing young woman. After September 11, the press focused on a more important matter—defeating terrorism at home and abroad. By early 2002, surveys indicated that the number of people

Many textbooks will include questions that encourage you to read critically. For example, the excerpt "Sensationalism in the Media" comes from the chapter entitled "The Media" in an American government textbook. The authors of this textbook begin every chapter by posing several questions for critical thinking. One of them is, "Can we trust the media to be fair?" Readers should consider their answers to such questions before, during, and after reading a chapter.

Exercise 24 Reading Critically

Critically read the excerpt from an American government textbook on pages 67–69. Record your thoughts and responses in the form of marginal notations.

Americans are often embarrassed by their low rate of participation in national elections. Data such as those shown in Table 6.1 are frequently used to make the point: whereas well over 80 percent of the people vote in many European elections, only about half of the people vote in American presidential elections (and a much smaller percentage vote in congressional contests). Many observers blame this low turnout on voter apathy and urge the government and private groups to mount campaigns to get out the vote.

There are only three things wrong with this view. First, it is a misleading description of the problem; second, it is an incorrect explanation of the problem; and third, it proposes a remedy that won't work.

A Closer Look at Nonvoting

First, let's look at how best to describe the problem. The conventional data on voter turnout here and abroad are misleading because they compute participation rates by two different measures. In this country only two-thirds of the voting-age population is registered to vote. To understand what this means,

131

132   *Chapter 6   Political Participation*

Table 6.1	Two Ways of Calculating Voter Turnout, 1996–2001 Elections, Selected Countries		
A Turnout as Percentage of Voting-Age Population		**B** Turnout as Percentage of Registered Voters	
Belgium	83.2%	Australia	95.2%
Denmark	83.1	Belgium	90.6
Australia	81.8	Denmark	86.0
Sweden	77.7	New Zealand	83.1
Finland	76.8	Germany	82.2
Germany	75.3	Sweden	81.4
New Zealand	74.6	Austria	80.4
Norway	73.0	France	79.7
Austria	72.6	Finland	76.8
France	72.3	Norway	75.0
Netherlands	70.1	Netherlands	73.2
Japan	59.0	UNITED STATES	63.4
United Kingdom	57.6	Japan	62.0
Canada	54.6	Canada	61.2
UNITED STATES	47.2	United Kingdom	59.4
Switzerland	34.9	Switzerland	43.2

Source: From the International Institute for Democracy and Electoral Assistance (IDEA), *Voter Turnout: A Global Survey* (Stockholm, Sweden, 2001). Reprinted with the permission of Cambridge University Press.

look at Table 6.1. In column A are several countries ranked in terms of the percentage of the **voting-age population** that voted in 1996–2001 national elections. As you can see, the United States, where 47.2 percent voted, ranked near the bottom; only Switzerland was lower. Now look at column B, where the same countries are ranked in terms of the percentage of **registered voters** who participated in these national elections. The United States, where 63.4 percent of registered voters turned out at the polls, is now fifth from the bottom.[1]

Second, let's consider a better explanation for the problem. Apathy on election day is clearly not the source of the problem. Of those who are registered, the overwhelming majority vote. The real source of the participation problem in the United States is that a relatively low percentage of the adult population is registered to vote.

Third, let's look at how to cure the problem. Mounting a get-out-the-vote drive wouldn't make much difference. What might make a difference is a plan that would get more people to register to vote. But doing that does not necessarily involve overcoming the "apathy" of unregistered voters. Some people may not register because they don't care about poli-

tics or their duty as citizens. But there are other explanations for being unregistered. In this country the entire burden of registering to vote falls on the individual voters. They must learn how and when and where to register; they must take the time and trouble to go someplace and fill out a registration form; and they must reregister in a new county or state if they happen to move. In most European nations registration is done for you, automatically, by the government. Since it is costly to register in this country and costless to register in other countries, it should not be surprising that fewer people are registered here than abroad.

In 1993 Congress passed a law designed to make it easier to register to vote. Known as the **motor-voter law,** the law requires states to allow people to register to vote when applying for driver's licenses and to provide registration through the mail and at some state offices that serve the disabled or provide public assistance (such as welfare checks). The motor-voter law took effect in 1995. In just two months, 630,000 new voters signed up in twenty-seven states. Even so, the results of the law so far have been mixed.

Only 49 percent of eligible voters went to the polls in 1996, and in North Dakota, where voters are not required to register, turnout was still only 56 percent.[2] In 1998 only 17.6 percent of the eligible electorate voted in primary elections, and a record-low 36.1 percent of the voting-age population cast ballots in the midterm congressional elections.[3] On the other hand, registration among the voting-age population rose to 70.1 percent in 1998, the highest in a nonpresidential year since 1970, and turnout was less depressed in states that had fully implemented the motor-voter law or instituted universal election-day registration programs.[4] Contrary to the fears of congressional Republicans (90 percent of whom opposed the motor-voter law) and the hopes of congressional Democrats (95 percent of whom supported it), the adoption of motor-voter programs has not changed the two-party balance of registrants, but it has increased independent registrations.[5] The motor-voter law has allowed a lot of people to register that way. In 1999–2000, 17.4 million voter registration applications were filed at motor vehicle offices, representing over a third of all such applications filed during that period (see Figure 6.1).

Still, there is scant evidence that the motor-voter law has had much of an impact on either voter

A Closer Look at Nonvoting **133**

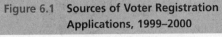

Figure 6.1   Sources of Voter Registration Applications, 1999–2000

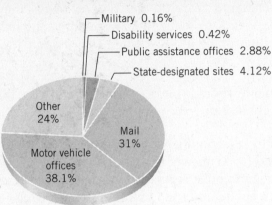

- Military 0.16%
- Disability services 0.42%
- Public assistance offices 2.88%
- State-designated sites 4.12%

Other 24%

Mail 31%

Motor vehicle offices 38.1%

Source: Federal Election Commission, *Executive Summary— Report to the Congress,* 2000.

turnout or election outcomes. A 2001 study found that turnout of motor voter registrants was lower than that of other new registrants, and concluded "that those who register when the process is costless are less likely to vote."[6]

A final point: voting is only one way of participating in politics. It is important (we could hardly be considered a democracy if nobody voted), but it is not all-important. Joining civic associations, supporting social movements, writing to legislators, fighting city hall—all these and other activities are ways of participating in politics. It is possible that, by these measures, Americans participate in politics *more* than most Europeans—or anybody else, for that matter. Moreover, it is possible that low rates of registration indicate that people are reasonably well satisfied with how the country is governed. If 100 percent of all adult Americans registered and voted (especially under a system that makes registering relatively difficult), it could mean that people were deeply upset about how things were run. In short it is not at all clear whether low voter turnout is a symptom of political disease or a sign of political good health.

The important question about participation is not how much participation there is but how different kinds of participation affect the kind of government we get. This question cannot be answered just by

MOTOR VOTER REGISTRATION INSTRUCTIONS

You must complete steps 1-3. Failure to provide this information may jeopardize your registration.

BOX 1   <u>Print</u> your name on the line in box # 1.

BOX 2   Please read the oath and then sign your name in the grey shaded area next to the RED X. This signature attests that you meet the qualifications of the oath.

BOX 3   Enter your daytime phone number, and date of birth.

BOX 4   If you are changing your address, or name, or have been registered to vote before, please write the name and address at which you were previously registered in box 4.

BOX 5   Do you want to be registered at the address on your current license or I.D. card?
  - If Yes, skip box #5.
  - If No, please write the address where you live in box #5. (You may not use a work address as your residence address.)

BOX 6   If your mailing address is different from the address where you live please write your mailing address in box #6. (You may not use a work address for mailing purposes.)

BOX 7   Please sign your name next to the RED X on the lower half of the form.

BOX 8   Please print your name.

OATH

"I declare that the facts relating to my qualifications as a voter recorded on this voter registration form are true. I am a citizen of the United States, I am not presently denied my civil rights as a result of being convicted of an infamous crime, I will have lived in this state, county, and precinct for thirty days immediately preceding the next election at which I offer to vote, and I will be at least eighteen years of age at the time of voting."

| ORIGINAL REGISTER OF VOTER | | | | |

"I declare that the facts relating to my qualifications as a voter recorded on this voter registration form are true. I am a citizen of the United States, I am not presently denied my civil rights as a result of being convicted of an infamous crime, I will have lived in this state, county, and precinct for thirty days immediately preceding the next election at which I offer to vote, and I will be at least eighteen years of age at the time of voting."

1.   2. SIGN HERE X

VOTER - PLEASE PRINT FULL NAME HERE   SIGNATURE OF VOTER – PLEASE SIGN WITHIN SHADED AREA

3. (AREA CODE) TELEPHONE NUMBER   4. PRINT FORMER NAME

DATE OF BIRTH (MONTH-DAY-YEAR)   PRINT FORMER ADDRESS

5. ADDRESS WHERE YOU LIVE   CITY OR TOWN   ZIP CODE

6. ADDRESS WHERE YOU RECEIVE YOUR MAIL   CITY OR TOWN   ZIP CODE

FOR OFFICE USE ONLY

REGISTRATION NUMBER   DATE OF REGISTRATION   Record Signing of Petitions Here (in Pencil)

PRECINCT CODE   PRECINCT NAME   DISTRICT/LEVY CODE

WARNING

Knowingly providing false information on this voter registration form or knowingly making a false declaration about your qualifications for registration is a class C felony that is punishable by imprisonment for up to five years, or by a fine not to exceed ten thousand dollars, or by both such imprisonment and fine. *(RCW 29.07.070)*

LAST NAME (Print)   FIRST NAME   INITIAL

REGISTRATION NUMBER   7. SIGN HERE X

COUNTY   SIGNATURE OF VOTER

8.   VOTER - PLEASE PRINT NAME HERE

STREET AND NUMBER OR RURAL ROUTE   REGISTRATION DATE

CITY   ZIP CODE

RECORD SIGNING OF PETITIONS HERE (in Pencil)

Motor Voter

Secretary of State Form VR –7/93

When you apply for a driver's license in the state of Washington, you are given this form so that you can register to vote at the same time. This "motor-voter" idea became the basis of a federal law passed in 1993.

Language and Learning

When you need to learn something new, use the power of language to do it. Language is an amazing tool for helping us understand what we know and for revealing what we don't know. Has anyone ever asked you to talk about a topic you'd thought about but never discussed before? As you searched for and said the words that expressed your thoughts or beliefs about that topic, you probably found that those thoughts and beliefs became clearer to you, too. As long as they stay only in our minds, ideas and opinions have a tendency to remain fuzzy, shadowy, and half-formed. When we communicate them to others—either orally or in writing—they assume more definite shape and form.

Therefore, when you read and study information in a textbook, you may not know for sure that you've grasped that information until you can talk about it or write about it.

Talking to Learn. Take advantage of opportunities to talk about what you're learning. Engage in the classroom discussions led by your instructor, and try to answer the questions he or she poses to the class. Form study groups with your classmates, and meet regularly to discuss the course material. Note the topics you aren't able to say much about, and spend more time reviewing those topics. You might even talk with friends and family about what you're learning. For example, if someone you know finds history interesting, talk to him or her about your Civil War studies.

Writing to Learn. Writing, too, requires you to find the language that helps solidify your knowledge about a subject. This writing does not have to be in the form of an assignment—such as an essay or a research paper—you submit for a grade. Informal types of writing can also be valuable learning tools. After reading a textbook section or chapter, put your book aside and try to write a summary of the information. Then, reread that section to check for and fill in any gaps in your knowledge.

Freewriting is another good way to explore and reinforce your understanding. For a set period of time, say 10 or 15 minutes, write as fast as you can about what you read, without stopping or pausing to correct or to censor anything. Don't worry about organization or grammar or spelling. Just concentrate on the topic itself and write down everything you can remember. This technique will reveal what you know and what you still need to learn.

Exercise 25 *Writing to Learn*

1. On a separate sheet of paper, freewrite for ten minutes about what you learned by reading "A Closer Look at Nonvoting," in Exercise 24.

2. What did this freewritng exercise reveal to you about what you learned? If you were going to be tested on the information in this section, what topics or details would you probably need to study more?

_____

_____

_____

_____

Part 3
Using Textbook Features and the Reading Strategies: Practice Exercises

Exercise 1 Economics: "Demand"

Actively read the excerpt from an economics textbook that follows, and then answer the questions below by circling the letter of the correct response.

1. What is the topic of this excerpt?
    a. Economics
    b. Bicycles
    c. Demand
    d. Price

2. How many key terms are highlighted and defined in this section?
    a. One
    b. Three
    c. Five
    d. Seven

3. Which of the following learning objectives corresponds to this section?
    a. Explain the law of supply.
    b. Define the term *demand*.
    c. List the steps involved in selling a bicycle to consumers.
    d. Discuss why people go into debt for things they don't really need.

The following sentences appear in the chapter. Circle the letter of the BEST meaning for each italicized word.

4. "Demand is a relationship between two economic *variables*...."
    a. Parts of a system
    b. Opinions
    c. Opposites
    d. Things prone to change

5. "...the quantity *consumers* are willing to buy depends on many other things besides the price of the good...."
    a. Business owners
    b. People who purchase and use goods and services
    c. Wealthy people
    d. People who save money

6. "Demand can be represented with a *numerical* table or a graph."
    a. Relating to numbers
    b. Relating to words
    c. Relating to economics
    d. Relating to computers

49

scissors are connected to form the scissors, they become an amazingly useful, yet simple, tool. So it is with the supply and demand model.

In this chapter, we first describe each of the three elements of the model. We then show how to use the model to answer a host of questions about price determination in a market economy.

Demand

demand: a relationship between **price** and **quantity demanded.**

price: the amount of money or other goods that one must pay to obtain a particular good.

quantity demanded: the quantity of a good that people want to buy at a given price during a specific time period.

Table 3.1
Demand Schedule for Bicycles (millions of bicycles per year)

Price	Quantity Demanded
$140	18
$160	14
$180	11
$200	9
$220	7
$240	5
$260	3
$280	2
$300	1

demand schedule: a tabular presentation of demand showing the price and quantity demanded for a particular good, all else being equal.

law of demand: the tendency for the quantity demanded of a good in a market to decline as its price rises.

To an economist, the term *demand*—whether the demand for health care or the demand for computers—has a very specific meaning. **Demand** is a relationship between two economic variables: (1) *the price of a particular good* and (2) *the quantity of the good consumers are willing to buy at that price during a specific time period*, all other things being equal. For short, we call the first variable the **price** and the second variable the **quantity demanded.** The phrase *all other things being equal*, or *ceteris paribus*, is appended to the definition of demand because the quantity consumers are willing to buy depends on many other things besides the price of the good; we want to hold these other things constant, or equal, while we examine the relationship between price and quantity demanded.

Demand can be represented with a numerical table or a graph. In either case, demand describes how much of a good consumers will purchase at each price. Consider the demand for bicycles in the United States. An example of the demand for bicycles is shown in Table 3.1. Several prices for a typical bicycle are listed in the first column of the table, ranging from $140 to $300. Of course, there are many kinds of bicycles—mountain bikes, racing bikes, children's bikes, and inexpensive one-speed bikes with cruiser brakes—so you need to think about the price of an average, or typical, bike.

Listed in the second column of Table 3.1 is the quantity demanded (in millions of bicycles) each year in the United States at the price in the first column. This is the total demand in the bicycle market. For example, at a price of $180 per bicycle, consumers would buy 11 million bicycles. That is, the quantity demanded would be 11 million bicycles each year in the United States, according to Table 3.1.

Observe that as the price rises, the quantity demanded by consumers goes down. If the price goes up from $180 to $200 per bicycle, for example, the quantity demanded goes down from 11 million to 9 million bicycles. On the other hand, if the price goes down, the quantity demanded goes up. If the price falls from $180 to $160, for example, the quantity demanded rises from 11 million to 14 million bicycles.

The relationship between price and quantity demanded in Table 3.1 is called a **demand schedule.** This relationship is an example of the law of demand. The **law of demand** says that the higher the price, the lower the quantity demanded in the market; and the lower the price, the higher the quantity demanded in the market. In other words, the law of demand says that the price and the quantity demanded are negatively related, all other things being equal.

The Demand Curve

Figure 3.1 represents demand graphically. It is a graph with the price of the good on the vertical axis and the quantity demanded of the good on the horizontal axis. It shows the demand for bicycles given in Table 3.1. Each of the nine rows in Table 3.1

For each of the following review questions, write your answer on the blanks provided.

7. Explain the relationship between price and quantity, as they relate to demand.

   _____

   _____

8. Explain the law of demand.

   _____

   _____

   _____

9. Give an example of a specific product that has recently experienced an increase in demand as its price went down.

   _____

   _____

   _____

Circle the letter of the correct response.

10. Which of the following conclusions based on Table 3.1 is accurate?
    a. As price rises, demand rises.
    b. As price falls, demand increases.
    c. The quantity is always half the amount of the price.
    d. Most people want to own $300 bicycles.

Exercise 2 Psychology: "Stress and Stressors"

Actively read the excerpt from a psychology textbook on pages 75–76 and then answer the questions by circling the letter of the correct response or writing the answer on the blank provided, as appropriate.

1. Following the excerpt is the outline for the chapter in which this section appears. Based on this outline, you can conclude that the section entitled "Stress and Stressors" is
   a. a major section of the chapter.
   b. a sub-section of the "Health Psychology" section.
   c. a sub-section of the "Stress Responses" section.
   d. equal in level to the "Stress, Illness, and the Immune System" section.

2. Before you actively read this excerpt, into what question did you transform the section heading?

   _____

   _____

This table shows five of the leading causes of death in the United States today, along with behavioral factors that contribute to their development.

table 13.1
Lifestyle Behaviors That Affect the Leading Causes of Death in the United States

Cause of Death	Contributing Behavioral Factor				
	Alcohol	**Smoking**	**Diet**	**Exercise**	**Stress**
Heart disease	x	x	x	x	x
Cancer	x	x	x		?
Stroke	x	x	x	?	?
Lung disease		x			
Accidents and Injury	x	x			x

Source: Data from USDHHS (1990); Centers for Disease Control and Prevention (1999a).

Running for Your Life Health psychologists have developed programs to help people increase exercise, stop smoking, eat healthier diets, and make other lifestyle changes that lower their risk of illness and death. They have even helped to insure community blood supplies by finding ways to make blood donation less stressful (Bonk, France, & Taylor, 2001).

century, the major causes of illness and death in the United States and Canada were acute infectious diseases, such as influenza, tuberculosis, and pneumonia. With these afflictions now less threatening, chronic illnesses—such as coronary heart disease, cancer, and diabetes—have joined accidents and injuries as the leading causes of disability and death (Guyer et al., 2000). Further, psychological, lifestyle, and environmental factors play substantial roles in determining whether a person will fall victim to these modern-day killers (Taylor, 1999). For example, lifestyle choices, such as whether a person smokes, affect the risk for the five leading causes of death for men and women in the United States (D'Agostino et al., 2001; Lichtenstein et al., 2000; see Table 13.1). Further, the psychological and behavioral factors that contribute to these illnesses can be altered by psychological interventions, including programs that promote nonsmoking and low-fat diets. As many as half of all deaths in the United States are due to potentially preventable lifestyle behaviors (National Cancer Institute, 1994).

Health psychologists have been active in helping people understand the role they can play in controlling their own health and life expectancy (Baum, Revenson, & Singer, 2001). For example, they have promoted early detection of disease by educating people about the warning signs of cancer, heart disease, and other serious illnesses and encouraging them to seek medical attention while lifesaving treatment is still possible. Health psychologists also study, and help people to understand, the role played by stress in physical health and illness.

Stress and Stressors

You have probably heard that death and taxes are the only two things you can be sure of in life. If there is a third, it must surely be stress. Stress is basic to life—no matter how wealthy, powerful, attractive, or happy you might be. It comes in many forms—a difficult exam, an automobile accident, waiting in a long line, a day on which everything goes wrong. Mild stress can be stimulating, motivating, and sometimes desirable. But as it becomes more severe, stress can bring on physical, psychological, and behavioral problems.

Stress is the negative emotional and physiological process that occurs as individuals try to adjust to or deal with **stressors**, which are environmental circumstances that disrupt, or threaten to disrupt, individuals' daily functioning and cause

stress The process of adjusting to circumstances that disrupt, or threaten to disrupt, a person's equilibrium.

stressors Events or situations to which people must adjust.

488   Chapter 13   Health, Stress, and Coping

figure 13.1

The Process of Stress

Stressful events, people's reactions to those events, and interactions between people and the situations they face are all important components of stress. Notice the two-way relationships in the stress process. For example, if a person has effective coping skills, stress responses will be less severe. Having milder stress responses will act as a "reward" that will strengthen those skills. Further, as coping skills (such as refusing unreasonable demands) improve, certain stressors (such as a boss's unreasonable demands) may become less frequent.

people to make adjustments (Taylor, 1999). In other words, stress involves a *transaction* between people and their environment. Figure 13.1 lists the main types of stressors and illustrates that when confronted by stressors, people respond physically (e.g., with nervousness, nausea, and fatigue), as well as psychologically.

As also shown in Figure 13.1, the transaction between people and their environment can be influenced by *stress mediators,* which include such variables as the extent to which people can predict and control their stressors, how they interpret the threat involved, the social support they get, and their stress-coping skills. (We discuss these mediators in greater detail later.) So stress is not a specific event but a *process* in which the nature and intensity of stress responses depend to a large degree on factors such as the way people think about stressors and the skills and resources they have to cope with them.

For humans, most stressors have both physical and psychological components. Students, for example, are challenged by psychological demands to do well in their courses, as well as by the physical fatigue that can result from a heavy load of classes, combined perhaps with a job and family responsibilities. Similarly, for victims of arthritis, AIDS, and other chronic illnesses, physical pain is accompanied by worry and other forms of psychological distress (Melzack, 1973; Salovey et al., 1992). Here, we focus on psychological stressors, which can stimulate some of the same physiological responses as physical stressors (Cacioppo et al., 1995).

Psychological Stressors

Any event that forces people to accommodate or change can be a psychological stressor. Accordingly, even pleasant events can be stressful (Brown & McGill, 1989). For example, the increased salary and status associated with a promotion may be desirable, but the upgrade usually brings new pressures as well (Schaubroeck, Jones, & Xie, 2001). Similarly, people often feel exhausted after a vacation. Still, it is typically negative events that have the most adverse psychological and physical effects (Kessler, 1997). These circumstances include catastrophic events, life changes and strains, chronic stressors, and daily hassles (Baum, Gatchel, & Krantz, 1997).

Catastrophic events are sudden, unexpected, potentially life-threatening experiences or traumas, such as physical or sexual assault, military combat, natural disasters, terrorist attacks, and accidents. *Life changes* and *strains* include divorce, illness in the family, difficulties at work, moving to a new place, and other circumstances that create demands to which people must adjust (Price, 1992; see Table 13.2). *Chronic stressors*—those that continue over a long period of time—include circumstances such as living near a noisy airport, having a serious illness, being unable to earn a decent living, residing in a high-crime neighborhood, being the victim of discrimination, and even enduring years of academic pressure (Evans, Hygge, & Bullinger, 1995; Levenstein, Smith, & Kaplan, 2001). *Daily hassles* include irritations, pressures, and annoyances that might not be significant stressors by themselves but whose cumulative effects can be significant (Evans & Johnson, 2000).

Health, Stress, and Coping

13

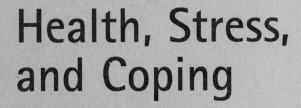

485

3. What technique did you use to mark the answers to the question as you read? Did you underline answers? Highlight them? Did you take notes in the margins?

    _____

    _____

    _____

The following sentences appear in the chapter. Circle the letter of the BEST meaning for each italicized word.

4. "Stress is the negative emotional and *physiological* process that occurs as individuals try to adjust to or deal with stressors…."
    a. Related to the mind
    b. Related to biological functions
    c. Related to stress
    d. Related to medicine

5. "Still, it is typically negative events that have the most *adverse* psychological and physical effects."
    a. Minor
    b. Rapid
    c. Irreversible
    d. Harmful

6. "Daily hassles include irritations, pressures, and annoyances that might not be significant stressors by themselves but whose *cumulative* effects can be significant."
    a. Immediate
    b. Decreasing over time
    c. Increasing or enlarging by accumulation
    d. Negative

Circle the letter of the correct response.

7. Based upon Figure 13.1, which of the following is an accurate conclusion?
    a. Daily hassles are a stress response.
    b. Stress mediators affect both stressors and stress responses.
    c. Chronic stressors always produce emotional behavioral responses.
    d. If a person does not have social support, then a life change will produce cognitive stress responses.

8. Environmental circumstances that disrupt, or threaten to disrupt, individuals' daily functioning and cause people to make adjustments are called
    a. stress.
    b. stressors.
    c. stress mediators.
    d. stress responses.

9. Which of the following is NOT a kind of psychological stressor?
   a. Catastrophic events
   b. Chronic stressors
   c. Stress mediators
   d. Life changes

10. Aretha had a tough week filled with many stressful events. Which one of them was a chronic stressor?
   a. A water pipe burst and filled her office with water. Most of the files she had been working on were totally ruined.
   b. On the subway on her way to work, a person splashed Aretha's suit jacket with a can of soda he was drinking.
   c. Her daughter was diagnosed with diabetes.
   d. Another poor company quarterly report meant that she would have to do without a much-needed raise.

Exercise 3 Communication: "Kinesics: Body Communication"

Actively read the excerpt from a communication textbook on pages 80–83, and then answer the questions by circling the letter of the correct response or writing the answer on the blank provided, as appropriate.

1. Describe the internal and external distractions you encountered as you read this passage. How did you overcome these distractions in order to concentrate on what you were reading?

   _____

   _____

   _____

2. The headings within this section indicate that
   a. Kinesics is a specific type of ocalics.
   b. Ocalics is a specific type of facsics.
   c. Ocalics is one specific type of kinesics.
   d. Kinesics and facsics are specific types of ocalics.

The following sentences appear in the chapter. Circle the letter of the BEST meaning for each italicized word.

3. "They are also so *subtle* that they can just pass by us as an observer."
   a. Meaningless
   b. Not obvious
   c. Invisible
   d. Unbelievable

64 Part One Foundations of Communication

Kinesics: Body Communication

Kinesics is the study of communication through the body and its body movements. We communicate through the gestures we use, the way we walk and stand, the expressions on our faces and in our eyes, the manner in which we combine these variables to open or close channels, and what we look like. Specific areas studied in the area of kinesics are facsics; ocalics; gestics; haptics; posture, walk, and stance; artifactics; and physical characteristics.

Facsics Facsics is the study of how the face communicates. "The 80 muscles of the face can create more than 7,000 expressions."[29] These expressions range from

Figure 3.3	**Categories of Nonverbal Communication**

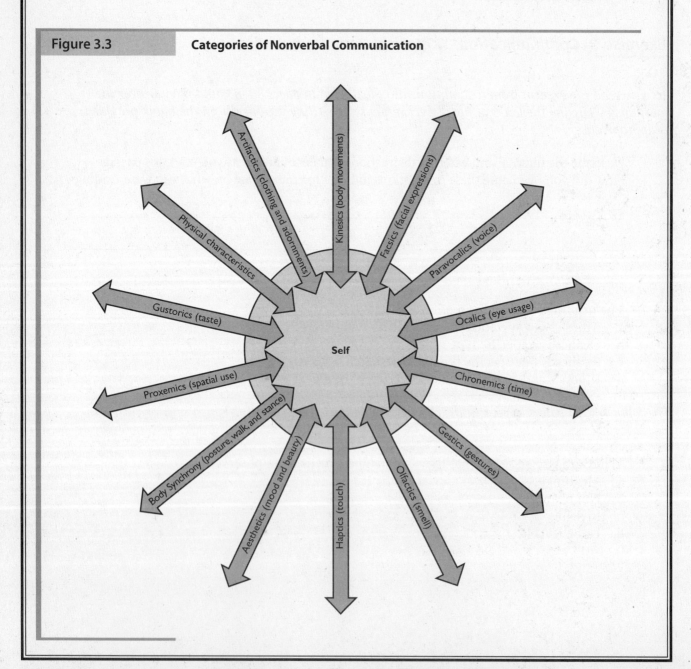

communicating our internal states such as anger or fear, to carrying messages to others of whether we want to interrupt what they are saying or are interested and want them to continue to speak. The face sends information about our personality, interests, responsiveness, and emotional states. How we perceive another person is often based on that person's facial expressions as we observe or interact with her.

Research on the face and its messages has been conducted through FACS (Facial Action Coding System). Through this process, we have more data about the face than about any other area of nonverbal communication.[30] What has been determined is that facial expressions are highly complex. Facial expressions are movements of such brief duration that if we don't watch carefully, we miss the message. They are also so subtle that they can just pass by us as an observer. An upturn of the corners of the mouth, nasal cavity expansions, an eyebrow arching, a dropping jaw, or open mouth are so subtle that they are often overlooked and the message is not conveyed.

Reading Body Language to Fight Terror

Learning to read body language is one skill FBI agents use to combat terror. Anxious people give off signals that trained personnel may be able to spot.

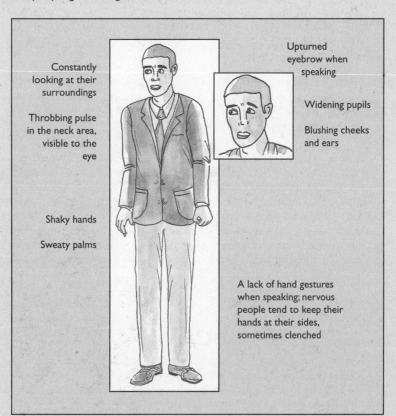

Source: Christopher Newton, "New FBI Agents Get Terrorism Training," *Cleveland Plain Dealer,* August 28, 2002, p. A14. Orginal source: Center for Nonverbal Communication.

66   Part One   Foundations of Communication

Research has established that nonverbal language is an important means of expression.

The FACS studies indicate that such emotions as anger, fear, disgust, sadness, happiness, surprise, and contempt may be universal signals. However, other research states that there is not enough evidence to prove this. Because each language system has its own words for these emotions, there would still be questions over the universal theory.[31]

Based on his early study of facsics, the leading FACS researcher summarized the importance of the face in communication when he said, "It's the one social fact that accurately reflects our subjective experiences. It's the only reflection of man's inner emotional life that is visible to the world." If anything, follow-up research has proved him to be correct.[32]

Ocalics   **Ocalics** is the study of how the eyes communicate. Winking, closing the eyes, and raising or lowering the eyelids and eyebrows can convey meaning.

The eye, unlike other organs of the body, is an extension of the brain.[33] Because of this, it is almost impossible for an individual to disguise eye meaning from someone who is a member of the same culture. Sayings such as "Look at the sparkle in her eye" and "He couldn't look me straight in the eye" have meaning. Of all our features, our eyes are the most revealing. Often they communicate without our even knowing it. For example, when the pupils of our eyes are dilated, we may appear friendlier, warmer, and more attractive.

A person's eye blinks have an effect on how he or she is perceived by others. For example, the slowness or rapidity of eye blinks can indicate nervousness. The normal blink rate for someone speaking is 31 to 50 blinks per minute. During the first presidential debate in 1996 between President Clinton and his Republican opponent, Bob Dole, polls indicated that Mr. Dole was considered to be very nervous. A review of the videotapes of the debate indicated that he had averaged 147 eye blinks per minute, almost three times the normal rate.[34]

A theory known as **pupilometrics** indicates that pupils dilate when the eyes are focused on a pleasurable object and contract when focused on an unpleasurable one.[35] Enlarged pupils signify interest, and contracted pupils reflect boredom. Thus, knowledgeable teachers often watch the pupils of their students' eyes to ascertain their interest in a particular lesson. The idea of wide-eyed wonder and interest is not new. In the late eighteenth century, European women placed a drug called belladonna in their eyes to keep their pupils large in order to make them look both interested and interesting.

Members of different social classes, generations, ethnic groups, and cultures use their eyes differently to express messages. European Americans often complain that they feel some foreigners stare at them too intensely or hold a glance too long. This is because a gaze of longer than ten seconds is likely to induce discomfort in a European American. But lengthy eye contact may be comfortable as long as the communicating people have sufficient distance between them. As you walk down a corridor, notice that you can look at someone for a long period of time until you suddenly feel uncomfortable and glance away. This usually happens at a distance of about ten feet.

When individuals in the European American culture are intent on hiding an inner feeling, they may try to avoid eye contact. Thus, the child who has eaten forbidden candy will not look at a questioning parent during the interrogation. (Euro-American children are often told, "Look me in the eye and say that.")

People in many cultures are very aware of the part played by eyes in communicating. This awareness has led some to try to mask their eyes. "Since people can't control the responses of their eyes," reported one source, "many Arabs wear dark glasses, even indoors."[36] This is especially true if they are negotiating.

Thus, in addition to watching a person's actions, an astute observer may ascertain what that person is doing by watching his eyes. For example, when 90 percent of people look up and to the left, they are recalling a visual memory they have experienced. Eyes up and to the right picture a future thought.[37]

4. "…when the pupils of our eyes are *dilated*, we may appear friendlier, warmer, and more attractive."
   a. Darkened
   b. Lightened
   c. Widened
   d. Reduced in size

5. "…knowledgeable teachers often watch the pupils of their students' eyes to *ascertain* their interest in a particular lesson."
   a. Stimulate
   b. Discover
   c. Deny
   d. Summarize

6. "…in addition to watching a person's actions, an *astute* observer may ascertain what that person is doing by watching his eyes."
   a. Imaginative
   b. Confident
   c. Rude
   d. Keenly aware

Circle the letter of the correct response.

7. The study of how the face communicates is called
   a. kinesics.
   b. facsics.
   c. ocalics.
   d. pupilometrics.

8. True or False: The eyes are an extension of the brain, so it is difficult to lie with the eyes.
   a. True
   b. False

9. True or False: Pupilometrics indicates that pupils contract when the eyes are focused on a pleasurable object and dilate when focused on an unpleasant one.
   a. True
   b. False

10. When you walk toward a person, you can usually look at him or her without feeling uncomfortable until you reach a distance of about
    a. 1 foot.
    b. 3 feet.
    c. 10 feet.
    d. 20 feet.

Exercise 4 Chemistry: "The Scientific Method"

Actively read the excerpt from a chemistry textbook on pages 85–87, and then answer the questions that follow by circling the letter of the correct response or writing the answer on the blank provided, as appropriate.

6 Chapter One   Chemical Foundations

nature. The first thing you did was collect relevant data. Then you made a prediction, and then you tested it by trying it out. This process contains the fundamental elements of science.

1. Making observations (collecting data)

2. Making a prediction (formulating a hypothesis)

3. Doing experiments to test the prediction (testing the hypothesis)

Scientists call this process the *scientific method*. We will discuss it in more detail in the next section. One of life's most important activities is solving problems—not "plug and chug" exercises, but real problems—problems that have new facets to them, that involve things you may have never confronted before. The more creative you are at solving these problems, the more effective you will be in your career and your personal life. Part of the reason for learning chemistry, therefore, is to become a better problem solver. Chemists are usually excellent problem solvers, because to master chemistry, you have to master the scientific approach. Chemical problems are frequently very complicated—there is usually no neat and tidy solution. Often it is difficult to know where to begin.

1.2 *The Scientific Method*

Science is a framework for gaining and organizing knowledge. Science is not simply a set of facts but also a plan of action—a *procedure* for processing and understanding certain types of information. Scientific thinking is useful in all aspects of life, but in this text we will use it to understand how the chemical world operates. As we have said in our previous discussion, the process that lies at the center of scientific inquiry is called the **scientific method.** There are actually many scientific methods, depending on the nature of the specific problem under study and on the particular investigator involved. However, it is useful to consider the following general framework for a generic scientific method (see Fig. 1.4):

Steps in the Scientific Method

➡ **1** *Making observations.* Observations may be *qualitative* (the sky is blue; water is a liquid) or *quantitative* (water boils at 100°C; a certain chemistry book weighs 2 kilograms). A qualitative observation does not involve a number. A quantitative observation (called a **measurement**) involves both a number and a unit.

➡ **2** *Formulating hypotheses.* A **hypothesis** is a *possible* explanation for an observation.

➡ **3** *Performing experiments.* An experiment is carried out to test a hypothesis. This involves gathering new information that enables a scientist to decide whether the hypothesis is valid—that is, whether it is supported by the new information learned from the experiment. Experiments always produce new observations, and this brings the process back to the beginning again.

To understand a given phenomenon, these steps are repeated many times, gradually accumulating the knowledge necessary to provide a possible explanation of the phenomenon.

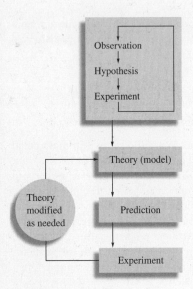

FIGURE 1.4
The fundamental steps of the scientific method.

Once a set of hypotheses that agrees with the various observations is obtained, the hypotheses are assembled into a theory. A **theory,** which is often called a **model,** is a set of tested hypotheses that gives an overall explanation of some natural phenomenon.

It is very important to distinguish between observations and theories. An observation is something that is witnessed and can be recorded. A theory is an *interpretation*—a possible explanation of *why* nature behaves in a particular way. Theories inevitably change as more information becomes available. For example, the motions of the sun and stars have remained virtually the same over the thousands of years during which humans have been observing them, but our explanations— our theories—for these motions have changed greatly since ancient times. (See the Chemical Impact on Observations, Theories, and the Planets on the Web site.

The point is that scientists do not stop asking questions just because a given theory seems to account satisfactorily for some aspect of natural behavior. They continue doing experiments to refine or replace the existing theories. This is generally done by using the currently accepted theory to make a prediction and then performing an experiment (making a new observation) to see whether the results bear out this prediction.

Always remember that theories (models) are human inventions. They represent attempts to explain observed natural behavior in terms of human experiences. A theory is actually an educated guess. We must continue to do experiments and to refine our theories (making them consistent with new knowledge) if we hope to approach a more nearly complete understanding of nature.

As scientists observe nature, they often see that the same observation applies to many different systems. For example, studies of innumerable chemical changes have shown that the total observed mass of the materials involved is the same before and after the change. Such generally observed behavior is formulated into a statement called a **natural law.** For example, the observation that the total mass of materials is not affected by a chemical change in those materials is called the **law of conservation of mass.**

Note the difference between a natural law and a theory. A natural law is a summary of observed (measurable) behavior, whereas a theory is an explanation of behavior. *A law summarizes what happens; a theory (model) is an attempt to explain why it happens.*

In this section we have described the scientific method as it might ideally be applied (see Fig. 1.5). However, it is important to remember that science does not always progress smoothly and efficiently. For one thing, hypotheses and observations are not totally independent of each other, as we have assumed in the description of the idealized scientific method. The coupling of observations and hypotheses occurs because once we begin to proceed down a given theoretical path, our hypotheses are unavoidably couched in the language of that theory. In other words, we tend to see what we expect to see and often fail to notice things that we do not expect. Thus the theory we are testing helps us because it focuses our questions. However, at the very same time, this focusing process may limit our ability to see other possible explanations.

It is also important to keep in mind that scientists are human. They have prejudices; they misinterpret data; they become emotionally attached to their theories and thus lose objectivity; and they play politics. Science is affected by profit motives, budgets, fads, wars, and religious beliefs. Galileo, for example, was forced to recant his astronomical observations in the face of strong religious resistance.

8   Chapter One   Chemical Foundations

Robert Boyle (1627–1691) was born in Ireland. He became especially interested in experiments involving air and developed an air pump with which he produced evacuated cylinders. He used these cylinders to show that a feather and a lump of lead fall at the same rate in the absence of air resistance and that sound cannot be produced in a vacuum. His most famous experiments involved careful measurements of the volume of a gas as a function of pressure. In his book *The Skeptical Chymist,* Boyle urged that the ancient view of elements as mystical substances should be abandoned and that an element should instead be defined as anything that cannot be broken down into simpler substances. This conception was an important step in the development of modern chemistry.

Lavoisier, the father of modern chemistry, was beheaded because of his political affiliations. Great progress in the chemistry of nitrogen fertilizers resulted from the desire to produce explosives to fight wars. The progress of science is often affected more by the frailties of humans and their institutions than by the limitations of scientific measuring devices. The scientific methods are only as effective as the humans using them. They do not automatically lead to progress.

1.3   *Units of Measurement*

Making observations is fundamental to all science. A quantitative observation, or *measurement,* always consists of two parts: a *number* and a scale (called a *unit*). Both parts must be present for the measurement to be meaningful.

In this textbook we will use measurements of mass, length, time, temperature, electric current, and the amount of a substance, among others. Scientists recognized long ago that standard systems of units had to be adopted if measurements were to be useful. If every scientist had a different set of units, complete chaos would result. Unfortunately, different standards were adopted in different parts of the world. The two major systems are the *English system* used in the United States and the *metric system* used by most of the rest of the industrialized world. This duality causes a good deal of trouble; for example, parts as simple as bolts are not interchangeable between machines built using the two systems. As a result, the United States has begun to adopt the metric system.

Soda is commonly sold in 2-liter bottles—an example of the use of SI units in everyday life.

TABLE 1.1   The Fundamental SI Units

Physical Quantity	Name of Unit	Abbreviation
Mass	kilogram	kg
Length	meter	m
Time	second	s
Temperature	kelvin	K
Electric current	ampere	A
Amount of substance	mole	mol
Luminous intensity	candela	cd

1. Write a brief definition for each of the following key terms in this section:

    scientific method: _____

    hypothesis: _____

    theory: _____

    model: _____

    natural law: _____

    law of conservation of mass :_____

2. How many steps are there in the scientific method?
    a. Two
    b. Three
    c. Four
    d. Ten

The following sentences appear in the chapter. Circle the letter of the best meaning for each italicized word.

3. "...it is useful to consider the following general framework for a *generic* scientific method."
    a. General, not specific
    b. Genuine, not fake
    c. Brief
    d. Effective

4. "...studies of *innumerable* chemical changes have shown that the total observed mass of the materials involved is the same before and after the change."
    a. Occurring instantly
    b. Significant
    c. Few
    d. Too many to be counted

5. "Galileo, for example, was forced to *recant* his astronomical observations in the face of strong religious resistance."
    a. Take back
    b. Change
    c. Prove
    d. Explain

Circle the letter of the correct response.

6. Based upon Figure 1.4 in the excerpt, which of the following conclusions is accurate?
    a. A theory is formed before a hypothesis is formed.
    b. Both a hypothesis and a theory are tested with experiments.
    c. A theory does not change, regardless of the results of an experiment.
    d. A theory is modified before an experiment is complete.

Write your answers to the following review and discussion questions on the blanks provided.

7. Summarize the steps of the scientific method.

    _____

    _____

    _____

8. Explain the difference between a law and a theory.

    _____

    _____

    _____

9. Is the scientific method suitable for solving problems only in the sciences? Explain.

    _____

    _____

    _____

10. The authors state, "The progress of science is often affected more by the frailties of humans and their institutions than by the limitations of scientific measuring devices." They illustrate this statement with the examples of Galileo, Lavoisier, and the creation of nitrogen fertilizers. Think of another example or two to illustrate this statement.

    _____

    _____

    _____

Exercise 5 *Humanities: "Impressionism"*

1. Before reading the following excerpt from a humanities textbook, write a paragraph on a separate sheet of paper about what you already know about Impressionism in art. Then, read the passage both actively and critically.

The following sentences appear in the chapter. Circle the letter of the BEST meaning for each italicized word or phrase.

2. "The Impressionists began a major *breach with* the Renaissance tradition...."
   a. Revival of
   b. Study of
   c. Break with
   d. Blending with

3. "They attempted to understand the *permutations* of light and color...."
   a. Mixtures
   b. Meanings
   c. Sources
   d. Changes

4. "...in contrast to the Realists, whose subjects were drawn from rural *toil* and lower-class life, Impressionists painted the middle class at leisure."
   a. Poverty
   b. Recreation
   c. Labor
   d. Towns

Write your answers to the following review and discussion questions on the blanks provided.

5. What were the basic artistic aims of Impressionism?

   _____

   _____

   _____

6. How were Impressionist artists like Realist artists? How were they different?

   _____

   _____

   _____

258 CHAPTER 22 Realism, Impressionism, and Later Romanticism in Art and Music

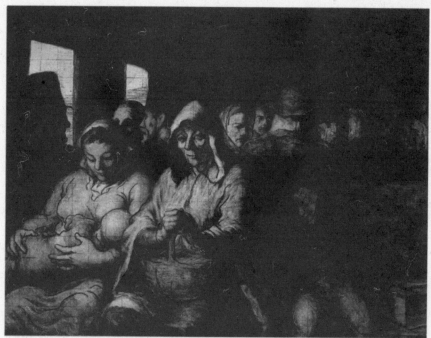

Figure 22.5   Honoré Daumier, *Third Class Carriage*, 1863–1865, 25 3/4″ x 35 1/2″ (65.4 x 90.2 cm), oil on canvas, The Metropolitan Museum of Art, New York.   The viewer is an anonymous fellow passenger in a crowded public transit carriage reserved for the poor. Rather than existing as portraits of individual people, these people represent the poor in spirit as well as the poor in possessions. *(The Metropolitan Musem of Art, H.O. Havemeyer Collection, Bequest of Mrs. H.O. Havemeyer, 1929 [29.100.129] Photograph © 1985 The Metropolitan Museum of Art)*

IMPRESSIONISM

The generation of French painters who followed the Realists is termed Impressionists. *Impressionism* was the logical extension of the Realists' preoccupation with light and color. Impressionists generally concluded that what they saw was not the object itself, but rather light reflecting from objects, forms, and surfaces. Intrigued by the impact that light has on objects, Impressionists left their studios for the countryside, where they painted landscapes or scenes of contemporary life under an open sky. The Impressionists began a major breach with the Renaissance tradition because their real subject was light rather than the scenes themselves. They attempted to understand the permutations of light and color, "to get an impression of," or to capture the moment when the eye perceives light on various surfaces during different times of the day. The Impressionists also violated the Renaissance traditions of perspective and three-dimensional space by acknowledging the two-dimensional surface of the painting. A contemporary observer explained the Impressionists' interest with painting scenes naturally:

[T]he Impressionist is . . . a modernist painter endowed with an uncommon sensibility of the eye. He is one who, forgetting the pictures amassed through the centuries in museums, forgetting his optical art school training—line, perspective, color—by dint of living and seeing frankly and primitively in the bright open air, that is, outside his poorly lighted studio, whether the city street, the country, or the interiors of houses, has succeeded in remaking for himself a natural eye, and in seeing naturally and painting as simply as he sees.[10]

Like the Realists, the Impressionists depicted ordinary experiences and everyday life. But in contrast to the Realists, whose subjects were drawn from rural toil and lower-class life, Impressionists painted the middle class at leisure.

The movement began in 1874 when several artists whose works were not in harmony with the ideals of the official Salon organized an independent exhibition of their work. One of the paintings exhibited was Claude Monet's *Impression—Sunrise*, from which the term "Impressionism" is derived. Between 1874 and 1886, the Impressionists held eight more of these independent exhibitions.

7. In what ways did Impressionism break with the Renaissance tradition?

    _____

    _____

    _____

8. From where did the term *Impressionism* originate?

    _____

    _____

    _____

9. Fill in the blanks in the following summary of this section of the chapter:

    Impressionism emerged as a logical extension of _____. However, while Realists

    focused on _____ themselves, the Impressionists attended to the effects of

    _____ and _____ on surfaces, thus breaking significantly with the

    _____ tradition. Further, although the Impressionists shared the Realists' interest

    in _____, they generally depicted _____ rather than _____.

10. Write a paragraph on a separate sheet of paper about what you learned from reading this
    material about Impressionism. Did any of the information surprise you? Did it contra-
    dict any of your previous knowledge about the topic?

Part 4

College Textbook Chapters with Exercises

Business: "Exploring the World of Business"

Applying the Reading Strategies

Write your responses to the following questions on your own paper.

1. Where are you as you begin to read this chapter? Describe your environment. Is this the ideal environment for reading? Why or why not? What external distractions might compete for your attention as you read, and how will you deal with these distractions?

2. Write a paragraph about what you already know or believe to be true about business in America, the topic of this chapter.

Previewing the Chapter

Preview the chapter entitled "Exploring the World of Business" on pages 95–131. Then, answer the questions that follow by circling the letter of the correct response.

3. How many learning objectives are there for this chapter?
   a. One
   b. Three
   c. Five
   d. Seven

4. On what topic does this whole chapter focus?
   a. International business
   b. American business
   c. Careers in business
   d. Companies in America

5. Which of the following is NOT something you should be able to do when you have finished reading the chapter?
   a. Describe two types of economic systems
   b. Outline four types of competition
   c. Explain how to be successful in international business
   d. Discuss future challenges for American business

6. True or False: This chapter provides definitions of key terms.
   a. True
   b. False

7. How many different historical periods does the author cover in the section about the development of American business?
   a. Three
   b. Seven
   c. Twelve
   d. Thirteen

8. The information in the Chapter Review is organized by
   a. headings within the chapter.
   b. the major sections of the chapter.
   c. the key terms.
   d. the learning objectives.

Reading the Chapter

Before you read the chapter entitled "Exploring the World of Business," turn all of the headings into questions. Then, read actively by either highlighting or underlining the answers to those questions. If you encounter an unfamiliar word, look it up in a dictionary and write its definition in the margin. The three "Check Your Understanding" sections that appear throughout the excerpted chapter, "Exploring the World of Business," include questions that will help you check your comprehension of the information provided in the chapter. They encourage you to practice the reading strategies you have learned from this text supplement, so stop to complete them before you continue reading.

1 Exploring the world of Business

This year, General Electric was chosen as America's most admired corporation for the third year in a row.

LEARNING OBJECTIVES

1 Discuss your future in the world of business.

2 Define *business* and identify potential risks and rewards.

3 Describe the two types of economic systems: capitalism and command economy.

4 Identify the ways to measure economic performance.

5 Outline the four types of competition.

6 Summarize the development of America's business system.

7 Discuss the challenges that American businesses will encounter in the future.

2

3

inside business

General Electric: America s Most Admired Company

EACH YEAR FOR THE last eighteen years, *Fortune* magazine has created a list of America's most admired companies. The process begins by identifying the companies that have the highest sales revenue. This year 1,025 U.S. companies and U.S. subsidiaries of foreign-held enterprises were placed on the *Fortune* list. Corporate executives then vote on the top companies in their respective industries to help *Fortune* create a "most admired" list for practically every industry—entertainment, trucking, and medical products, to name a few. Eight specific criteria that include innovation, quality of management, employee talent, financial soundness, use of corporate assets, long-term investment value, social responsibility, and quality of products and services are used to help determine the best of the best. Then the list of top ten companies is chosen by securities analysts, corporate board members, and executives. This year, General Electric was chosen as America's Most Admired Corporation. What makes this year's award even more important is that this year is the fourth year in a row that General Electric has won this coveted award.

By now, you may be asking yourself: How could a company that makes light bulbs win this prestigious award? Although most of us know General Electric, or simply GE, as a manufacturer of light bulbs, the company is also a corporate giant consisting of over twenty different core businesses. It all started back in 1878 when Thomas Edison founded the Electric Light Company. A merger with the Thomson-Houston Electric Company before the turn of the century created the General Electric Corporation—the name we know today. This new company invented and manufactured electrical devices that ranged from the small filaments that are still used in light bulbs to the first steam turbine generator powerful enough to supply electricity to an entire city. Since then GE has expanded into many other areas of business that range from broadcasting to financial services to silicone manufacturing. The company even built the first nuclear power plant.

While General Electric is admired by many business executives and enjoys tremendous financial success, America's most admired company is not one to sit back and rest on past performance. A program of lofty standards, called *growth initiatives,* is used to examine every facet of production and service. One growth initiative, called the *Sixth Sigma,* is a rigid process of defining, measuring, analyzing, improving, and controlling quality. Because of the Sixth Sigma, managers and employees are empowered to improve on every product the company sells, from jet engines to medical equipment.

Another growth initiative states GE's firm resolution to become the global leader in each of its core business areas. Although lesser companies often want to just sell their products or services around the world, GE doesn't just stop with selling its products or services. This award-winning company also helps the people in other nations develop their resources including raw materials and "intellectual capital." For example, GE employs over thirty thousand people and has made large investments in building manufacturing plants in Mexico. America's Most Admired Corporation is also urging its suppliers to build facilities in Mexico. And GE's global commitment doesn't stop with Mexico. Currently, the firm employs over 340,000 employees in 100 different countries around the globe.

So what if the company wins an award and is recognized as a global leader? Has time and money been invested well? Consider the following facts. The company has paid quarterly dividends to stockholders every year since 1899. One share of General Electric purchased before 1926 is now worth $245,760. Maybe, what's more important is the fact that General Electric is the "darling" of Wall Street. Financial analysts continue to recommend the stock as a "best bet" for the future.[1]

4

Part I **The Environment of Business**

In today's competitive business environment, it's common to hear of profitable companies. It is less common to hear of profitable companies that are held in high regard by their competitors. That's what is so astonishing about General Electric being chosen by *Fortune* magazine as America's Most Admired Corporation for four years in a row. What's even more astonishing is that General Electric doesn't just concentrate on earning profits. The company is committed to giving back resources to the communities in which it operates. Its public service program, Elfun, consists of more than 40,000 GE employees and retirees who have just donated an annual record of 1.3 million volunteer hours working for community service projects such as food and renovation programs for the poor and also supporting mentoring programs at schools to help students and teachers in science, engineering, and math. In reality, General Electric is an excellent example of what American business should be doing.

Perhaps the most important characteristic of our economic system is the freedom of individuals to start a business, to work for a business, and to buy or sell ownership shares in the business. While business always entails risks, it can also have its rewards. For Michael Dell, the chairman, CEO, and founder of Dell Computer Corporation, there has been the satisfaction of succeeding in a very competitive industry—not to mention some very substantial financial rewards.

free enterprise the system of business in which individuals are free to decide what to produce, how to produce it, and at what price to sell it

Within certain limits, imposed mainly to ensure public safety, the owners of a business can produce any legal good or service they choose and attempt to sell it at the price they set. This system of business, in which individuals decide what to produce, how to produce it, and at what price to sell it, is called **free enterprise.** Our free-enterprise system ensures, for example, that Dell Computer can buy parts from Intel, software from Lotus Development Corporation, and manufacture its own computers. Our system gives Dell's owners and stockholders the right to make a profit from the company's success; it gives Dell's management the right to compete with Compaq and IBM; and it gives computer buyers the right to choose.

In this chapter, we look briefly at what business is and how it got that way. First, we discuss your future in business and explore some important reasons for studying business. Then we define *business,* noting how business organizations satisfy needs and earn profits. Next we examine how capitalism and command economies answer four basic economic questions. Then our focus shifts to how the nations of the world measure economic performance and the four types of competitive situations. Next we go back into American history for a look at the events that helped shape today's business system. We conclude this chapter with a discussion of the challenges that businesses face.

Your Future in the World of Business

LEARNING OBJECTIVE

1 Discuss your future in the world of business.

What do you want?
Why do you want it?
Write it down!

During a segment on the Oprah Winfrey television show, Joe Dudley, one of the world's most successful Black business owners, gave the above advice to anyone who wants to succeed in business. And his advice is an excellent way to begin our discussion of what free enterprise is all about. What's so amazing about Dudley's success is that he grew up in a rural farmhouse with no running water and began his career selling Fuller Brush products door-to-door. He went on to develop his own line of hair-care products and open a chain of beauty schools and beauty supply stores. Today, Dudley is president of Dudley Products, Inc.—one of the largest minority-owned companies in the nation. Not only a successful business owner, he is the winner of the Horatio Alger Award—an award given to outstanding individuals who have succeeded in the face of adversity.[2]

Opportunity! It's only eleven letters, but no other word provides a better description of the current business environment. While many people would say that Joe Dudley was just lucky or happened to be in the right place at the right time, the truth

5

is that he became a success because he had a dream and worked hard to turn his dream into a reality. He would be the first to tell you that you have the same opportunities that he had. In fact, employment opportunities for entry-level workers, investment opportunities, and career advancement opportunities have never been greater. However, people who are successful must adapt to changes in their environment. Consider just some of the changes that have occurred since the previous edition of *Business* was published.

All work and no play? Not for this entrepreneur. Jeff Bonforte, founder and CEO of idrive.com, knows that starting a high-tech company is hard work and requires long hours, but that it can be a lot of fun. It can also be very rewarding. Bonforte is now worth an estimated $5 to $10 million.

- Today the economy is healthy and we have experienced the longest period of sustained economic growth in our history.
- There is a large increase in the number of new, start-up companies especially in the technology and information industries.
- The increased use of the Internet has created new jobs that did not exist even three years ago.
- Unemployment numbers are at record lows and employers are now recruiting new employees.
- An increasing number of people work at home for all or part of the work week.

For the person that has the required abilities and skills, it is an excellent time to start a career. And yet, employers and our capitalistic economic system are more demanding than ever before. Ask yourself: What can I do that will make employers want to pay me a salary? What skills do I have that employers need? With these two questions in mind, we begin the next section with another basic question: Why Study Business?

Why Study Business?

Education is a unique purchase—one of the few things you can buy that will last your lifetime. It can't rust, corrode, break down, or wear out. Education can't be stolen, burned, repossessed, or destroyed. Education is a purchase that becomes a permanent part of you. Once you have it, no one can take it away.[3]

In this section, we explore what you may expect to get out of this business course and text. You will find at least four quite compelling reasons for studying business.

To Become a Better-Informed Consumer and Investor
The world of business surrounds us. You cannot buy a home, a new Trans Am from the local Pontiac dealer, a Black & Decker sander at the Home Depot, a pair of jeans at the Gap, or a hot dog from a street vendor without entering a business transaction. These and thousands of similar transactions describe the true nature of the American business system.

Using the Internet

Your Internet connection to more business information begins at **Houghton Mifflins College Division** web site. Enter the web site URL **http://www.college.hmco.com**. Select the student tab and then go to "Business." Select the text web site or the resource center to find quick access to business journals and web sites that explore many topics discussed in the text chapters and more. This site will simplify your search for information on the Internet. Use it often to keep up to date with current developments in the fast-paced world

6

spotLight

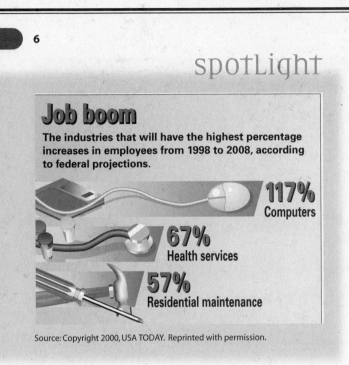

Job boom

The industries that will have the highest percentage increases in employees from 1998 to 2008, according to federal projections.

117% Computers

67% Health services

57% Residential maintenance

Source: Copyright 2000, USA TODAY. Reprinted with permission.

Because you will no doubt engage in business transactions almost every day of your life, one very good reason for studying business is to become a more fully informed consumer. Your knowledge of business will enable you to make intelligent buying decisions and to spend your money more wisely. This same basic understanding of business will also make you a better-informed investor.

For Help in Choosing a Career   What do you want to do with the rest of your life? Someplace, sometime, someone has probably asked you that same question. And like many people, you may find it a difficult question to answer. This business course will introduce you to a wide array of employment opportunities. In private enterprise, these range from small, local businesses owned by one individual to large companies like American Express and Marriott International that are owned by thousands of stockholders. There are also employment opportunities with federal, state, county, and local governments and with not-for-profit organizations like the Red Cross and Save the Children. For help deciding what career might be right for you, read Appendix A: Careers in Business. Also, you might want to read information about researching a career and the steps necessary to perform a job search that are posted on the web site that accompanies this edition of *Business*. To view this information:

1. Make an Internet connection and go to http://college.hmco.com/business/
2. Locate the Student Center site and click to enter.
3. Then scroll down on the Student Center page and click on *career section*.

One thing to remember as you think about what your ideal career might be is that a person's choice of a career is ultimately just a reflection of what he or she values and holds most important. Because people have different values, they choose different careers; what will give one individual personal satisfaction may not satisfy another. For example, one person may dream of becoming a millionaire before the age of thirty. Another may choose a career that has more modest monetary rewards but that provides the opportunity to help others. One person may be willing to work long hours and seek additional responsibility in order to get promotions and pay raises. Someone else may prefer a less demanding job with little stress and more free time. What you choose to do with your life will be based on what you feel is most important.

To Be a Successful Employee   Deciding on the type of career you want is only a first step. To get a job in your chosen field and to be successful at it, you will have to develop a plan, or road map, that ensures that you have the skills and knowledge the job requires. Today's employers are looking for job applicants who can *do something*, not just fill a spot on an organizational chart. You will be expected to have both the technical skills needed to accomplish a specific task and the ability to work well with many types of people in a culturally diverse work force. These skills, together with a working knowledge of the American business system, can give you an inside edge when you are interviewing with a prospective employer.

This course, your instructor, and all the resources available at your college or university can help you acquire the skills and knowledge you will need for a successful career. But don't underestimate your part in making your dream a reality. It will take hard work, dedication, perseverance, and time management to achieve your goals. Time management is especially important because it will help you accomplish the tasks that you

7

consider most important. As an added bonus, it is also a skill that employers value. Communication skills are also important. Today, most employers are looking for employees who can compose a business letter and get it in mailable form. They also want employees who can talk with customers and use e-mail to communicate to people within and outside of the organization. Employers will also be interested in any work experience you may have had in cooperative work/school programs, during summer vacations, or in part-time jobs during the school year. These things can make a difference when it is time to apply for the job you really want.

Home or office? Today more and more successful employees—like Carla Patterson, a field representative for Nebraska's Department of Economic Development—are working at home.

To Start Your Own Business   Some people prefer to work for themselves, and they open their own businesses. To be successful, business owners must possess many of the same skills that successful employees have. And they must be willing to work hard and put in long hours.

It also helps if your small business can provide a product or service that customers want. For example, Mark Cuban started a small Internet company called Broadcast.com that now provides hundreds of live and on-demand audio and video programs ranging from rap music to sporting events to business events over the Internet. This new, high-tech startup company quickly became a major player in electronic business or what many refer to as e-business. **E-business** is the organized effort of individuals to produce and sell, for a profit, the products and services that satisfy society's needs *through the facilities available on the Internet.* When Cuban sold Broadcast.com to Yahoo! Inc., he became a billionaire. Today he is an expert on how the Internet and e-business will affect society in the future and believes that many small technology firms will fail over the next ten years. According to Cuban, there is a real need for all companies—not just technology companies—to provide something that their customers want. If they don't do that, their company could very well fail.[4] For more information on how two very successful firms use e-business, read the Adapting to Change boxed feature.

e-business the organized effort of individuals to produce and sell, for a profit, the products and services that satisfy society's needs through the facilities available on the Internet

Unfortunately, many small-business firms fail; 70 percent of them fail within the first five years. The material in Chapter 6 and selected topics and examples throughout this text will help you decide whether you want to open your own business. Before proceeding to the next section, take a few minutes to familiarize yourself with the text by reading the material below.

Special Note to Students

It's important to begin reading this text with one thing in mind: *this business course doesn't have to be difficult.* In fact, we've done everything possible to eliminate the problems that students encounter in a typical class. All the features in each chapter have been evaluated and recommended by instructors with years of teaching experience. In addition, business students were asked to critique each chapter component. Based on this feedback, the text includes the following features:

8

E-Business Is Here to Stay

ALL ACROSS THE GLOBE, E-BUSINESS IS changing the way in which companies process purchasing orders, ship merchandise, and handle customer requests. And for companies that use e-business to increase productivity and sales, profits also increase. While doing business electronically used to be reserved for only high-tech companies, over the last few years it has become apparent that those companies that refuse to join the e-business revolution will be left behind. Consider how e-business is changing the way that Charles Schwab and Wal-Mart do business.

Charles Schwab Discount Brokerage

Today, Charles Schwab is recognized as one of the most successful discount firms in the brokerage business. The reason for this success is based on two concepts: customer service and the use of technology. Technology enables investors to not only trade online but also to research potential investments online. Back in 1975, when Schwab opened his first office, employees were taught that customer service was a top priority. To help ensure that employees were willing to help the firm's customers get top quality service, his employees were paid salaries, not commissions—a practice unheard of in the brokerage business. As a result, employees were able to spend more time with customers helping them learn how to make investment decisions. When the technology became available, it was possible for the company to extend this same philosophy to investors who wanted to trade online. Today, both stock market rookies and experienced investors use the Schwab system to trade stocks online at reduced commissions. More importantly, these same investors use research tools provided online to learn more about the financial fundamentals required to become better investors.

Wal-Mart

When the late Sam Walton opened his first Wal-Mart store in 1962, company growth was his primary objec-

adapting to change

tive. In order to succeed he implemented all of the emerging technology available at the time. Over the years, his objective was achieved; Wal-Mart became the number 1 retailer in the world employing over 1,140,000 employees in almost 4,000 stores. Although the road to success has been phenomenal, it has not been without a few bumps along the way. During the mid-1990s, for example, the retailer experienced inventory problems and a sales slump. According to some analysts, it almost seemed like the retail giant lost its competitive edge. Corporate executives investigating the problem discovered that both managers and employees were not as technology-literate as they should be. They also discovered that just because the technology had been made available, it didn't mean that the managers and employees were using it. To remedy the problem both managers and employees received advanced training which eventually enabled Wal-Mart to correct problems and increase sales. Today, the company owns an elite information system which can automatically transmit data via satellite to all stores and corporate headquarters. Inventory is no longer an issue; suppliers are connected to the network and receive orders immediately. Wal-Mart recently expanded its network by adding an online ordering system for consumers. Wal-Mart.com is a virtual store and a complete companion to its physical stores.

E-Business: A Career Perspective

Companies who have the willingness to make the e-business conversion create extraordinary opportunities and have incredible advantages over their competitors. And while it's obvious e-business is here to stay, the largest stumbling block for companies using improved technology is not purchasing the new equipment, but training people or finding people who can use it. Today, companies are looking for employees who have the computer skills required to not only use new technology, but also improve on existing technology. In fact, many employers believe skilled talent is indispensable. Excellent jobs are available for those who have a vision on how to use improved technology.

■ *Learning objectives* appear at the beginning of each chapter. All objectives signal important concepts to be mastered within the chapter.

■ *Inside Business* is a chapter-opening case that highlights how successful companies do business on a day-to-day basis. These short cases were chosen to illustrate the key concepts and ideas described in each chapter.

■ *Margin notes* are used throughout the text to reinforce both learning objectives and key terms.

■ *Boxed features* highlight ethical behavior, change in the workplace, global issues, and the impact of technology. In addition, a boxed feature entitled Exploring Business highlights a wide range of contemporary business issues.

- *Spotlight* features highlight interesting facts about business and society and often provide a real-world example of an important concept within a chapter.
- *Using the Internet* features provide useful web addresses that relate to chapter material.
- *End-of-chapter materials* provide questions about the opening case, a chapter summary, a list of key terms, review and discussion questions, and a video case. The last section of every chapter is entitled Building Skills for Career Success and includes exercises devoted to exploring the Internet, developing critical thinking skills, building team skills, researching different careers, and improving communication skills.

In addition to the text, a number of student supplements will help you explore the world of business. We're especially proud of two items that are available with this edition of *Business*. The set of student CDs packaged with every new text purchased through your college bookstore will help you review important concepts with audio material that you can use at your convenience. We're also proud of the web site that accompanies this edition. Here you will find a computerized study guide, along with many other tools designed to help ensure your success in this course. If you want to take a look at the Internet support materials available for this edition of *Business,* go to: http://college.hmco.com/business and click on Text Web Sites.

As authors, we realize that you are our customers. We want you to be successful. And we want you to appreciate business and how it affects your life as an employee and a consumer. Since a text should always be evaluated by the students and instructors who use it, we would welcome and sincerely appreciate your comments and suggestions. Please feel free to contact us by using one of the following e-mail addresses:

Bill Pride	w-pride@tamu.edu
Bob Hughes	rjh8410@dcccd.edu
Jack Kapoor	kapoorj@cdnet.cod.edu

Business: A Definition

LEARNING OBJECTIVE

2 Define *business* and identify potential risks and rewards.

Business is the organized effort of individuals to produce and sell, for a profit, the goods and services that satisfy society's needs. The general term *business* refers to all such efforts within a society (as in "American business") or within an industry (as in "the steel business"). However, *a business* is a particular organization, such as Dudley Products, Inc., American Airlines, Inc., or Cracker Barrel Old Country Stores. To be successful, a business must perform three activities. It must be organized. It must satisfy needs. And it must earn a profit.

business the organized effort of individuals to produce and sell, for a profit, the goods and services that satisfy society's needs

The Organized Effort of Individuals

For a business to be organized, it must combine four kinds of resources: material, human, financial, and informational. *Material* resources include the raw materials used in manufacturing processes, as well as buildings and machinery. For example, Sara Lee Corporation needs flour, sugar, butter, eggs, and other raw materials to produce the food products it sells worldwide. In addition, this Chicago-based company needs human, financial, and informational resources. *Human* resources are the people who furnish their labor to the business in return for wages. The *financial* resource is the money required to pay employees, purchase materials, and generally keep the business operating. And *information* is the resource that tells the managers of the business how effectively the other resources are being combined and used (see Figure 1.1).

Today, businesses are usually classified as one of three specific types. *Manufacturing businesses* are organized to process various materials into tangible goods, such as delivery trucks or towels. For example, Intel produces computer chips that are in turn sold to companies that manufacture computers. *Service businesses*

10

figure 1.1

Combining Resources
A business must effectively combine all four resources to be successful.

produce services, such as haircuts, legal advice, or tax preparation. And some firms— called *marketing intermediaries*—are organized to buy products from manufacturers and then resell them. Sony Corporation is a manufacturer that produces stereo equipment, among other things. These products may be sold to a marketing intermediary such as Kmart Corporation, which then resells them to consumers in its retail stores. **Consumers** are individuals who purchase goods or services for their own personal use.

consumers individuals who purchase goods or services for their own personal use

Satisfying Needs

The ultimate objective of every firm must be to satisfy the needs of its customers. People generally don't buy goods and services simply to own them; they buy products and services to satisfy particular needs. People rarely buy an automobile solely to store it in a garage; they do, however, buy automobiles to satisfy their need for transportation. Some of us may feel this need is best satisfied by an air-conditioned BMW with stereo compact-disc player, automatic transmission, power seats and windows, and remote-control side mirrors. Others may believe a Ford Focus with a stick shift and an AM radio will do just fine. Both products are available to those who want them, along with a wide variety of other products that satisfy the need for transportation. To satisfy their customers' needs for information, Ford has joined up with Microsoft's *Carpoint* web site http://carpoint.msn.com/home/New.asp to help consumers find decision-critical information about their products and dealers from the comfort, convenience, and privacy of their own homes and offices. Ford and Microsoft hope to transform the site into a complete build-to-order system that will link customer orders for options directly with their supplier system. This way, customers get the products they want and Ford reduces the risks associated with guessing the inventories of cars its dealers should stock.[5]

And you think you've got books! For a company like Amazon.com, books are a way of life. In this warehouse facility, employees process orders and ship books to satisfy customers' needs.

When firms lose sight of their customers' needs they are likely to find the going rough. But when businesses understand their customers' needs and work to satisfy those needs, they are usually successful. Arkansas-based Wal-Mart Stores, Inc., provides the products its customers want and offers excellent prices. This highly successful discount-store organization continues to open new stores in the United States, Argentina, Brazil, Canada, China, Germany, and Mexico.

11

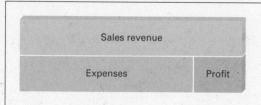

figure 1.2

The Relationship Between Sales Revenue and Profit
Profit is what remains after all business expenses have been deducted from sales revenue.

Business Profit

A business receives money (sales revenue) from its customers in exchange for goods or services. It must also pay out money to cover the expenses involved in doing business. If the firm's sales revenue is greater than its expenses, it has earned a profit. More specifically, as shown in Figure 1.2, **profit** is what remains after all business expenses have been deducted from sales revenue. (A negative profit, which results when a firm's expenses are greater than its sales revenue, is called a *loss*.)

The profit earned by a business becomes the property of its owners. So in one sense, profit is the reward business owners receive for producing goods and services that consumers want.

Profit is also the payment that business owners receive for assuming the considerable risks of ownership. One of these is the risk of not being paid. Everyone else—employees, suppliers, and lenders—must be paid before the owners. A second risk that owners run is the risk of losing whatever they have invested into the business. A business that cannot earn a profit is very likely to fail, in which case the owners lose whatever money, effort, and time they have invested. Internet-based book and CD retailer Amazon.com Inc. currently spends over $115 million each month to keep the company on track toward the eventual day when the firm will sell enough merchandise to generate profits for its shareholders. To date, Amazon's six years of operating losses total more than $1.2 billion, scaring away some who fear the firm will never reach the promised profit goals set by visionary founder Steve Bezos.[6] When a business is profitable, some businesses choose to give back a portion of their profits to the communities they serve. For information on how three different companies help children, read the Examining Ethics boxed feature.

To satisfy society's needs, and make a profit, a business must operate within the parameters of a nation's economic system. In the next section, we describe two different types of economic systems and how they affect not only businesses but also the people within a nation.

profit what remains after all business expenses have been deducted from sales revenue

Types of Economic Systems

Economics is the study of how wealth is created and distributed. By *wealth* we mean anything of value, including the products produced and sold by business. *How wealth is distributed* simply means "who gets what." The way in which people deal with the creation and distribution of wealth determines the kind of economic system, or **economy,** that a nation has.

Over the years, the economic systems of the world have differed in essentially two ways: (1) the ownership of the factors of production and (2) how they answer four basic economic questions that direct a nation's economic activity. **Factors of production** are the resources used to produce goods and services. There are four such factors:

- *Natural resources*—elements in their natural state that can be used in the production process. Typical examples include crude oil, forests, minerals, land, water, and even air.

LEARNING OBJECTIVE

3 Describe the two types of economic systems: capitalism and command economy.

economics the study of how wealth is created and distributed

economy the system through which a society answers the two economic questions—how wealth is created and distributed

factors of production natural resources, labor, capital, and entrepreneurship

Check Your Understanding

The following sentences appear in the chapter. Circle the letter of the BEST meaning for each italicized word.

9. "Because you will no doubt engage in business *transactions* almost every day of your life, one very good reason for studying business is to become a more fully informed consumer."
   a. Exchanges
   b. Studies
   c. Calculations
   d. Transfers

10. "You will be expected to have … the ability to work well with many types of people in a culturally *diverse* work force."
    a. Competitive
    b. Interesting
    c. Different
    d. Inferior

11. "To satisfy society's needs, and make a profit, a business must operate within the *parameters* of a nation's economic system."
    a. Boundaries or limits
    b. Time frame
    c. Goals
    d. Mathematical equations

Circle the letter of the correct response.

12. Which of the following is an accurate conclusion based on the "Job Boom" visual aid?
    a. The federal government predicts that the computer industry will have the highest percentage of increase in employees.
    b. Federal projections indicate that the computer and health services industries will add about the same number of jobs.
    c. According to federal projections, the residential maintenance industry will grow faster than any other industry.
    d. The federal government says that the residential maintenance industry will grow much faster than the health services industry.

13. On the blanks provided, write a brief definition for each of the following key terms:

    free enterprise: _____

    e-business: _____

    business: _____

    consumers: _____

    profit: _____

On the blanks provided, write your answers to the following review questions for the section of the business textbook you just read.

14. What reasons would you give if you were advising someone to study business?

_____

_____

_____

15. What factors affect a person's choice of careers?

_____

_____

_____

16. Describe the four resources that must be combined to organize and operate a business. How do they differ from the economist's factors of production?

_____

_____

_____

17. What distinguishes consumers from other buyers of goods and services?

_____

_____

_____

18. Describe the relationship among profit, business risk, and the satisfaction of customers' needs.

_____

_____

_____

12

Corporations That Give Back To Communities

... McDonald's and Ronald McDonald House Charities are committed to continuing our efforts in support of children and families around the world.... We remain dedicated to one of McDonald's fundamental values, which is to give back to communities we serve.

JACK GREENBERG, MCDONALD'S
CHAIRMAN AND CEO

BECAUSE OF ITS CONCERN FOR THE WELL BEING and education of children, its environmental programs in recycling, reducing waste, and conserving energy, *Fortune* magazine ranked McDonald's number 1 in social responsibility—one of eight criteria used to select America's Most Admired Corporation for 1999. Is the recognition deserved? Before you answer this question, consider the following.

Today, McDonald's is viewed as a pioneer in recognizing the need for social responsibility in the corporate world, but the firm's history of social responsibility began with one project—a Ronald McDonald house. Back in 1974, McDonald's created a home-away-from-home for families of seriously ill children receiving treatment at nearby hospitals in Philadelphia. Named in honor of the clown that is the firm's symbol of happiness, McDonald's is now responsible for establishing over 200 Ronald McDonald houses in 32 countries and has awarded more than $225 million in grants to children's programs worldwide. What a success story!

examining ethics

While many people think that corporations are only interested in earning profits, McDonald's is not alone in its desire to give back part of their profits to communities. In fact, many business organizations are giving back resources to the communities they serve. Some corporate responsibility programs even go the extra mile and get their customers involved. One such program—Campbell Soup Company's Labels for Education program has been in operation for over twenty-six years. This program provides a way for people in the community to help local schools by collecting Campbell Soup product labels. Once enough labels are collected, then the school can redeem the labels for computers, software, sports equipment, research materials, and other types of equipment that the school needs. Like the Campbell Soup Labels for Education program, the Randalls/Tom Thumb Good Neighbor Program involves the firm's customers. Customers apply for a Reward Card which allows them to receive special discounts on select merchandise purchased in either a Randalls or Tom Thumb grocery story. At the time of application, customers can designate any nonprofit youth organization to receive cash donations based on the dollar value of the customers' total purchases.

Issues to Consider

1. As a stockholder, do you feel it is right for management to use corporate funds to sponsor social responsibility programs?
2. Is it ethical for a corporation to promote the sale of their products or services in return for a corporate promise to contribute to youth-oriented programs?

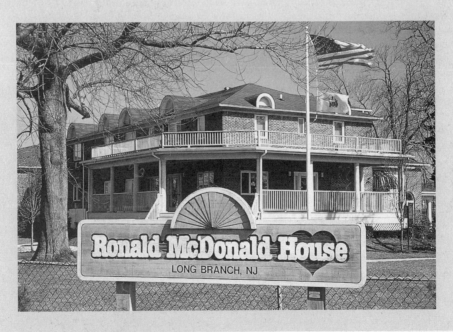

Ronald McDonald House
LONG BRANCH, NJ

- *Labor*—human resources such as managers and workers.
- *Capital*—money, facilities, equipment, and machines used in the operation of organizations. While most people think of capital as just money, it can also be the manufacturing equipment on a Ford automobile assembly line or a computer used in the corporate offices of Ace Hardware.
- *Entrepreneurship*—the willingness to take risks and the knowledge and ability to use the other factors of production efficiently. An **entrepreneur** is a person who risks his or her time, effort, and money to start and operate a business.

A nation's economic system significantly affects all the economic activities of its citizens and organizations. This far-reaching impact becomes more apparent when we consider that a country's economic system provides answers to four basic economic questions.

1. What goods and services—and how much of each—will be produced?
2. How will these goods and services be produced?
3. For whom will these goods and services be produced?
4. Who owns and who controls the major factors of production?

Capitalism

Capitalism is an economic system in which individuals own and operate the majority of businesses that provide goods and services. Capitalism stems from the theories of the eighteenth-century Scottish economist Adam Smith. In his book *Wealth of Nations*, published in 1776, Smith argued that a society's interests are best served when the individuals within that society are allowed to pursue their own self-interest.

Adam Smith's laissez-faire capitalism is based on four fundamental issues. First, Smith argued that the creation of wealth is properly the concern of private individuals, not of government. Second, the resources used to create wealth must be owned by private individuals. Smith argued that the owners of resources should be free to determine how these resources are used. They should also be free to enjoy the income, profits, and other benefits they might derive from the ownership of these resources. Third, Smith contended that economic freedom ensures the existence of competitive markets that allow both sellers and buyers to enter and exit as they choose. This freedom to enter or leave a market at will has given rise to the term *market economy*. A **market economy** (sometimes referred to as a *free-market economy*) is an economic system in which businesses and individuals make the decisions about what to produce and what to buy, and the market determines how much is sold and at what prices. Finally, in Smith's view, the role of government should be limited to providing defense against foreign enemies, ensuring internal order, and furnishing public works and education. With regard to the economy, government should act only as rule maker and umpire.

In other words, Smith believed that each person should be allowed to work toward his or her *own* economic gain, without interference from government. The French term *laissez faire* describes Smith's capitalistic system and implies that there shall be no interference in the economy. Loosely translated, it means "let them do" (as they see fit).

Capitalism in the United States

Our economic system is rooted in the laissez-faire capitalism of Adam Smith. However, our real-world economy is not as "laissez faire" as Smith would have liked because government participates as more than umpire and rule maker. Ours is, in fact, a **mixed economy,** one that exhibits elements of both capitalism and socialism.

entrepreneur a person who risks time, effort, and money to start and operate a business

capitalism an economic system in which individuals own and operate the majority of businesses that provide goods and services

market economy an economic system in which businesses and individuals decide what to produce and buy, and the market determines quantities sold and prices

mixed economy an economy that exhibits elements of both capitalism and socialism

Saturn: A true success story. There are no guarantees that Saturn will be successful just because it operates in a capitalistic society. However, companies like Saturn that produce goods and services that customers *really* want have a much better chance of being successful.

14

In today's economy, the four basic economic questions discussed at the beginning of this section of Chapter 1 are answered through the interaction of households, businesses, and governments. The interactions among these three groups are shown in Figure 1.3.

Households   Households are consumers of goods and services, as well as owners of some of the factors of production. As *resource owners,* the members of households provide businesses with labor, land, buildings, and capital. In return, businesses pay wages, rent, and dividends and interest, which households receive as income.

As *consumers,* household members use their income to purchase the goods and services produced by business. Today almost two-thirds of our nation's total production consists of **consumer products:** goods and services purchased by individuals for personal consumption. (The remaining one-third is purchased by businesses and governments.) This means that consumers, as a group, are the biggest customer of American business.

Businesses   Like households, businesses are engaged in two different exchanges. They exchange money for resources and use these resources to produce goods and services. Then they exchange their goods and services for sales revenue. This sales revenue, in turn, is exchanged for additional resources, which are used to produce and sell more goods and services. So the circular flow of Figure 1.3 is continuous.

Along the way, of course, business owners would like to remove something from the circular flow in the form of profits. And households try to retain some income as savings. But are profits and savings really removed from the flow? Usually not! When the economy is running smoothly, households are willing to invest their savings in businesses. They can do so directly, by buying ownership shares in businesses or by lending money to businesses. They can also invest indirectly, by placing their savings in bank accounts; banks then invest these savings as part of their normal business operations. In either case, savings usually find their way back into the circular flow in order to finance business activities.

consumer products goods and services purchased by individuals for personal consumption

figure 1.3

The Circular Flow in Our Modified Capitalist System
Our economic system is guided by the interaction of buyers and sellers, with the role of government being taken into account.

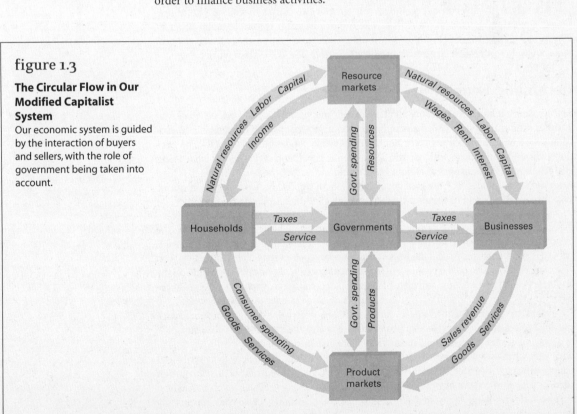

When business profits are distributed to business owners, these profits become household income. (Business owners are, after all, members of households.) And, as we saw, household income is retained in the circular flow as either consumer spending or invested savings. So business profits, too, are retained in the business system, and the circular flow is complete. How, then, does government fit in?

Governments   The framers of our Constitution desired as little government interference with business as possible. At the same time, the Preamble to the Constitution sets forth the responsibility of government to protect and promote the public welfare. Local, state, and federal governments discharge this responsibility through regulation and the provision of services. Government regulations of business are discussed in detail in various chapters of this book. The numerous services are important but either (1) would not be produced by private business firms or (2) would be produced only for those who could afford them. Typical services include national defense, police and fire protection, education, and construction of roads and highways. To pay for all these services, governments collect a variety of taxes from households (such as personal income taxes and sales taxes) and from businesses (corporate income taxes).

Figure 1.3 shows this exchange of taxes for government services. It also shows government spending of tax dollars for resources and products required to provide these services. In other words, governments, too, return their incomes to the business system through the resource and product markets.

Actually, with government included, our circular flow looks more like a combination of several flows. And in reality it is. The important point is that, together, the various flows make up a single unit—a complete economic system that effectively provides answers to the basic economic questions. Simply put, the system works.

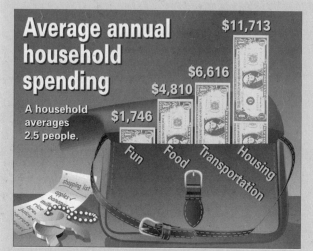

spotLight

Average annual household spending

A household averages 2.5 people.

$1,746 $4,810 $6,616 $11,713

Fun   Food   Transportation   Housing

Source: Copyright 2000, USA TODAY. Reprinted with permission.

Command Economies

Before we discuss how to measure a nation's economic performance, we look quickly at another economic system called a command economy. A **command economy** is an economic system in which the government decides what goods and services will be produced, how they will be produced, who gets available goods and services, and what prices will be charged. The answers to all four basic economic questions are determined, at least to some degree, through centralized government planning. Today, two types of economic systems—*socialism* and *communism*—serve as examples of command economies.

command economy an economic system in which the government decides what will be produced, how it will be produced, who gets what is produced, and the prices of what is produced

Socialism   In a *socialist* economy, the key industries are owned and controlled by the government. Such industries usually include transportation, utilities, communications, banking, and industries producing important materials such as steel. Land, buildings, and raw materials may also be the property of the state in a socialist economy. Depending on the country, private ownership of smaller businesses is permitted to varying degrees. People usually may choose their own occupations, but many work in state-owned industries.

What to produce and how to produce it are determined in accordance with national goals, which are based on projected needs and the availability of resources—at least for government-owned industries. The distribution of goods and services—who gets what—is also controlled by the state to the extent that it controls rents and wages. Among the professed aims of socialist countries are the equitable distribution of income, the elimination of poverty, the distribution of social services (such as medical care) to all who need them, and elimination of the economic waste that supposedly accompanies capitalistic competition.

16

Britain, France, Sweden, and India are democratic countries whose economies include a very visible degree of socialism. Other, more authoritarian countries may actually have socialist economies; however, we tend to think of them as communist because of their almost total lack of freedom.

Communism   If Adam Smith was the father of capitalism, Karl Marx was the father of communism. In his writings during the mid-nineteenth century, Marx advocated a classless society whose citizens together owned all economic resources. All workers would then contribute to this *communist* society according to their ability and would receive benefits according to their need.

Since the breakup of the Soviet Union and economic reforms in China and most of the eastern European countries, the best remaining examples of communism are North Korea and Cuba. Today these so-called communist economies seem to practice a strictly controlled kind of socialism. Almost all economic resources are owned by the government. The basic economic questions are answered through centralized state planning, which sets prices and wages as well. In this planning, the needs of the state generally outweigh the needs of individual citizens. Emphasis is placed on the production of goods the government needs rather than on the products that consumers might want, so there are frequent shortages of consumer goods. Workers have little choice of jobs, but special skills or talents seem to be rewarded with special privileges. Various groups of professionals (bureaucrats, university professors, and athletes, for example) fare much better than, say, factory workers.

LEARNING OBJECTIVE

4 Identify the ways to measure economic performance.

Measuring Economic Performance

productivity the average level of output per worker per hour

One way to measure a nation's economic performance is to assess its productivity. **Productivity** is the average level of output per worker per hour. An increase in productivity results in economic growth because a larger number of goods and services are produced by a given labor force. Although U.S. workers produce more than many workers in other countries, the rate of growth in productivity has declined in the United States and has been surpassed in recent years by workers in Japan and the United Kingdom. Productivity improvements are expected to improve dramatically as more economic activity is transferred onto the Internet, reducing costs for servicing customers and handling routine ordering functions between businesses. The resulting time and money savings allow businesses to increase their profits and turn their efforts to other business opportunities. We discuss productivity in detail in Chapter 9.

Economic Indicators

gross domestic product (GDP) the total dollar value of all goods and services produced by all people within the boundaries of a country during a one-year period

In addition to productivity, a measure called gross domestic product can be used to measure the economic well-being of a nation. **Gross domestic product (GDP)** is the total dollar value of all goods and services produced by all people within the boundaries of a country during a one-year period. For example, the value of automobiles produced by employees in both an American-owned General Motors plant and a Japanese-owned Toyota plant *in the United States* are both included in the GDP for the United States. The U.S. gross domestic product was $9,256.1 billion in 1999.[7]

inflation a general rise in the level of prices

The gross domestic product figure facilitates comparisons between the United States and other countries, since it is the standard used in international guidelines for economic accounting. It is also possible to compare the GDP for one nation over several different time periods. This comparison allows observers to determine the extent to which a nation is experiencing economic growth. To make accurate comparisons of the GDP for different years, we must adjust the dollar amounts for inflation. **Inflation** is a general rise in the level of prices. By using inflation-adjusted figures, we are able to measure the *real* gross domestic product for a nation. In effect, it is now possible to compare the products and services produced by a nation in constant dollars—dollars that will purchase the same amount of goods and services. Figure 1.4 depicts the GDP

17

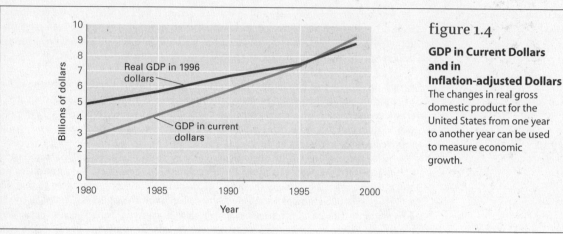

figure 1.4

GDP in Current Dollars and in Inflation-adjusted Dollars
The changes in real gross domestic product for the United States from one year to another year can be used to measure economic growth.

Source: U.S. Department of Commerce web site (www.doc.gov) on May 8, 2000.

of the United States in current dollars and the *real* GDP in inflation-adjusted dollars. Note that between 1980 and 1999, America's real GDP grew from $4,900.9 billion to $8,848.2 billion.

In addition to gross domestic product, there are other economic measures that can be used to evaluate a nation's economy. Although there are many economic measures, some of the more significant terms are described in Table 1.1. Like the GDP, these measures can be used to compare one economic statistic over different periods of time. For current statistical information about the government, you may want to access the U.S. Department of Commerce web site (www.doc.gov/).

The Business Cycle

A nation's economy fluctuates rather than grows at a steady pace every year. These fluctuations are generally referred to as the **business cycle,** that is, the recurrence of periods of growth and recession in a nation's economic activity. The changes that result

business cycle the recurrence of periods of growth and recession in a nation's economic activity

table 1.1	**Common Measures Used to Evaluate a Nation s Economic Health**
Economic Measure	**Description**
1. Balance of Trade	The total value of a nation's exports minus the total value of its imports over a specific period of time.
2. Consumer Price Index	A monthly index that measures the changes in prices of approximately three hundred goods and services purchased by a typical consumer.
3. Inflation Rate	An economic statistic that tracks the increase in prices of goods and services over a period of time. This measure is usually calculated on a monthly or annual basis.
4. Prime Interest Rate	The lowest interest rate that banks charge their most creditworthy customers.
5. Producer Price Index	A monthly index that measures prices at the wholesale level.
6. Productivity Rate	An economic measure that tracks the increase and decrease in the average level of output per worker.
7. Unemployment Rate	The percentage of a nation's labor force unemployed at any time.

18

Part I **The Environment of Business**

recession two consecutive three-month periods of decline in a country's gross domestic product

depression a severe recession that lasts longer than a recession

monetary policies Federal Reserve's decisions that determine the size of the supply of money in the nation and the level of interest rates

fiscal policy government influence on the amount of savings and expenditures; accomplished by altering the tax structure and by changing the levels of government spending

federal deficit a shortfall created when the federal government spends more in a fiscal year than it receives

national debt the total of all federal deficits

from either growth or recession affect the amount of products and services that consumers are willing to purchase, and as a result the amount of products and services produced. Generally, the business cycle consists of four states: prosperity, recession, depression, and recovery.

During *prosperity,* unemployment is low and total income is relatively high. As long as the economic outlook remains prosperous, consumers are willing to buy products and services. In fact, businesses often expand and offer new products and services during prosperity in order to take advantage of the consumer's increased buying power.

Economists define a **recession** as two consecutive three-month periods of decline in a country's gross domestic product. Because unemployment rises during a recession, total buying power declines. The pessimism that accompanies a recession often stifles both consumer and business spending. As buying power decreases, consumers tend to become more value-conscious and reluctant to purchase frivolous items. In response to a recession, many businesses focus on the products and services that provide the most value to their customers.

Economists define a **depression** as a severe recession that lasts longer than a recession. A depression is characterized by extremely high unemployment rates, low wages, reduced purchasing power, lack of confidence in the economy, and a general decrease in business activity. To offset the effects of recession and depression, the federal government uses both monetary and fiscal policies. **Monetary policies** are the Federal Reserve's decisions that determine the size of the supply of money in the nation and the level of interest rates. Through **fiscal policy,** the government can influence the amount of savings and expenditures by altering the tax structure and changing the levels of government spending.

Although the federal government collects almost $2 trillion in annual revenues, the government spends more than it receives in most years, resulting in the **federal deficit.** Since 1980, there has been a federal deficit every year except 1998 and 1999. The total of all federal deficits is called the **national debt.** Today, the U.S. national debt is about $5.6 trillion or about $21,000 for every man, woman, and child in the United States.

Some experts believe that effective use of monetary and fiscal policies can speed up recovery and even eliminate depressions from the business cycle. *Recovery* is the movement of the economy from depression or recession to prosperity. High unemployment rates decline, income increases, and both the ability and the willingness to buy rise. Greater demand for products and services results.

Types of Competition

5 Outline the four types of competition.

competition rivalry among businesses for sales to potential customers

Our free-market economic system ensures that businesses make the decisions about what to produce, how to produce it, and what price to charge for the product. Mattel Inc., for example, can introduce new versions of its famous Barbie doll, license the Barbie name, change the doll's price and method of distribution, and attempt to produce and market Barbie in other countries or over the Internet at www.mattel.com. Our system also allows customers the right to choose between Mattel's products and those produced by competitors.

Competition like that between Mattel and other toy manufacturers is a necessary and extremely important by-product of a free-market economy. Because many individuals and groups can open businesses, there are usually a number of firms offering similar products. In other words, business firms must compete with each other for sales. Business **competition,** then, is essentially a rivalry among businesses for sales to potential customers. In a free-market economy, competition works to ensure the efficient operation of business. Competition also ensures that a firm will survive only if it serves its customers well. Economists recognize four different degrees of competition, ranging from ideal, complete competition to no competition at all. These are pure competition, monopolistic competition, oligopoly, and monopoly.

Pure Competition

Pure competition is the market situation in which there are many buyers and sellers of a product, and no single buyer or seller is powerful enough to affect the price of that product. Note that this definition includes several important ideas. First, we are discussing the market for a single product—say, bushels of wheat. Second, all sellers offer essentially the same product for sale; a buyer would be just as satisfied with seller A's wheat as with that offered by seller B or seller Z. Third, all buyers and sellers know everything there is to know about the market (including, in our example, the prices that all sellers are asking for their wheat). And fourth, the overall market is not affected by the actions of any one buyer or seller.

> **pure competition** the market situation in which there are many buyers and sellers of a product, and no single buyer or seller is powerful enough to affect the price of that product

When pure competition exists, every seller should ask the same price that every other seller is asking. Why? Because if one seller wanted 50 cents more per bushel of wheat than all the others, that seller would not be able to sell a single bushel. Buyers could—and would—do better by purchasing wheat from the competition. On the other hand, a firm willing to sell below the going price would sell all its wheat quickly. But that seller would lose sales revenue (and profit), because buyers are actually willing to pay more.

In pure competition, then, sellers—and buyers as well—must accept the going price. But who or what determines this price? Actually, everyone does. The price of each product is determined by the actions of *all buyers and all sellers together,* through the forces of supply and demand.

The Basics of Supply and Demand   The **supply** of a particular product is the quantity of the product that *producers are willing to sell at each of various prices.* Producers are rational people, so we would expect them to offer more of a product for sale at higher prices and to offer less of the product at lower prices, as illustrated by the supply curve in Figure 1.5.

> **supply** the quantity of a product that producers are willing to sell at each of various prices

The **demand** for a particular product is the quantity that *buyers are willing to purchase at each of various prices.* Buyers, too, are usually rational, so we would expect them—as a group—to buy more of a product when its price is low and to buy less of the product when its price is high, as depicted by the demand curve in Figure 1.5. This is exactly what happens when the price of wheat rises dramatically. People buy other grains or do without and reduce their purchases of wheat. They buy more wheat only when the price drops.

> **demand** the quantity of a product that buyers are willing to purchase at each of various prices

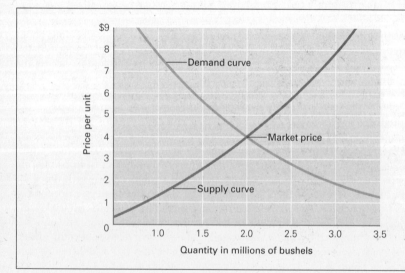

figure 1.5

Supply Curve and Demand Curve
The intersection of a supply curve and a demand curve indicates a single price and quantity at which suppliers will sell products and buyers will purchase them.

20

market price the price at which the quantity demanded is exactly equal to the quantity supplied

The Equilibrium, or Market, Price   There is always one certain price at which the demanded quantity of a product is exactly equal to the produced quantity of that product. Suppose producers are willing to *supply* 2 million bushels of wheat at a price of $4 per bushel, and buyers are willing to *purchase* 2 million bushels at a price of $4 per bushel. In other words, supply and demand are in balance, or *in equilibrium,* at the price of $4. Economists call this price the market price. The **market price** of any product is the price at which the quantity demanded is exactly equal to the quantity supplied. If suppliers produce 2 million bushels, then no one who is willing to pay $4 per bushel will have to go without wheat, and no producer who is willing to sell at $4 per bushel will be stuck with unsold wheat.

In theory and in the real world, market prices are affected by anything that affects supply and demand. The *demand* for wheat, for example, might change if researchers suddenly discovered that it offered a previously unknown health benefit. Then buyers would demand more wheat at every price. Or, the *supply* of wheat might change if new technology permitted the production of greater quantities of wheat from the same amount of acreage. Other changes that can affect competitive prices are shifts in buyer tastes, the development of new products, fluctuations in income due to inflation or recession, or even changes in the weather that affect the production of wheat.

Pure competition is quite rare in today's world. Some specific markets (such as auctions of farm products) may come close, but no real market totally exhibits perfect competition. Many real markets, however, are examples of monopolistic competition.

Monopolistic Competition

monopolistic competition a market situation in which there are many buyers along with a relatively large number of sellers who differentiate their products from the products of competitors

Monopolistic competition is a market situation in which there are many buyers along with a relatively large number of sellers. The various products available in a monopolistically competitive market are very similar in nature, and they are all intended to satisfy the same need. However, each seller attempts to make its product different from the others by providing unique product features, an attention-getting brand name, unique packaging, or services such as free delivery or a "lifetime" warranty. For example, Hanes originally differentiated L'eggs pantyhose from numerous competing brands through unique branding and packaging.

product differentiation the process of developing and promoting differences between one's products and all similar products

Product differentiation is the process of developing and promoting differences between ones products and all similar products. It is a fact of life for the producers of many consumer goods, from soaps to clothing to personal computers. An individual producer like Hanes sees what looks like a mob of competitors, all trying to chip away at its market. By differentiating each of its products from all similar products, the producer obtains some limited control over the market price of its product. Under pure competition, the price of all pantyhose brands would simply be the market price of all similar pantyhose products.

Oligopoly

oligopoly a market situation (or industry) in which there are few sellers

An **oligopoly** is a market situation (or industry) in which there are few sellers. Generally these sellers are quite large, and sizable investments are required to enter into their market. For this reason, oligopolistic industries tend to remain oligopolistic. Examples of oligopolies are the automobile, car rental, and farm implement industries.

Because there are few sellers in an oligopoly, each seller has considerable control over price. At the same time, the market actions of each seller can have a strong effect on competitors' sales. If General Motors, for example, reduces its automobile prices, Ford, Chrysler, Toyota, and Nissan usually do the same to retain their market shares. As a result, similar products eventually have similar prices. In the absence of much price competition, product differentiation becomes the major competitive weapon; this is very evident in the advertising of the major auto manufacturers. For instance, when General

21

Motors began offering low-interest financing for all of its cars, Ford, Chrysler, and Toyota also launched competitive financing deals.

Monopoly

A **monopoly** is a market (or industry) with only one seller. Because only one firm is the supplier of a product, it would seem that it has complete control over price. However, no firm can set its price at some astronomical figure just because there is no competition; the firm would soon find it had no customers or sales revenue, either. Instead, the firm in a monopoly position must consider the demand for its product and set the price at the most profitable level.

Classic examples of monopolies in the United States are public utilities. Each utility firm operates in a **natural monopoly,** an industry that requires a huge investment in capital and within which any duplication of facilities would be wasteful. Natural monopolies are permitted to exist because the public interest is best served by their existence, but they operate under the scrutiny and control of various state and federal agencies. While many public utilities are still classified as natural monopolies, there is increased competition in many industries. For example, the breakup of AT&T has increased the amount of competition in the telecommunications industry. And there have been increased demands for consumer choice when choosing a company that provides electrical service to both homes and businesses.

A legal monopoly—sometimes referred to as a *limited monopoly*—is created when the federal government issues a copyright, patent, and trademark. A copyright, patent, or trademark exists for a specific period of time and can be used to protect the owners of written materials, ideas, or product brands from unauthorized use by competitors that have not shared in the time, effort, and expense required for their development. Because Microsoft owns the copyright on its popular Windows software, it enjoys a limited monopoly position. Competitors cannot take the windows software, change the name, and sell it as their product without Microsoft's approval.

Except for natural monopolies and monopolies created by copyrights, patents, and trademarks, federal laws prohibit both monopolies and attempts to form monopolies. A recent amendment to the Sherman Antitrust Act of 1890 made any such attempt a criminal offense, and the Clayton Antitrust Act of 1914 prohibited a number of specific actions that could lead to monopoly. The goal of these and other antitrust laws is to ensure the competitive environment of business and thereby to protect consumers. Although both the Sherman and Clayton acts were enacted many years ago, they still provide a legal basis for encouraging competition and the possible breakup of a company that has a monopoly position. In fact, the Sherman act provided the legal basis for the recent court case involving the United States Department of Justice vs. Microsoft. Although Judge Thomas Penfield Jackson issued "findings of fact" stating Microsoft used its monopoly in personal computer (PC) operating systems to stifle competition to the detriment of consumers, Microsoft has responded through appeals to higher courts. Microsoft is likely to argue that it enjoys industry dominance because consumers choose their products voluntarily and that the court has no right to remove its proprietary right to continue selling its products that have contributed to American technological dominance in the PC field globally.[8]

How do you spell monopoly? This is one word that Bill Gates and the folks at Microsoft know how to spell. Embroiled in multiple lawsuits and legal battles, Microsoft argues that it has become one of the most successful companies in the world because it operates in a capitalistic society that encourages business firms to pursue excellence. On the other hand, opponents argue that Microsoft is too successful and takes advantage of its monopoly position in the computer software industry.

monopoly a market (or industry) with only one seller

natural monopoly an industry requiring huge investments in capital and within which duplication of facilities would be wasteful and thus not in the public interest

Check Your Understanding

The following sentences appear in the chapter. Circle the letter of the BEST meaning for each italicized word.

19. "A nation's economy *fluctuates* rather than grows at a steady pace every year."
    a. Decreases
    b. Expands
    c. Shrinks
    d. Rises and falls

20. "The *pessimism* that accompanies a recession often stifles both consumer and business spending."
    a. Cheerfulness
    b. Fear
    c. Tendency to stress the negative
    d. Belief in a divine power

21. "As buying power decreases, consumers tend to become more value-conscious and reluctant to purchase *frivolous* items."
    a. Worthless
    b. Trivial or silly
    c. Sentimental
    d. Large

22. "Business competition, then, is essentially a *rivalry* among businesses for sales to potential customers."
    a. Act of trying to surpass another
    b. Illegal act
    c. Argument
    d. Act of friendship

23. Natural monopolies are permitted to exist because the public interest is best served by their existence, but they operate under the *scrutiny* and control of various state and federal agencies."
    a. Authority
    b. Observation
    c. Charity
    d. Understanding
    Circle the letter of the correct response

24. What conclusion can you draw from Figure 1.4 in the preceding section of the business chapter?
    a. The GDP has been decreasing since 1980.
    b. The GDP has been increasing since 1980.
    c. The GDP in 1995 was over 10 billion dollars.
    d. The GDP for 1985 and 1990 were the same.

On the blanks provided, write your answers to the following review questions for the section of the business textbook you just read.

25. What are the four basic economic questions? How are they answered in a capitalist economy?

_____

_____

_____

26. Describe the four fundamental issues required for a laissez-faire capitalist economy.

_____

_____

_____

27. Why is the American economy called a mixed economy?

_____

_____

_____

28. Based on Figure 1.3 in the preceding section of the business chapter, outline the economic interactions between government and business in our business system. Outline those between government and households.

_____

_____

_____

29. How does capitalism differ from socialism and communism?

_____

_____

_____

30. Define *gross domestic product*. Why is this economic measure significant?

_____

_____

_____

31. Choose three of the economic measure described in Table 1.1 in the preceding section of the business chapter and describe why these indicators are important when measuring a nation's economy.

_____

_____

_____

32. Identify and compare the four forms of competition.

_____

_____

_____

33. Explain how the equilibrium, or market price, of a product is determined.

_____

_____

_____

Discuss the following questions with a partner or group, and then collaborate to write a response to each question on your own paper.

34. Does an individual consumer really have a voice in answering the basic economic questions?

35. In our business system, how is government involved in answering the four basic economic questions? Does government participate in the system or interfere with it?

22

The Development of American Business

LEARNING OBJECTIVE

6 Summarize the development of America's business system.

Our American business system developed together with the nation itself. Both have their roots in the knowledge, skills, and values that the earliest settlers brought to this country. Refer to Figure 1.6 for an overall view of the relationship between our history, the development of our business system, and some major inventions that influenced them both.

figure 1.6

Time Line of American Business
Notice that invention and innovation naturally led to changes in transportation. This trend in turn caused a shift to more of a manufacturing economy.

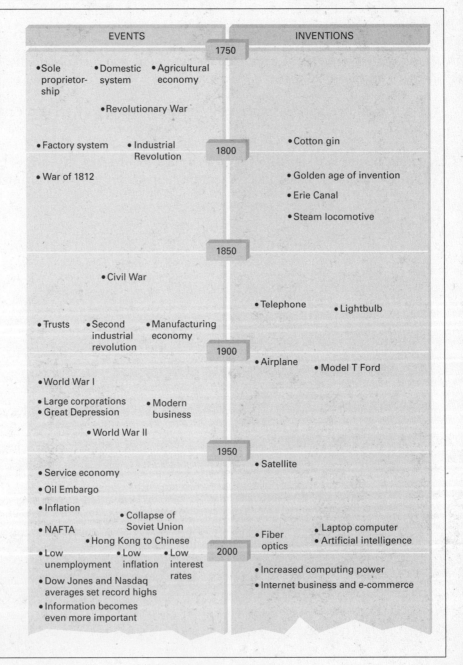

EVENTS		INVENTIONS
	1750	
• Sole proprietorship • Domestic system • Agricultural economy		
• Revolutionary War		
• Factory system • Industrial Revolution	1800	• Cotton gin
• War of 1812		• Golden age of invention
		• Erie Canal
		• Steam locomotive
	1850	
• Civil War		
		• Telephone • Lightbulb
• Trusts • Second industrial revolution • Manufacturing economy	1900	
		• Airplane • Model T Ford
• World War I		
• Large corporations • Modern business		
• Great Depression		
• World War II		
	1950	
		• Satellite
• Service economy		
• Oil Embargo		
• Inflation		
• NAFTA • Collapse of Soviet Union		• Fiber optics • Laptop computer • Artificial intelligence
• Hong Kong to Chinese		
• Low unemployment • Low inflation • Low interest rates	2000	• Increased computing power
• Dow Jones and Nasdaq averages set record highs		• Internet business and e-commerce
• Information becomes even more important		

The Colonial Period

The first settlers in the New World were concerned mainly with providing themselves with basic necessities—food, clothing, and shelter. Almost all families lived on farms, and the entire family worked at the business of surviving.

The colonists did indeed survive, and eventually they were able to produce more than they consumed. They used their surplus for trading, mainly by barter, among themselves and with the English trading ships that called at the colonies. **Barter** is a system of exchange in which goods or services are traded directly for other goods and/or services—without using money. As this trade increased, small-scale business enterprises began to appear. Most of these businesses produced farm products. Other industries that had been founded by 1700 were shipbuilding, lumbering, fur trading, rum manufacturing, and fishing. International trade with England grew, but British trade policies heavily favored British merchants.

barter a system of exchange in which goods or services are traded directly for other goods and/or services—without using money

As late as the Revolutionary War period, 90 percent of the population were still living on farms and were engaged primarily in activities to meet their own needs. Some were able to use their skills and their excess time to work under the domestic system of production. The **domestic system** was a method of manufacturing in which an entrepreneur distributed raw materials to various homes, where families would process them into finished goods. The goods were then offered for sale by the merchant entrepreneur.

domestic system a method of manufacturing in which an entrepreneur distributed raw materials to various homes, where families would process them into finished goods to be offered for sale by the merchant entrepreneur

The Industrial Revolution

In 1790 a young English apprentice mechanic named Samuel Slater decided to sail to America. At this time, British law forbade the export of machinery, technology, and skilled workers. To get around the law, Slater painstakingly memorized the plans for Richard Arkwright's water-powered spinning machine, which had revolutionized the British textile industry, and left England disguised as a farmer. A year later, he set up a textile factory in Pawtucket, Rhode Island, to spin raw cotton into thread. Slater's ingenuity resulted in America's first use of the **factory system** of manufacturing, in which all the materials, machinery, and workers required to manufacture a product are assembled in one place. The Industrial Revolution in America was born.

factory system a system of manufacturing in which all the materials, machinery, and workers required to manufacture a product are assembled in one place

The invention of the cotton gin in 1793 by Eli Whitney greatly increased the supply of cotton for the textile industry. And by 1814 Francis Cabot Lowell had established a factory in Waltham, Massachusetts, to spin, weave, and bleach cotton, all under one roof. In doing so, Lowell seems to have used a manufacturing technique called specialization. **Specialization** is the separation of a manufacturing process into distinct tasks and the assignment of different tasks to different individuals. The purpose of specialization is to increase the efficiency of industrial workers; Lowell's workers were able to produce 30 miles of cloth each day.

specialization the separation of a manufacturing process into distinct tasks and the assignment of different tasks to different individuals

The three decades from 1820 to 1850 were the golden age of invention and innovation in machinery. Elias Howe's sewing machine became available to convert materials into clothing. The agricultural machinery of John Deere and Cyrus McCormick revolutionized farm production. At the same time, new means of transportation greatly expanded the domestic markets for American products. The Erie Canal was opened in the 1820s. Soon afterward, thanks to Robert Fulton's engine, steamboats could move upstream against the current and use the rivers as highways for hauling bulk goods. During the 1830s and 1840s, the railroads began to extend the existing transportation system to the West carrying goods and people much farther than was possible by waterways alone.

Many business historians view the period from 1870 to 1900 as the second industrial revolution; certainly, many characteristics of our modern business system took form during these three decades. In this period, for example, the nation shifted from a farm economy to a manufacturing economy. The developing coal and oil industries provided fuel for light, heat, and energy. During this time, the United States became not only an industrial giant but a leading world power as well.

24

Early Twentieth Century

Industrial growth and prosperity continued well into the twentieth century. Henry Ford's moving automotive assembly line, which brought the work to the worker, refined the concept of specialization and helped spur on the mass production of consumer goods. By the 1920s the automobile industry had begun to influence the entire economy. The steel industry, which supplies materials to the auto industry, grew along with it. The oil and chemical industries grew just as fast. And the emerging airplane and airline industries promised convenient and faster transportation.

Fundamental changes occurred in business ownership and management as well. The largest businesses were no longer owned by one individual; instead, ownership was in the hands of thousands of corporate shareholders who were willing to invest in—but not to operate—a business.

Certain modern marketing techniques are products of this era, too. Large corporations developed new methods of advertising and selling. Time payment plans made it possible for the average consumer to purchase costly durable goods such as automobiles, appliances, and home furnishings. Advertisements counseled the public to "buy now and pay later." Capitalism and our economy seemed strong and healthy, but it was not to last.

The Great Depression

The Roaring Twenties ended with the sudden crash of the stock market in 1929 and the near collapse of the economy. The Great Depression that followed in the 1930s was a time of misery and human suffering. The unemployment rate varied between 16 and 25 percent in the years 1931 through 1939, and the value of goods and services produced in America fell by almost half. People lost their faith in business and its ability to satisfy the needs of society without government interference.

After Franklin D. Roosevelt became president in 1933, the federal government devised a number of programs to get the economy moving again. In implementing these programs, the government got deeply involved in business for the first time. Many business people opposed this intervention, but they reluctantly accepted the new government regulations.

Recovery and Beyond

The economy was on the road to recovery when World War II broke out in Europe in 1939. The need for vast quantities of war materials—first for our allies and then for the American military as well—spurred business activity and technological development. This rapid economic pace continued after the war, and the 1950s and 1960s witnessed both increasing production and a rising standard of living. **Standard of living** is a loose, subjective measure of how well-off an individual or a society is, mainly in terms of want-satisfaction through goods and services.

standard of living a loose, subjective measure of how well-off an individual or a society is, mainly in terms of want-satisfaction through goods and services

The Late Twentieth Century

In the mid-1970s, however, a shortage of crude oil led to a new set of problems for business. As the cost of petroleum products increased, a corresponding increase took place in the cost of energy and the cost of goods and services. The result was inflation at a rate well over 10 percent per year during the early 1980s. Interest rates also increased dramatically, so both businesses and consumers reduced their borrowing. Business profits fell as the consumer's purchasing power was eroded by inflation and high interest rates. By the mid-1980s, many of these problem areas showed signs of improvement. Unfortunately, many managers now had something else to worry about—corporate mergers and takeovers. In addition, a large number of bank failures, coupled with an increasing number of bankruptcies, again made people uneasy about our business system.

By the 1990s, the U.S. economy began to show signs of improvement and economic growth. Unemployment numbers, inflation, and interest—all factors that affect business—were now at record lows. In turn, business took advantage of this economic prosperity to invest in information technology, cut costs, and increase flexibility and efficiency. (To see the excellent returns that investments in information technology have provided, read the Talking Technology boxed feature.) These changes in our economy have led some economists to believe that we now have a *New Economy* fueled by faster economic growth and increased demand for new products. If there exists a centerpiece of the New Economy, then the Internet is surely it. Initially created in America and now part of a globally connected telecommunications network of people and organizations around the world, the Internet is still dominated by American commercial interests including computer hardware, software, and Internet content providers. As further evidence of the financial health of the new economy, the stock market has enjoyed the longest period of sustained economic growth in our history. Both the Dow Jones Industrial Average and the Nasdaq Stock Index—two measures that investors use to measure stock market performance—have reached record highs. For individual

Talking Technology

Looking for a Good Investment? Try a Computer Industry

JUST SAY THE WORD COMPUTERS TO investors, and they sit up and take notice. When *Fortune* magazine released their report card on corporate America in the spring of 2000, three different computer industries were bunched at the very top when ranked on return to shareholders. Check out the numbers below—they're guaranteed to get your attention.

Fortune Ranking	Specific Industry	Return to Shareholders for One Year
1	Computer Peripherals	80.1 percent
3	Computer and Data Services	47.3 percent
6	Computers and Office Equipment	28.5 percent

In addition to the top industry rankings above, three major corporations that were leaders in the computers and office equipment industry were also among the top twenty corporations in the first *Fortune* 500 list of the twenty-first century. Let's look at this year's winners.

International Business Machines

Ranked Number 6 on *Fortune's* list of top twenty, IBM—sometimes referred to as Big Blue—markets over 40,000 products and is the world's largest computer firm. It is a major provider of technical support to business accounts. Today, IBM is promoting its networking products and has intensified sales of its stand-alone computer parts. Based in Armonk, New York, IBM has 291,000 employees with sales revenues of more than $87 million in 1999. Chairman and CEO Louis Gerstner, Jr., became head of IBM in 1993.

Hewlett-Packard Company

Ranked number 13 on *Fortune's* list of top twenty corporations, Hewlett-Packard is the world's second largest computer company and is based in Palo Alto, California. Today HP is re-creating itself as a speedy Internet specialist providing web servers, software, and services to corporate customers. With more than 29,000 products on the market, it had sales revenues that total nearly $50 million for 1999. It employs approximately 124,000 employees. Appointed by the board in 1999, Carleton S. "Carley" Florina is the first woman CEO and president of a top *Fortune* 500 Corporation—"not a bad way to start a new century."

Compaq Computer Corporation

Ranked number 20 on *Fortune's* list of top twenty corporations, Compaq is the third largest computer firm in the world. This Houston-based company has 71,000 employees and generated revenues of $38.5 million in 1999. It was the first company to introduce a computer based on Intel's 386 computer chip in 1986. Their laptop computer was an immediate success in 1988. Today, personal computers account for over half of its sales. Its primary head-to-head competitor is Dell Computer, and both companies are challenging each other for the top spot among PC makers. In 1999, Compaq chose Michael D. Capellas as president and CEO.

investors, it has been a bumpy ride at times, but the financial rewards have justified the added risk of investing in stocks and mutual funds. As we enter a new millennium, many of those same economists and investors are wondering how long it will last.

The New Millennium

Quick test! Answer the following questions:

1. Do you own a cell phone?
2. Do you own a computer or use a computer at work?
3. How much time do you spend surfing the Internet?

Three quick questions, but they serve as a crude measuring stick to determine the importance of information technology in the world today. As we begin the new millennium, information technology will continue to fuel the new economy. There will be more investment spending on information technology and Internet usage will increase at even faster rates. The importance of e-business—a topic that we will continue to explore throughout this text—will increase dramatically. In addition to information technology, the growth of service businesses and increasing opportunities for global trade will also impact the way American firms do business in the twenty-first century. Because they employ over half of the American work force, service businesses are a very important component of our economy. As a result, service businesses must find ways to improve productivity and cut costs while at the same time providing jobs for even a larger portion of the work force.

American businesses are beginning to realize that to be successful, they must enter the global marketplace. In short, American firms must meet the needs not only of American consumers but also of foreign consumers. And foreign firms are now selling record amounts of products and services to American consumers. Indeed, the world—as far as business is concerned—is becoming smaller. (Both our service economy and our place in the global marketplace are discussed more fully later in the text.)

The Challenges Ahead

LEARNING OBJECTIVE

7 Discuss the challenges that American businesses will encounter in the future.

There it is—the American business system in brief. When it works well, it provides jobs for those who are willing to work, a standard of living that few countries can match, and many opportunities for personal advancement. But, like every other system devised by humans, it is not perfect. Our business system may give us prosperity, but it also gave us the Great Depression of the 1930s and the economic problems of the 1970s and the late 1980s.

Obviously, the system can be improved. It may need no more than a bit of fine-tuning, or it may require more extensive overhauling. Certainly there are plenty of people who are willing to tell us exactly what *they* think the American economy needs. But these people provide us only with conflicting opinions. Who is right and who is wrong? Even the experts cannot agree.

The experts do agree, however, that several key issues will challenge our economic system over the next few decades. Some of the questions to be resolved:

■ How much government involvement in our economy is necessary for its continued well-being? In what areas should there be less involvement? In what areas, more?
■ How can we encourage economic growth and at the same time continue to conserve natural resources and protect our environment?

27

Today it seems that everyone is wired. One of the fastest growing segments of the economy is telecommunications. At this career fair, a human resource specialist for CellNet Data Systems talks with a job applicant about the qualities and skills necessary for success in high-tech companies.

- How can we meet the challenges of managing culturally diverse work forces to meet the needs of a culturally diverse marketplace?
- How can we evaluate the long-term economic costs and benefits of existing and proposed government programs?
- How can we hold down inflation and yet stimulate the economy to provide jobs?
- How can we preserve the benefits of competition in our American economic system?
- How can we meet the needs of the less fortunate?
- How can we make American manufacturers more productive and more competitive with foreign producers who have lower labor costs?
- How can we best market American-made products in foreign nations?
- How can we ensure that domestic business organizations will keep pace with the technological advancements of firms in other countries?
- How can we finance additional investment spending on information technology?
- How can we encourage an entrepreneurial spirit in large, established corporations?

The answers to these questions are anything but simple. In the past, Americans have always been able to solve their economic problems through ingenuity and creativity. Now, as we begin the twenty-first century, we need that same ingenuity and creativity not only to solve our current problems but also to compete in the global marketplace.

According to economic experts, if we as a nation can become more competitive, we may solve many of our current domestic problems. As an added bonus, increased competitiveness will also enable us to meet the economic challenges posed by other industrialized nations of the world. The way we solve these problems will affect our own future, our children's future, and that of our nation. Within the American economic and political system, the answers are ours to provide.

The American business system is not perfect by any means, but it does work reasonably well. We discuss some of its problems in Chapter 2, as we examine the role of business as part of American society.

RETURN TO inside Business

ACCORDING TO MANAGEMENT EXPERTS, a business must do two things to be
successful. First, it must put the customer first—by listening, understanding, and
providing customer service. Second, a company—both its managers and employees—must act with speed and flexibility. The General Electric Company scores A+
on both counts. For the past four years, General Electric has received *Fortune* magazine's Most Admired Corporation Award because of its ability to see an opportunity and turn it into a product or service that its customers want.

What does the future hold for GE? Well, to begin with, the General Electric
Company is not one to sit back and rest on past performance. Like most large
firms, GE is concerned about sales and profits, but corporate management real-
izes that sales and profits will increase when a business meets customer needs. To
that end, corporate management is always looking for ways to meet customer
needs and at the same time perfect the methods it uses for generating ideas, planning, and product manufacturing. This huge corporate giant is on the lookout for
ways to expand its core businesses. For example, one of GE's most aggressive
growth initiatives is to develop methods for conducting e-business within its core
businesses. Until the beginning of 1999, GE's use of the Internet was almost non-
existent. At that time, GE's chief executive officer, Jack Welch, and its board of
directors decided that the company needed to use the Internet to attract new customers. General Electric's new e-business strategy not only attracted new customers, generating millions of dollars in sales revenue, it evolved into a system
that enabled the company to offer innovative services to its existing customers. To
see how America's Most Admired Corporation uses the Internet to meet customer
needs and increase sales, go to www.ge.com.

Questions

1. Today General Electric is one of the largest and most respected firms in the world. What
   factors led to GE's success?
2. It would be easy for General Electric to sit back and rest on past performance. After all,
   it is the Most Admired Corporation in America and the darling of Wall Street. And
   yet, Jack Welch and other corporate managers want to maintain their position in a very
   competitive business world. What steps is General Electric taking to maintain their

chapter review

SUMMARY

1 Discuss your future in the world of business.

Opportunity! It's only eleven letters, but no other word provides a better description of our current business environment. And yet, employers and our capitalistic economic system are more demanding than ever before. As you begin

this course, ask yourself: What can I do that will make
employers want to pay me a salary? What skills do I have
that employers need? By studying business, you can become
a better-informed consumer and investor. By introducing
you to a wide range of employment opportunities, a business course can also help you decide on a career. The kind of
career you choose will ultimately depend on your own values and what you feel is most important in life. But deciding
on the kind of career you want is only a first step. To get a
job in your chosen field and to be successful at it, you will

have to develop a plan, or road map, that ensures you have the skills and knowledge the job requires. A sound working knowledge of business can also enable you to start your own business.

2 Define *business* and identify potential risks and rewards.

Business is the organized effort of individuals to produce and sell, for a profit, the goods and services that satisfy society's needs. Four kinds of resources—material, human, financial, and informational—must be combined to start and operate a business. The three general types of businesses are manufacturers, service businesses, and marketing intermediaries. Profit is what remains after all business expenses are deducted from sales revenue. It is the payment that owners receive for assuming the risks of business—primarily the risks of not receiving payment and of losing whatever has been invested in the firm. Most often, a business that is operated to satisfy its customers earns a reasonable profit.

3 Describe the two types of economic systems: capitalism and command economy.

Economics is the study of how wealth is created and distributed. An economy is a system through which a society decides those two issues. An economic system must answer four questions: What goods and services will be produced? How will they be produced? For whom will they be produced? Who owns and who controls the major factors of production? Capitalism (on which our economic system is based) is an economic system in which individuals own and operate the majority of businesses that provide goods and services. Capitalism stems from the theories of Adam Smith. Smith's pure laissez-faire capitalism is an economic system in which these decisions are made by individuals and businesses as they pursue their own self-interest. In a laissez-faire capitalist system, the factors of production are owned by private entities, and all individuals are free to use their resources as they see fit; prices are determined by the workings of supply and demand in competitive markets; and the economic role of government is limited to protecting competition.

Our economic system today is a mixed economy. Although our present business system is essentially capitalist in nature, government takes part, along with households and businesses. In the circular flow (Figure 1.3) that characterizes our business system, households and businesses exchange resources for goods and services, using money as the medium of exchange. Government collects taxes from businesses and households and purchases products and resources with which to provide services.

In a command economy, government, rather than individuals, owns the factors of production and provides the answers to the three other economic questions. Socialist and communist economies are—at least in theory—command economies. In the real world, however, communists seem to practice a strictly controlled kind of socialism.

4 Identify the ways to measure economic performance.

One way to evaluate the performance of an economic system is to assess changes in productivity, which is the average level of output per worker per hour. Gross domestic product (GDP) can also be used to measure a nation's economic well being and is the total dollar value of all goods and services produced by all people within the boundaries of a country during a one-year period. This figure facilitates comparisons between the United States and other countries, since it is the standard used in international guidelines for economic accounting. It is also possible to adjust GDP for inflation and thus to measure real GDP. In addition to gross domestic product, there are other economic indicators that can be used to measure a nation's economy. These include a nation's balance of trade, consumer price index, inflation rate, prime interest rate, producer price index, productivity rate, and unemployment rate.

A nation's economy fluctuates rather than grows at a steady pace every year. These fluctuations are generally referred to as the business cycle. Generally, the business cycle consists of four states: prosperity, recession, depression, and recovery. Some experts believe that effective use of monetary policy (the Federal Reserve's decisions that determine the size of the supply of money) and fiscal policies (the government's influence on the amount of savings and expenditures) can speed up recovery and even eliminate depressions for the business cycle.

5 Outline the four types of competition.

Competition is essentially a rivalry among businesses for sales to potential customers. In a free-market economy, competition works to ensure the efficient and effective operation of business. Competition also ensures that a firm will survive only if it serves its customers well. Economists recognize four degrees of competition. Ranging from most to least competitive, the four degrees are pure competition, monopolistic competition, oligopoly, and monopoly. The factors of supply and demand generally influence the price that consumers pay producers for goods and services.

6 Summarize the development of America's business system.

Since its beginnings in the seventeenth century, American business has been based on private ownership of property and freedom of enterprise. And from this beginning, through the Industrial Revolution of the early nineteenth century, to the phenomenal expansion of American industry in the nineteenth and early twentieth centuries, our government maintained an essentially laissez-faire attitude toward business. However, during the Great Depression of the 1930s, the federal government began to provide a number of social services to its citizens. Government's role in business has expanded considerably since that time.

30

During the 1970s a shortage of crude oil led to higher prices and inflation. Business profits fell as the consumer's purchasing power was eroded by inflation and high interest rates. By the mid-1980s, corporate mergers and takeovers, bank failures, and an increasing number of bankruptcies made people uneasy about our business system. By the 1990s, the U.S. economy began to show signs of improvement and economic growth. Unemployment numbers, inflation, and interest—all factors that affect business—were now at record lows. Fueled by investment in information technology, the stock market enjoyed the longest period of sustained economic growth in our history. As we enter the new millennium, information technology will continue to fuel a new economy. Increased use of the Internet and e-business are now changing the way that firms do business in the twenty-first century. Other factors that affect the way firms do business include the increasing importance of services and global trade.

---

7 | **Discuss the challenges that American businesses will encounter in the future.**

Today, American businesses face a number of significant challenges. Among the issues to be contended with are the level of government involvement in business; the extent of business's environmental and social responsibilities; the effective management of cultural diversity in the workplace; the problem of holding down inflation while stimulating the economy; competition with foreign producers; technological innovation; and the problem of encouraging the entrepreneurial spirit in large, established corporations. If we as a nation can become more competitive, we may solve many of our domestic economic problems. As an added bonus, increased competitiveness will enable us to meet the challenges posed by foreign nations.

KEY TERMS

You should now be able to define and give an example relevant to each of the following terms:

free enterprise (4)
e-business (7)
business (9)
consumers (10)
profit (11)
economics (11)
economy (11)
factors of production (11)
entrepreneur (13)
capitalism (13)
market economy (13)
mixed economy (13)
consumer products (14)
command economy (15)
productivity (16)
gross domestic product (GDP) (16)

inflation (16)
business cycle (17)
recession (18)
depression (18)
monetary policies (18)
fiscal policy (18)
federal deficit (18)
national debt (18)
competition (18)
pure competition (19)
supply (19)
demand (19)
market price (20)
monopolistic competition (20)
product differentiation (20)
oligopoly (20)
monopoly (21)
natural monopoly (21)
barter (23)
domestic system (23)
factory system (23)
specialization (23)
standard of living (24)

REVIEW QUESTIONS

1. What reasons would you give if you were advising someone to study business?
2. What factors affect a person's choice of careers?
3. Describe the four resources that must be combined to organize and operate a business. How do they differ from the economist's factors of production?
4. What distinguishes consumers from other buyers of goods and services?
5. Describe the relationship among profit, business risk, and the satisfaction of customers' needs.
6. What are the four basic economic questions? How are they answered in a capitalist economy?
7. Describe the four fundamental issues required for a laissez-faire capitalist economy.
8. Why is the American economy called a mixed economy?
9. Based on Figure 1.3, outline the economic interactions between government and business in our business system. Outline those between government and households.
10. How does capitalism differ from socialism and communism?
11. Define gross domestic product. Why is this economic measure significant?
12. Choose three of the economic measures described in Table 1.1 and describe why these indicators are important when measuring a nation's economy.
13. Identify and compare the four forms of competition.
14. Explain how the equilibrium, or market price, of a product is determined.
15. Trace the steps that led from farming for survival in the American colonial period to today's mass production.

31

16. What do you consider the most important challenges that will face people in the United States in the years ahead?

DISCUSSION QUESTIONS

1. What factors caused American business to develop into a mixed economic system rather than some other type of system?
2. Does an individual consumer really have a voice in answering the basic economic questions?
3. Is gross domestic product a reliable indicator of a nation's standard of living? What might be a better indicator?
4. Discuss this statement: "Business competition encourages efficiency of production and leads to improved product quality."
5. In our business system, how is government involved in answering the four basic economic questions? Does government participate in the system or interfere with it?

VIDEO CASE

Motorola s Total Commitment to Employees

Because everyone wants to find the "perfect" position, choosing a career can be a traumatic experience, to say the least. Many job applicants express concern about being hired to work in dead-end positions with no potential. They worry that employers may be more concerned about finding someone willing to work for low wages than about helping employees grow professionally. If you have had similar concerns, take heart: some firms do value employees and the contributions they make to their operations. One such firm is Motorola. A leading provider of wireless communications, semiconductors, and advanced electronic systems, Motorola credits its employees with making it the largest producer of cellular phones, pagers, and mobile radios in the world.

How important are employees to Motorola's success? According to Robert Galvin, the chairman of Motorola's executive committee, people are the firm's most important asset. Given this attitude, it is not surprising that very few employees leave Motorola until they reach retirement age. The firm was one of the first major corporations to offer a cafeteria for employees, and its profit-sharing plan has served as a model for other companies. But there is something more to Motorola's ability to retain people beyond its above-average compensation, medical benefits, and company-sponsored day-care centers. The secret to attracting and keeping some of the best people in the industry is Motorola's commitment to making people the most effective employees they can be.

For Motorola, the employment process begins with recruiting people who have the emotional, psychological, and physical skills the organization needs. But recruiters also look for employees who can think creatively and who

can use their mental agility in decision making. Once hired, employees are not just encouraged to develop professionally to reach their career potential; they are expected to do so. All employees are required to take at least five days of training each year. Workers who do poorly on reading and mathematics tests enroll in remedial classes. Manufacturing workers attend classes in quality control, idea sharing, and teamwork. And all employees can take courses in product design, risk taking, and managing change. In short, Motorola is willing to invest both time and money to provide its employees with state-of-the-art training programs.

Although Motorola—or for that matter any organization—may use financial, material, or informational resources to accomplish its goals, people are the ones who get the job done. As Robert Galvin points out, people in an organization like Motorola have one fundamental purpose, and that is to provide total customer satisfaction. The ability to provide total customer satisfaction, which depends on Motorola's most important asset—its dedicated employees—is what has enabled Motorola to maintain its leadership position in the very competitive electronics industry.[9]

Questions

1. To be successful, most businesses use material, financial, human, and informational resources. Robert Galvin, chairman of Motorola's executive committee, has said that people are his firm's most important asset. Do you think human resources are really that important?
2. Motorola's state-of-the-art training programs cost the company both time and money. As a stockholder in this corporation, would you feel this is a good use of corporate assets? Why or why not?
3. Motorola's recruiters look for people who can think creatively and use their mental agility in decision making. In your own words, describe what you think "creative thinking" and "mental agility" mean. Why would these traits be important to a firm like Motorola?
4. Once hired, Motorola's employees are not just encouraged to develop professionally to reach their career potential; they are expected to do so. Would you want to work for a company like Motorola? Explain your answer.

32

Building skills for career success

1. Exploring the Internet

The World Wide Web, or web, is a global network of corporate, government, institutional, and individual computers accessible to users who can connect to its grid. Your school or firm is most likely connected to the Web, or you may have private access through a commercial service provider like America Online.

To familiarize you with the wealth of information available through the Internet and its usefulness to business students, this exercise focuses on information services available from a few popular "search engines" used to explore the web. Each of the remaining chapters in the text also contains an Internet exercise that is in some way associated with the topics covered in the chapter. After completing these exercises, you will not only be familiar with a variety of sources of business information, you will also be better prepared to locate information you might need in the future.

To use one of these search engines, enter its "Internet address" in your web browser or choose from a list of search engines that may be posted on your school's startup screen. Ask your teacher or technician for help if you have any trouble. The addresses of some search engines are as follows:

http://www.altavista.com
http://www.yahoo.com
http://www.lycos.com

Visit the text web site for updates to this exercise.

Assignment

1. Examine the way in which two search engines present categories of information on their opening screens. Explore the articles in the business and economics categories. Which search engine was better to use, in your opinion? Why?
2. Think of a business topic you would like to know more about; for example, "gross domestic product" or another concept introduced in this chapter. Using your preferred search engine, explore a few articles and reports provided on your topic. Briefly summarize your findings.

2. Developing Critical Thinking Skills

Under capitalism, competition is a driving force that allows the market economy to work, affecting the supply of goods and services in the marketplace and the prices consumers pay for those goods and services. Have you thought about how competition has a daily impact on your life and your buying habits? Let's see how competition works by pretending you want to buy a new car.

Assignment

1. Brainstorm the following questions:
   a. How will you decide on the make and model of car you want to buy, where to buy the car, and how to finance it?
   b. How is competition at work in this scenario?
   c. What are the pros and cons of competition as it affects the buyer?
2. Record your ideas.
3. Write a summary of the key points you learned about how competition works in the marketplace.

3. Building Team Skills

Over the past few years, employees have been expected to function as productive team members instead of working alone. People often believe they can work effectively in teams, but this is not always true. Being an effective team member requires skills that encourage other members to participate in the team endeavor. College classes that function as teams are more interesting and more fun to attend, and students generally learn more about the topics in the course. If your class is to function as a team, it is important to begin building the team early in the semester. One way to begin creating a team is to learn something about each student in the class. This helps team members feel comfortable with each other and fosters a sense of trust.

Assignment

1. Find a partner, preferably someone you do *not* know.
2. Each partner has five minutes to answer the following questions:
   a. What is your name and where do you work?
   b. What interesting or unusual thing have you done in your life? (Do not talk about work; rather, focus on things like hobbies, travel, family, and sports.)
   c. Why are you taking this course and what do you expect to learn? (Satisfying a degree requirement is not an acceptable answer.)
3. Introduce your partner to the class. Use one to two minutes, depending on the size of the class.

4. Researching Different Careers

In this chapter, *entrepreneurship* is defined as the willingness to take risks and the knowledge and ability to use the other factors of production efficiently. An *entrepreneur* is a person who risks his or her time, effort, and money to start and operate a business. Often people believe these terms apply only to small business operations, but recently employees with entrepreneurial attitudes have advanced more rapidly in large companies.

Assignment

1. Go to the local library or use the Internet to research how large firms, especially corporations, are rewarding employees who have entrepreneurial skills.
2. Find answers to the following questions:
   a. Why is an entrepreneurial attitude important in corporations today?
   b. What makes an employee with an entrepreneurial orientation different from other employees?
   c. How are these employees being rewarded, and are the rewards worth the effort?
3. Write a two-page report that summarizes your findings.

5. Improving Communication Skills

Most jobs today require good writing skills. Written communications in the workplace range from the simple task of jotting down telephone messages to the more complex tasks of writing memos, newspaper articles, policy manuals, and technical journals. Regardless of the type of communication, the writer must convey the correct information to the reader in a clear, concise, and courteous manner. This involves using effective writing skills, which can be improved through practice. You can begin improving your skills by writing in a journal on a regular basis.

Assignment

1. Each week during the semester, write your thoughts and ideas in a journal. Include business terms you learned during the week and give an example of how each term is used in the business world. Also, do one of the following:
   a. Ask someone, preferably a person working in business, a question based on a topic in the class assignment for the week. Record the answers, and comment on your perceptions about the topic.
   b. Read a newspaper article relating to a topic covered in the class assignment for the week. Summarize your thoughts on the topic in your journal, specifically discussing what you learned.
2. Ask your instructor for guidelines and due dates for the completed journal and the summary you will prepare at the end of the semester.

Check Your Understanding

The following sentences appear in the chapter. Circle the letter of the best meaning for each italicized word.

36. "Slater's *ingenuity* resulted in America's first use of the factory system of manufacturing...."
    a. Dishonesty
    b. Cleverness
    c. Anger
    d. Good fortune

37. "The three decades from 1820 to 1850 were the golden age of invention and *innovation* in machinery."
    a. Protection against something evil
    b. Affection
    c. Introduction of something new
    d. Freedom from sin

38. "Standard of living is a loose, *subjective* measure of how well-off an individual or society is...."
    a. Based upon personal beliefs and feelings
    b. Based on factual information
    c. Derived from guesswork
    d. Random

On the blanks provided, write your answers to the following review questions for the section of the business textbook you just read.

39. Trace the steps that led from farming for survival in the American colonial period to today's mass production.

_____

_____

_____

40. What do you consider the most important challenges that will face people in the United States in the years ahead?

_____

_____

Discuss the following questions with a partner or group, and then collaborate to write a response to each question on your own page.

41. What factors caused American business to develop into a mixed economic system rather than some other type of system?

42. Is gross domestic product a reliable indicator of a nation's standard of living? What might be a better indicator?

43. Discuss this statement: "Business competition encourages efficiency of production and leads to improved product quality."

44. Complete one of the five assignments in the section entitled "Building Skills for Career Success."

An Introduction to Physical Science: "Atmospheric Effects"

Applying the Reading Strategies

Write your response to the following question on your own paper.

1. Freewrite or brainstorm lists of words and phrases for ten minutes in order to clear your mind in preparation for reading.

Previewing the Chapter

Preview the chapter entitled "Atmospheric Effects" on pages 135–170, and then answer the following questions by circling the letter of the correct response.

2. On what topics does this chapter focus?
   a. Rain and storms
   b. Weather, climate, and pollution
   c. Keeping the environment clean
   d. The planet Earth

3. Into how many major sections is this chapter divided?
   a. Two
   b. Three
   c. Five
   d. Eight

4. Where are the learning goals of this chapter located?
   a. In a list at the beginning of the chapter
   b. In a list at the end of the chapter
   c. In the margins throughout the chapter
   d. Within the text of the chapter

5. True or False: In this chapter, key terms are defined in the margins.
   a. True
   b. False

6. Which of the following is NOT an action you should be able to perform after reading this chapter?
   a. Distinguish among the various types of precipitation
   b. Identify various types of local and tropical storms
   c. Define *climate* and identify climatic changes
   d. Identify the major types of water pollution

7. Locate the list of key terms in the chapter. In this chapter, they are known as
   a. key terms.
   b. vocabulary.
   c. important terms.
   d. words to know.

8. Based on the chapter outline, you can reasonably conclude that this chapter will NOT cover
   a. tornadoes.
   b. smog.
   c. how the moon affects ocean tides.
   d. sources of air pollution.

9. Into what two major categories does the author divide storms?
   a. Local storms and tropical storms
   b. Thunder and lightning
   c. Tornadoes and hurricanes
   d. Thunderstorms and tropical storms

Reading the Chapter

Before you read the chapter entitled "Atmospheric Effects," turn all of the headings and subheadings into questions. Then, read actively by either highlighting or underlining the answers to those questions. If you encounter an unfamiliar word, look it up in a dictionary and write its definition in the margin.

The three "Check Your Understanding" sections that appear throughout the excerpted chapter, "Atmospheric Effects," include questions that will help you check your comprehension of the information provided in the chapter. They encourage you to practice the reading strategies you have learned from this text supplement, so stop to complete them before you continue reading.

20

Atmospheric Effects

And pleas'd the Almighty's orders to perform
Rides in the whirlwind and directs the storm.

Joseph Addison (1672–1719)

Photo: Lightning—a most spectacular atmospheric effect.

522

It is not just farmers who are concerned with the daily and future weather conditions. Readily available weather reports and forecasts help us decide such things as how we should dress for the day, whether to take an umbrella along, and whether a weekend picnic should be canceled. The weather changes frequently, because the lower atmosphere is a very dynamic place.

The air we now breathe may have been far out over the Pacific Ocean a week ago. As air moves into a region, it brings with it the temperature and humidity of previous locations. Cold, dry, arctic air may cause a sudden drop in the temperature of the regions in its path. Warm, moist air from the Gulf of Mexico may bring heat and humidity and make the summer seem unbearable.

Thus moving air transports the physical characteristics that influence the weather and produce changes. A large mass of air can influence the region for a considerable period of time, or it can have only a brief effect. The movement of air masses depends heavily on the Earth's air circulation structure and seasonal variations.

When air masses meet, variations of their properties may trigger storms along their common boundary. Thus the types of storms depend on the properties of the air masses involved. Also, variations within a single air mass can give rise to storms locally. Storms can be violent and sometimes destructive. They remind us of the vast amount of energy contained in the atmosphere and also of its capability. As we shall see in this chapter, the variations of our weather are closely associated with air masses and their movements and interactions.

An unfortunate issue in atmospheric science is pollution. Various pollutants are being released into the atmosphere, thereby affecting our health, living conditions, and environment.

Climate also may be affected by pollution. For example, we hear about *acid rain*. Government restrictions have helped reduce this problem, but what about the "ozone hole" and CFCs? These topics will be considered in this chapter.   ■

20.1 Condensation and Precipitation

LEARNING GOALS

▼ Explain how precipitation is formed.

▼ Distinguish among the various types of precipitation.

In the preceding chapter's section on cloud formation, we noted that condensation occurs in an air mass when the dew point is reached. However, it is quite possible for an air mass containing water vapor to be cooled below the dew point without condensation occurring. In this state, the air mass is said to be *supersaturated,* or *supercooled*.

How, then, are visible droplets of water formed? You might think that the collision and coalescing of water molecules would form a droplet. But this event would require the collision of millions of molecules. Moreover, only after a small droplet has reached a critical size will it have sufficient binding force to retain additional molecules. The probability of a droplet forming by this process is quite remote.

Instead, water droplets form around microscopic foreign particles called *hygroscopic nuclei* that are already present in the air. These particles are in the form of dust, combustion residue (smoke and soot), salt from seawater evaporation, and so forth. Because foreign particles initiate the formation of droplets that eventually fall as precipitation, condensation provides a mechanism for cleansing the atmosphere.

Liquid water may be cooled below the freezing point (supercooled) without the formation of ice if it does not contain the proper type of foreign particles

to act as ice nuclei. For many years scientists believed that ice nuclei could be just about anything, such as dust. However, research has shown that "clean" dust—that is, dust without biological materials from plants or bacteria—will not act as ice nuclei. This discovery is important because precipitation involves ice crystals, as will be discussed shortly.

Because cooling and condensation occur in updrafts, the formed droplets are readily suspended in the air as a cloud. For precipitation, larger droplets or drops must form. This condition may be brought about by two processes: (1) coalescence and/or (2) the Bergeron process.

Coalescence

Coalescence is the formation of drops by the collision of droplets, the result being that larger droplets grow at the expense of smaller ones. The efficiency of this process depends on the variation in the size of the droplets.

Raindrops vary in size, reaching a maximum diameter of approximately 7 mm. A drop 1 mm in diameter would require the coalescing of a million droplets of 10-μm (micrometer) diameter but only 1000 droplets of 100-μm diameter. Thus we see that having larger droplets greatly enhances the coalescence process.

Bergeron Process

The **Bergeron process,** named after the Swedish meteorologist who suggested it, is probably the more important process for the initiation of precipitation. This process involves clouds that contain ice crystals in their upper portions and have become supercooled in their lower portions (● Fig. 20.1).

Mixing or agitation within such a cloud allows the ice crystals to come into contact with the supercooled vapor. Acting as nuclei, the ice crystals grow larger from the vapor condensing on them. The ice crystals melt into large droplets in the warmer, lower portion of the cloud and coalesce to fall as precipitation. Air currents are the normal mixing agents.

Note that there are three essentials in the Bergeron process: (1) ice crystals, (2) supercooled vapor, and (3) mixing. *Rainmaking* is based on the essentials of the Bergeron process.

The early rainmakers were mostly charlatans. With much ceremony, they would beat on drums or fire

524 Chapter 20 ATMOSPHERIC EFFECTS

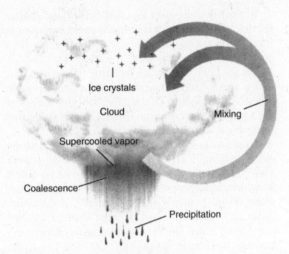

FIGURE 20.1 The Bergeron Process
The essence of the Bergeron process is the mixing of ice crystals and supercooled vapor, which produces water droplets and initiates precipitation.

cannons and rockets into the air. Explosives may have supplied the agitation or mixing for rainmaking, assuming that the other two essentials of the Bergeron process were present.

However, modern rainmakers use a different approach. There are usually enough air currents present for mixing, but the ice crystal nuclei may be lacking. To correct this, they "seed" clouds with silver iodide crystals or dry-ice pellets (solid CO_2).

The silver iodide crystals have a structure similar to that of ice and provide a substitute for ice crystals. Silver iodide crystals are produced by a burning process. The burning may be done on the ground, with the iodide crystals being carried aloft by the rising warm air, or the burner may be attached to an airplane and the process carried out in a cloud to be seeded.

Dry-ice pellets are seeded into a cloud from an airplane. The pellets do not act as nuclei but serve another purpose. The temperature of solid dry ice is $-79°C$ ($-110°F$), and it quickly sublimes—that is, goes directly from the solid to the gaseous phase. Rapid cooling associated with the sublimation triggers the conversion of supercooled cloud droplets into ice crystals. Precipitation may then occur if this part of the Bergeron process has been absent.

Also, the latent heat released from the ice crystal formation is available to set up convection cycles for mixing. Seeding may also come to be widely used for initiating the precipitation of fog, which frequently hinders airport operations.

Types of Precipitation

Precipitation can occur in the form of rain, snow, sleet, hail, dew, or fog depending on atmospheric conditions. *Rain* is the most common form of precipitation in the lower and middle latitudes. The formation of large water drops that fall as rain has been described previously.

If the dew point is below $0°C$, the water vapor freezes on condensing, and the ice crystals that result fall as *snow*. In cold regions, these ice crystals may fall individually. In warmer regions, the ice crystals become stuck together, forming a snowflake that may be as much as 2 to 3 cm across. Because ice crystallizes in a hexagonal (six-sided) pattern, snowflakes are hexagonal (see Fig. 2 on page 96).

Frozen rain, or pellets of ice in the form of *sleet*, occurs when rain falls through a cold surface layer of air and freezes or, more often, when the ice pellets fall directly from the cloud without melting before striking the ground. Large pellets of ice, or *hail*, result from successive vertical descents and ascents in vigorous convection cycles associated with thunderstorms. Additional condensation on successive cycles into supercooled regions that are below freezing may produce layered-structure hailstones the size of golf balls and baseballs. When hailstones are cut in two, the layers of ice can be observed, much like the rings in tree growth (● Fig. 20.2).

Dew is formed by atmospheric water vapor condensing on various surfaces. The land cools quickly at night, particularly with no cloud cover, and the temperature may fall below the dew point. Water vapor then condenses on available surfaces such as blades of grass, giving rise to the "early morning dew."

If the dew point is below freezing, the water vapor condenses in the form of ice crystals as *frost*. Frost is *not* frozen dew but, rather, results from the direct change of water vapor into ice (the reverse of sublimation, called *deposition*).

Interestingly, research has shown that frost is a result of bacteria-seeded ice formation. Without two common types of bacteria on leaf surfaces, water will not freeze at $0°C$ but can be supercooled to $-6°$ to $-8°C$. These bacteria exist on plants, fruit trees, and so on and serve as nuclei for frost formation.

FIGURE 20.2 Hailstones
The successive vertical ascents of ice pellets into supercooled air and regions of condensation produce large, layered "stones" of ice. The layered structure can be seen in these cross sections.

With frost damage to crops and fruits exceeding $1 billion annually, scientists are exploring techniques to prevent the formation of bacteria-seeded frost. One method involves the development of genetically engineered bacteria, which are altered such that they can no longer trigger ice formation.

Researchers believe that a protein on the surface of the bacterium acts as the seed for the formation of frost ice crystals. They hope that "frost-free" bacteria can be made by genetically removing the gene that serves as the blueprint for this protein.

RELEVANCE QUESTION: *By late morning or early afternoon the morning dew you observe is gone. Where does it go?*

20.2 Air Masses

LEARNING GOALS

▼ Define *air masses*, and tell how they are classified.

▼ Identify fronts and their effects on local weather.

As we know, the weather changes with time. However, we often experience several days of relatively uniform weather conditions. Our general weather conditions depend in large part on vast air masses that move across the country.

When a large body of air takes on physical characteristics that distinguish it from the surrounding air, it is referred to as an **air mass**. The main distinguishing characteristics are *temperature* and *moisture content*.

A mass of air remaining for some time over a particular region, such as a large body of land or water, takes on the physical characteristics of the surface of the region. The region from which an air mass derives its characteristics is called its **source region**.

An air mass eventually moves from its source region, bringing its characteristics to regions in its path and thus bringing changes in the weather. As an air mass travels, its properties may become modified because of local variations. For example, if Canadian polar air masses did not become warmer as they travel southward, Florida would experience some extremely cold temperatures.

Whether an air mass is termed *cold* or *warm* is relative to the surface over which it moves. Quite logically, if an air mass is warmer than the land surface, it is referred to as a *warm air mass*. If the air is colder than the surface, it is called a *cold air mass*. Remember, though, that these terms are relative. *Warm* and *cold* do not always imply warm and cold weather. A "warm" air mass in winter may not raise the temperature above freezing.

Air masses are classified according to the surface and general latitude of their source regions:

Surface	Latitude
Maritime (m)	Arctic (A)
Continental (c)	Polar (P)
	Tropical (T)
	Equatorial (E)

The surface of the source region, abbreviated by a small letter, gives an indication of the moisture content of an air mass. An air mass forming over a body of water (maritime) would naturally be expected to have a greater moisture content than one forming over land (continental).

The general latitude of a source region, abbreviated by a capital letter, gives an indication of the temperature of an air mass. For example, "mT" designates a maritime tropical air mass, which would be expected to be a warm, moist one. The air masses that affect the weather in the United States are listed in Table 20.1, along with their source regions, and are illustrated in ● Fig. 20.3.

The movement of air masses is influenced to a great extent by the Earth's general circulation patterns

526 Chapter 20 ATMOSPHERIC EFFECTS

TABLE 20.1 Air Masses That Affect the Weather of the United States

Classification	Symbol	Source Region
Maritime arctic	mA	Arctic regions
Continental arctic	cA	Greenland
Maritime polar	mP	Northern Atlantic and Pacific oceans
Continental polar	cP	Alaska and Canada
Maritime tropical	mT	Caribbean Sea, Gulf of Mexico, and Pacific Ocean
Continental tropical	cT	Northern Mexico, southwestern United States

(Section 19.4). Because the conterminous United States lies predominantly in the westerlies zone, the general movement of air masses—and hence of the weather—is from west to east across the country. Global circulation zones vary to some extent in latitude with the seasons, and the polar easterlies may also move air masses into the eastern United States during the winter.

The boundary between two air masses is called a **front**. A *warm front* is the boundary of an advancing warm air mass over a colder surface, and a *cold front* is the boundary of a cold air mass moving over a warmer surface. These boundaries, called *frontal zones*, may vary in width from a few miles to over 160 km (100 mi). It is along fronts, which divide air masses of different physical characteristics, that drastic changes in weather occur. Turbulent weather and storms usually characterize a front.

The degree and rate of weather change depend on the difference in temperature of the air masses and on the degree of vertical slope of a front. A cold front moving into a warmer region causes the lighter,

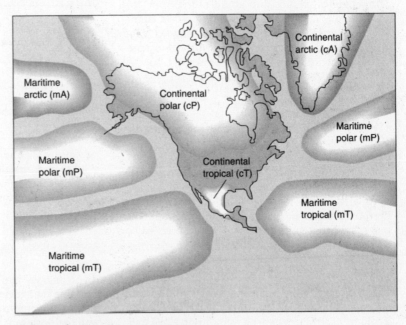

FIGURE 20.3 Air-Mass Source Regions
The map shows the source regions for the air masses of North America.

warm air to be displaced upward over the front (● Fig. 20.4). The lighter air of the advancing warm front cannot displace the heavier, colder air as readily, and generally it moves slowly up and over the colder air.

Heavier, colder air is associated with high pressure, and this downward divergent air flow in a high-pressure region generally gives a cold front greater speed than a warm front. A cold front may have an average speed of 30 to 40 km/h (20 to 25 mi/h), whereas a warm front averages about 15 to 25 km/h (10 to 15 mi/h).

Cold fronts have sharper vertical boundaries than warm fronts, and warm air is displaced upward faster by an advancing cold front. As a result, cold fronts are accompanied by more violent or sudden changes in weather. The sudden decrease in temperature is often described as a "cold snap." Dark altocumulus clouds often mark a cold front's approach (Fig. 20.4). The sudden cooling and the rising warm air may set off rainstorm or snowstorm activity along the front.

A warm front also may be characterized by precipitation and storms. Because the approach of a warm front is more gradual, it is usually heralded by a period of lowering clouds. Cirrus and mackerel scale (cirrocumulus) clouds drift ahead of the front, followed by alto clouds. As the front approaches, cumulus or cumulonimbus clouds that result from the rising air produce precipitation and storms. Most precipitation occurs before the front passes.

The graphical symbol for a cold front is

and for a warm front is

The side of the line with the symbol indicates the direction of advance.

As a faster-moving cold front advances, it may overtake a warm air mass and push it upward. The boundary between these two air masses is called an *occluded front* and is indicated by

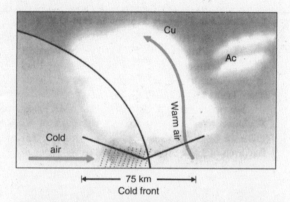

That is, the cold front occludes, or cuts off, the warm air from the ground along the occluded front. When a cold front advances under a warm front, a *cold front occlusion* results. When a warm front advances up and over a cold front, the air ahead is colder than the

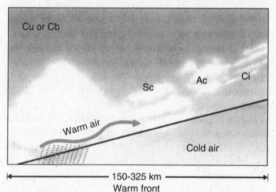

FIGURE 20.4 Side Views of Cold and Warm Fronts
Note in the upper diagram the sharp, steep boundary that is characteristic of cold fronts. The boundary of a warm front, as shown in the lower diagram, is less steep. As a result, different cloud types are associated with the approach of the two types of fronts. (See the table on page 517 for cloud abbreviations.)

advancing air, and the occluded front is referred to as a *warm front occlusion.*

Sometimes fronts traveling in opposite directions meet. The opposing fronts may balance each other so that no movement occurs. This case is referred to as a *stationary front* and is indicated by

Air masses and fronts move across the country bringing changes in weather. Dynamic situations give rise to cyclonic disturbances around low-pressure and high-pressure regions. As we saw in Chapter 19, these disturbances are called *cyclones* and *anticyclones*, respectively (see Fig. 19.20).

528   Chapter 20   ATMOSPHERIC EFFECTS

As a low or cyclone moves, it carries with it rising air currents, clouds, possibly precipitation, and generally bad weather. Hence lows or cyclones are usually associated with poor weather, whereas highs or anticyclones are usually associated with good weather. The lack of rising air and cloud formation in highs gives clear skies and fair weather. Because of their influence on the weather, the movements of highs and lows are closely monitored.

We usually think of a source region as being relatively hot or cold. But significant variations can occur within a source region at a particular latitude, giving rise to abnormal weather conditions. A classic example, El Niño, is discussed in the chapter's first Highlight on page 530.

RELEVANCE QUESTION: *Which types of air masses (see Table 20.1) generally affect your weather?*

20.3 Storms

LEARNING GOALS

▼ Identify various types of local and tropical storms.

▼ Describe the aspects of lightning safety and tornado safety.

Storms are atmospheric disturbances that may develop locally within a single air mass or may be due to frontal activity along the boundary of air masses. Several types of storms, distinguished by their intensity and violence, will be considered. These will be divided generally into local storms and tropical storms.

Local Storms

There are several types of local storms. A heavy downpour is commonly referred to as a *rainstorm*. Storms with rainfalls of 1 to 3 inches per hour are not uncommon.

A *thunderstorm* is a rainstorm distinguished by thunder and lightning, and sometimes hail. The **lightning** associated with a thunderstorm is a discharge of electrical energy. In the turmoil of a thundercloud or "thunderhead," there is a separation of charge associated with the breaking up and movement of water droplets. This gives rise to an electric potential. When this is of sufficient magnitude, lightning occurs.

FIGURE 20.5 Lightning
Lightning discharges can occur between a cloud and the Earth, between clouds, and within a cloud.

Lightning can take place entirely within a cloud (intracloud or cloud discharges), between two clouds (cloud-to-cloud discharges), between a cloud and the Earth (cloud-to-ground or ground discharges), or between a cloud and the surrounding air (air discharges). See ● Fig. 20.5.

Lightning has reportedly even occurred in clear air, apparently giving rise to the expression "a bolt from the blue." When lightning occurs below the horizon or behind clouds, it often illuminates the clouds with flickering flashes. This commonly occurs on a still summer night and is known as *heat lightning*.

Although the most frequently occurring form of lightning is the intracloud discharge, of greatest concern is lightning between a cloud and the Earth. The shorter the distance from a cloud to the ground, the more easily the electric discharge takes place. For this reason, lightning often strikes trees and tall buildings. It is inadvisable, therefore, to take shelter from a thunderstorm under a tree. A person in the vicinity of a lightning strike may experience an electric shock that causes breathing to fail. In such a case, mouth-to-mouth resuscitation or some other form of artificial respiration should be given immediately, and the person should be kept warm as a treatment for shock. (See the following discussion of lightning safety.)

Check Your Understanding

The following sentences appear in the chapter. Circle the letter of the BEST meaning for each italicized word.

10. "You might think that the collision and *coalescing* of water molecules would form a droplet."
    a. Striking
    b. Evaporating
    c. Separating
    d. Uniting

11. "The *probability* of a droplet forming by this process is quite remote."
    a. Percentage
    b. Likelihood
    c. Certainty
    d. Occurrence

12. "The probability of a droplet forming by this process is quite *remote*."
    a. Far
    b. Near
    c. Slight
    d. Possible

13. "Mixing or *agitation* within such a cloud allows the ice crystals to come into contact with the supercooled vapor."
    a. Violent movement
    b. Expansion
    c. Floating
    d. Hostile behavior

14. "The early rainmakers were mostly *charlatans*."
    a. Frauds
    b. Powerful magicians
    c. Generous people
    d. Leaders

15. "*Turbulent* weather and storms usually characterize a front."
    a. Swollen
    b. Violently disturbed
    c. Fast-moving
    d. Very cold

Circle the letter of the correct response.

16. Based on Table 20.1 in the preceding section of the physical science chapter, which of the following conclusions is accurate?
    a. The continental arctic air mass affects the weather of the United States more than the other air masses.
    b. The continental polar air mass originates in Alaska and Canada.
    c. The maritime tropical air mass originates in Mexico.
    d. The Pacific Ocean is the source of only the maritime polar air mass.

17. Based on Figure 20.1 in the preceding section of the physical science chapter, you can conclude that
    a. ice crystals are in the upper portion of a cloud.
    b. the ice crystals freeze to form precipitation.
    c. the lower portion of the cloud is colder than the upper portion.
    d. supercooled vapor is outside the cloud.

For each of the following review questions for the section of the physical science textbook you just read, either circle the letter of the correct response or write your answer on the blanks provided, as appropriate.

18. When the temperature of the air is below the dew point without precipitation, the air is said to be what?
    a. Stable
    b. Supercooled
    c. Sublimed
    d. Coalesced

19. Which of the following is NOT essential to the Bergeron process?
    a. Silver iodide
    b. Mixing
    c. Supercooled vapor
    d. Ice crystals

20. Describe the three essentials of the Bergeron process and how they are related to methods of modern rainmaking.

_____

_____

_____

21. Is frost frozen dew? Explain. How are large hailstones formed?

_____

_____

_____

22. Which of the following air masses would be expected to be cold and dry?
    a. cP
    b. mA
    c. cT
    d. mE

23. A cold front advancing under a warm front is called a
    a. warm front.
    b. stationary front.
    c. cold front occlusion.
    d. warm front occlusion.

24. How are air masses classified? Explain the relationship between air-mass characteristics and source regions.

_____

_____

_____

25. Give the source region(s) of the air mass(es) that affect the weather in your area.

_____

_____

_____

26. What is a front? List the meteorological symbols for four types of fronts.

_____

_____

_____

27. Describe the weather associated with warm fronts and with cold fronts. What is the significance of the sharpness of their vertical boundaries?

_____

_____

_____

Discuss the following questions with a partner or group, and then collaborate to write a response to each question on your own paper.

28. By late morning or early afternoon, the morning dew you observe is gone. Where does it go?

_____

_____

_____

29. Which types of air masses (see Table 20.1 in the preceding section of the physical science chapter) generally affect your weather?

_____

_____

_____

528   Chapter 20   ATMOSPHERIC EFFECTS

As a low or cyclone moves, it carries with it rising air currents, clouds, possibly precipitation, and generally bad weather. Hence lows or cyclones are usually associated with poor weather, whereas highs or anticyclones are usually associated with good weather. The lack of rising air and cloud formation in highs gives clear skies and fair weather. Because of their influence on the weather, the movements of highs and lows are closely monitored.

We usually think of a source region as being relatively hot or cold. But significant variations can occur within a source region at a particular latitude, giving rise to abnormal weather conditions. A classic example, El Niño, is discussed in the chapter's first Highlight on page 530.

RELEVANCE QUESTION: *Which types of air masses (see Table 20.1) generally affect your weather?*

20.3 Storms

LEARNING GOALS

▼ Identify various types of local and tropical storms.

▼ Describe the aspects of lightning safety and tornado safety.

Storms are atmospheric disturbances that may develop locally within a single air mass or may be due to frontal activity along the boundary of air masses. Several types of storms, distinguished by their intensity and violence, will be considered. These will be divided generally into local storms and tropical storms.

Local Storms

There are several types of local storms. A heavy downpour is commonly referred to as a *rainstorm*. Storms with rainfalls of 1 to 3 inches per hour are not uncommon.

A *thunderstorm* is a rainstorm distinguished by thunder and lightning, and sometimes hail. The **lightning** associated with a thunderstorm is a discharge of electrical energy. In the turmoil of a thundercloud or "thunderhead," there is a separation of charge associated with the breaking up and movement of water droplets. This gives rise to an electric potential. When this is of sufficient magnitude, lightning occurs.

FIGURE 20.5 Lightning
Lightning discharges can occur between a cloud and the Earth, between clouds, and within a cloud.

Lightning can take place entirely within a cloud (intracloud or cloud discharges), between two clouds (cloud-to-cloud discharges), between a cloud and the Earth (cloud-to-ground or ground discharges), or between a cloud and the surrounding air (air discharges). See ● Fig. 20.5.

Lightning has reportedly even occurred in clear air, apparently giving rise to the expression "a bolt from the blue." When lightning occurs below the horizon or behind clouds, it often illuminates the clouds with flickering flashes. This commonly occurs on a still summer night and is known as *heat lightning*.

Although the most frequently occurring form of lightning is the intracloud discharge, of greatest concern is lightning between a cloud and the Earth. The shorter the distance from a cloud to the ground, the more easily the electric discharge takes place. For this reason, lightning often strikes trees and tall buildings. It is inadvisable, therefore, to take shelter from a thunderstorm under a tree. A person in the vicinity of a lightning strike may experience an electric shock that causes breathing to fail. In such a case, mouth-to-mouth resuscitation or some other form of artificial respiration should be given immediately, and the person should be kept warm as a treatment for shock. (See the following discussion of lightning safety.)

Lightning Safety

If you are outside during a thunderstorm and feel an electric charge, as evidenced by hair standing on end or skin tingling, what should you do? *Fall to the ground fast!* Lightning may be about to strike.

Statistics show that lightning kills, on average, 200 people a year in the United States and injures another 550. Most deaths and injuries occur at home. Indoor casualties occur most frequently when people are talking on the telephone, working in the kitchen, doing laundry, or watching TV. During severe lightning activity, the following safety rules are recommended:

Stay indoors away from open windows, fireplaces, and electrical conductors such as sinks and stoves.

Avoid using the telephone. Lightning may strike the telephone lines outside.

Do not use electrical plug-in equipment such as radios, TVs, and lamps.

Should you be caught outside, seek shelter in a building. If no buildings are available, seek protection in a ditch or ravine. Getting wet is a lot better than being struck by lightning.

A lightning stroke's sudden release of energy explosively heats the air, producing the compressions we hear as **thunder.** When heard at a distance of about 100 m (330 ft) or less from the discharge channel, thunder consists of one loud bang, or "clap." When heard at a distance of 1 km (0.62 mi) from the discharge channel, thunder generally consists of a rumbling sound punctuated by several large claps. In general, thunder cannot be heard at distances of more than 25 km (16 mi) from the discharge channel.

Because lightning strokes generally occur near the storm center, the resulting thunder provides a method of approximating the distance to the storm. Light travels at approximately 300,000 km/s (186,000 mi/s), and so the lightning flash is seen instantaneously. Sound, however, travels at approximately $\frac{1}{3}$ km/s ($\frac{1}{5}$ mi/s), so a time lapse occurs between an observer's seeing the lightning flash and hearing the thunder. By counting the seconds between seeing the lightning and hearing the thunder (by saying, "one-thousand-one, one-thousand-two," etc.), you can estimate your distance from the lightning stroke or the storm.

EXAMPLE 20.1

Estimating the Distance of a Thunderstorm

Suppose some campers notice an approaching thunderstorm in the distance. Lightning is seen, and the thunder is heard 5.0 s later. Approximately how far away is the storm in (a) kilometers and (b) miles?

SOLUTION

We know that the approximate or average speed of sound is $\bar{v} = \frac{1}{3}$ km/s $= \frac{1}{5}$ mi/s. Then the distance (d) that the sound travels in a time (t) is given by Eq. 2.1 $(d = \bar{v}t)$.

(a) Using the metric speed,

$$d = \bar{v}t = (\tfrac{1}{3} \text{ km/s})(5.0 \text{ s}) = 1.6 \text{ km}$$

(b) You could convert the distance in (a) to miles (and, in fact, you may recognize the conversion right away), but let's compute it.

$$d = \bar{v}t = (\tfrac{1}{5} \text{ mi/s})(5.0 \text{ s}) = 1.0 \text{ mi}$$

(Recall that 1 mi = 1.6 km.)

CONFIDENCE EXERCISE 20.1

If thunder is heard 3 s after the flash of a lightning stroke is seen, approximately how far away, in kilometers and miles, is the lightning?

If the temperature of the Earth's surface is below 0°C and raindrops do not freeze before striking the ground, the rain will freeze on striking cold surface objects. Such an **ice storm** builds up a layer of ice on objects exposed to the freezing rain. The ice layer may build up to over half an inch in thickness, depending on the magnitude of the rainfall. Viewed in sunlight, the ice glaze produces beautiful winter scenes as the ice-coated landscape glistens in the Sun. However, damage to trees and power lines often detracts from the beauty.

Snow is made up of ice crystals that fall from ice clouds. A *snowstorm* is an appreciable accumulation of snow. What may be considered a severe snowstorm in some regions may be thought of as a light snowfall in areas where snow is more prevalent.

When a snowstorm is accompanied by high winds and low temperatures, the storm is referred to

530 Chapter 20 ATMOSPHERIC EFFECTS

highlight El Niño and La Niña

El Niño, an occasional disruption of the ocean-atmosphere system in the tropical Pacific Ocean, has important weather consequences for many parts of the world. Originally recognized by fishermen off the Pacific coast of South America, the appearance at irregular intervals of unusually warm water near the beginning of the year was named *El Niño*, which means "the little boy" or "the Christ child" in Spanish. The name reflects the tendency of El Niño to arrive at Christmastime.

Under normal conditions, the Pacific trade winds blow generally from east to west near the equator (see Fig. 19.21) and pile up warm surface water in the western Pacific Ocean near Indonesia and the Australian continent. As a result of this warm water, the atmosphere is heated, and conditions favorable for convection and precipitation occur (Fig. 1).

This surface flow results in cooler water temperatures off the coast of South America because of the upwelling of cold water from deeper levels. The cold water is nutrient-rich and supports an abundance of fish and, thereby, a fishing industry. With an atmospheric circulation as shown in Fig. 1, the Pacific coast of South America is relatively dry because of little precipitation. (Why?)

At irregular intervals, typically every 3 to 5 years, the normal trade winds relax, and the warm pool of water in the western Pacific is free to move back eastward along the equator toward the South American continent (El Niño conditions). The displacement of warm water affects the atmospheric convection cycles, as shown in Fig. 2.

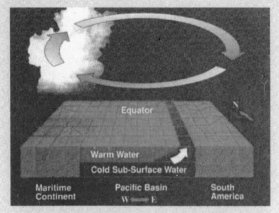

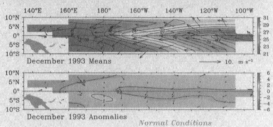

FIGURE 1 Normal Pacific Conditions.
The trade winds generally blow from east to west, causing warm surface water currents. These conditions give rise to precipitation in the western Pacific and to cooler water temperatures in the eastern Pacific along the coast of South America.

The convection and precipitation shift to the central and eastern Pacific and usually result in heavier than normal rains over northern Peru and Ecuador. The mechanism for precipitation for Indonesia and Australia is no longer there, and this area often experiences drought during an El Niño.

Twenty-three El Niños have occurred since 1900, and the cause of this relatively frequent event, which lasts about 18 months, is not known. The 1982–1983 El Niño was one of the worst, being responsible for the loss of as many as 2000 lives and for the displacement of thousands from their homes. Indonesia and Australia suffered droughts and bush fires. Peru was hit with heavy rainfall—11 feet in areas where 6 inches was normal! The warm

---

as a *blizzard*. The winds whip the fallen snow into blinding swirls. Visibility may be reduced to a few inches. For this reason, a blizzard is often called a *blinding* snowstorm.

The swirling snow causes a loss of one's direction, and people have gotten lost only a few feet from their homes. The wind may blow the snow across level terrain, forming huge drifts against some obstructing object. Drifting is common on the flat prairies of the western United States.

The **tornado** is the most violent of storms. Although it may have less *total* energy than some other storms, the concentration of its energy in a relatively small region gives the tornado great destructive

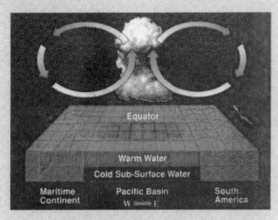

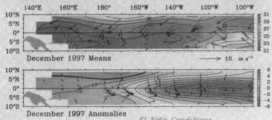

FIGURE 2 El Niño Conditions.

At irregular intervals, the normal trade winds relax, and warm surface water moves back eastward, causing changes in weather patterns.

water spread along the coast to the United States, and the West Coast was drenched with rain. Sharks were observed off the Oregon coast as a result of the unseasonably warm sea temperatures. Also, more hurricanes occurred in the Pacific than in the Atlantic.

Another severe El Niño occurred in 1998, with much the same effects. The normal weather patterns were disrupted around the country. At the time of this writing (2002), it is believed that another El Niño is forming.

At various times, the reverse conditions of El Niño are found. That is, the eastern Pacific surface waters are colder than usual, and cold water extends farther westward than usual (Fig. 3). This condition is called *La Niña* ("the little girl" in Spanish) and occurs after some, but not all, El Niño years. Strong La Niñas cause unusual weather conditions around the country. For example, during a La Niña year, winter temperatures are usually warmer than normal in the southeastern United States and cooler than normal in the Northwest.

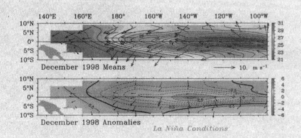

FIGURE 3 La Niña Conditions.

At various times, cold water extends farther westward than usual, which affects coastal weather patterns.

potential. Characterized by a whirling, funnel-shaped cloud that hangs from a dark cloud mass, the tornado is commonly referred to as a *twister* (●Fig. 20.6).

Tornadoes occur around the world but are most prevalent in the United States and Australia. In the United States, most tornadoes occur in the Deep South and in the broad, relatively flat basin between the Rockies and the Appalachians. But no state is immune. The peak months of tornado activity are April, May, and June, with southern states usually hit hardest in winter and spring, and northern states in spring and summer. A typical time of occurrence is between 3:00 and 7:00 P.M. on an unseasonably warm, sultry spring afternoon. However, tornadoes

532 Chapter 20 ATMOSPHERIC EFFECTS

(a)

(b)

FIGURE 20.6 Tornado Destruction

(a) A tornado funnel touching down with a town in its path. (b) The high-speed winds of a tornado can push in the windward wall of a house, lift off the roof, push the other walls outward and mangle steel structures as shown here. Imagine all of the debris that was flying around during the tornado.

have occurred in every month at all times of day and night.

Most tornadoes travel from southwest to northeast, but the direction of travel can be erratic and may change suddenly. They usually travel at an average speed of 48 km/h (30 mi/h). The wind speed of a major tornado may vary from 160–480 km/h (100–300 mi/h). The wind speed of the devastating 1999 Oklahoma tornado was measured by Doppler radar to be 502 km/h (312 mi/h), the highest ever recorded.

Because of many variables, the complete mechanism of tornado formation is not known. One essential component, however, is rising air, which occurs in thunderstorm formation and in the collision of cold and warm air masses.

As the ascending air cools, clouds are formed that are swept to the outer portions of the cyclonic motion and outline its funnel form. Because clouds form at certain heights (Section 19.5), the outlined funnel may appear well above the ground. Under the right conditions, a full-fledged tornado develops. The winds increase and the air pressure near the center of the vortex is reduced as the air swirls upward. When the funnel is well developed, it may "touch down," or be seen extending up from the ground, as a result of dust and debris picked up by the swirling winds.

The system for a tornado alert has two phases. A **tornado watch** is issued when atmospheric conditions indicate that tornadoes may form. A **tornado warning** is issued when a tornado has actually been sighted or indicated on radar.

The similarity between the terms *watch* and *warning* can be confusing. Remember that you should *watch* for a tornado when the conditions are right, but when you are given a *warning*, the situation is dangerous and critical—no more watching.

Care should be taken after a tornado has passed. There may be downed power lines, escaping natural gas, and dangerous debris. (See the following discussion of tornado safety.)

Tornado Safety

Knowing what to do in the event of a tornado is critically important. If a tornado is sighted, if the ominous roar of one is heard at night, or if a tornado warning is issued for your particular locality, *seek shelter fast!*

The basement of a home or building is one of the safest places to seek shelter.

Avoid chimneys and windows, because there is great danger from debris and flying glass.

Get under a sturdy piece of furniture, such as an overturned couch, or into a stairwell or closet, and *cover your head.*

In a home or building without a basement, seek the lowest level in the central portion of the structure and the shelter of a closet or hallway.

If you live in a mobile home, evacuate it. Seek shelter elsewhere.

Tropical Storms

The term *tropical storm* refers to the massive disturbances that form over tropical oceanic regions. A tropical storm becomes a **hurricane** when its wind speed exceeds 118 km/h (74 mi/h). The hurricane is known by different names in different parts of the world. For example, in southeast Asia it is called a *typhoon,* and in the Indian Ocean, a *cyclone* (● Fig. 20.7).

Regardless of the name, this type of storm is characterized by high-speed rotating winds, whose energy is spread over a large area. A hurricane may be 480 to 960 km (300 to 600 mi) in diameter and may have wind speeds of 118 to 320 km/h (74 to 200 mi/h).

Hurricanes form over tropical oceanic regions where the Sun heats huge masses of moist air, and an ascending spiral motion results. When the moisture of the rising air condenses, the latent heat provides additional energy, and more air rises up the column. This latent heat is the chief source of a hurricane's energy and is readily available from the condensation of the evaporated moisture from its source region.

Unlike a tornado, a hurricane gains energy from its source region. As more and more air rises, the hurricane grows, with clouds and increasing winds that blow in a large spiral around a relatively calm, low-pressure center—the *eye* of the hurricane (● Fig. 20.8). The eye may be 32 to 48 km (20 to 30 mi) wide, and ships sailing into this area have found that it is usually calm and clear, with no indication of the surrounding storm. The air pressure is reduced 6% to

FIGURE 20.7 Tropical Storm Regions of the World

Tropical storms are known by different names in different parts of the world. The average tropical storm activities by month are shown in the graphs.

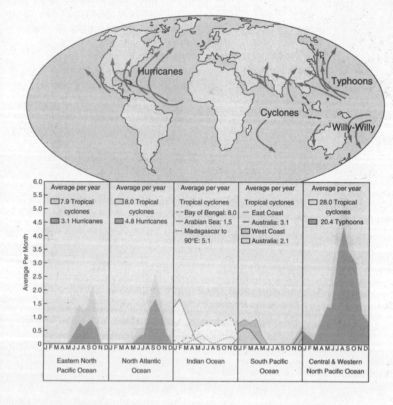

534   Chapter 20   ATMOSPHERIC EFFECTS

FIGURE 20.8 Hurricane Paths and Eyes

(a) A computer-enhanced infrared image of Hurricane Floyd moving along the eastern coast of the United States in September, 1999. As Fig. 20.7 shows, hurricanes that form in the Atlantic Ocean generally travel northwest until they are blown eastward by the prevailing westerlies. As a result, hurricanes can strike coastal areas around the Gulf of Mexico and the southeastern United States, both coming and going. (b) A radar profile of a hurricane. Note the generally clear eye about 35 to 55 miles from the radar station and the vertical buildup of clouds near the sides of the eye.

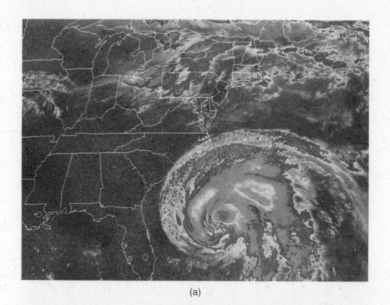

(a)

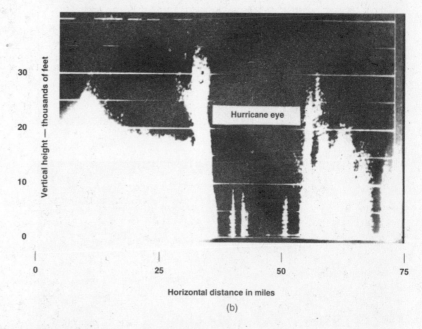

(b)

8% near the eye. Hurricanes move rather slowly, at a few miles per hour.

Although the tornado is labeled the most violent of storms, the hurricane is the most energetic. One method for estimating the energy production of a hurricane uses the amount of rain produced within an average hurricane per day and the latent heat of condensation (Section 5.3) released. This gives an energy (power × time) production of 6.0×10^{11} kWh, which is equivalent to about 200 times the worldwide electrical generating capacity—an incredible amount of energy. Another method of estimation, which uses the kinetic energy of the winds generated in a hurricane, puts this figure at 1.5×10^{9} kWh, which is on the order of about half the worldwide electrical generating capacity. Although it is considerably smaller, this is still an enormous amount of energy production within the area of a hurricane (see Fig. 20.8). With such tremendous amounts of energy, hurricanes can be particularly destructive. Hurricane winds do much damage, but oddly enough, drowning is the greatest cause of hurricane deaths. As the eye of a hurricane comes ashore, or *makes landfall*, a great dome of water called a **storm surge**, often over 80 km (50 mi) wide, comes sweeping across the coastline. It brings huge waves and storm tides that may reach 5 m (17 ft) or more above normal (Fig. 20.9). The storm surge comes suddenly, often flooding coastal lowlands. Nine out of ten casualties are caused by the storm surge.

The torrential rains that accompany the hurricane commonly produce flooding as the storm moves inland. As its winds diminish, floods constitute a hurricane's greatest threat.

You may have heard of hurricanes being classified into categories—for example, a Category 2 hurricane or a Category 4 hurricane. These categories come from the Saffir-Simpson scale (Table 20.2).* Note the maximum speed, minimum pressure, and height of storm surge for each category.

A terrible cyclone came out of the Indian Ocean in the spring of 1991 and struck Bangladesh with a 20-foot wall of water and winds of 145 mi/h. The flooding and devastation in the low-lying regions where the storm made landfall were enormous. Over 125,000 people lost their lives.

---

*Developed in 1969 by Herbert Saffir, a consulting engineer, and Robert Simpson, director of the National Hurricane Center.

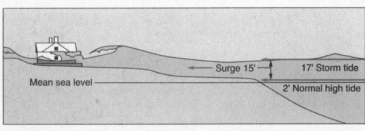

(a)

(b)

FIGURE 20.9 Hurricane Storm Surge and Damage
(a) The drawing illustrates a storm surge coming ashore at high tide. (b) An aerial view of housing destruction after a hurricane.

536   Chapter 20 ATMOSPHERIC EFFECTS

TABLE 20.2 Saffir-Simpson Hurricane Scale

Saffir-Simpson Category	Maximum Sustained Wind Speed *mph*	Minimum Surface Pressure *mb*	Storm Surge	
			ft	*m*
1	74–95	Greater than 980	3–5	1.0–1.7
2	96–110	979–965	6–8	1.8–2.6
3	111–130	964–945	9–12	2.7–3.8
4	131–155	944–920	13–18	3.9–5.6
5	156+	Less than 920	19+	5.7+

Category	Winds	Effects
One	74–95 mph	No real damage to building structures. Damage primarly to unanchored mobile homes, shrubbery, and trees. Some coastal road flooding and minor pier damage.
Two	96–110 mph	Some roofing material, door, and window damage to buildings. Considerable damage to vegetation, mobile homes, and piers. Coastal and low-lying escape routes flood 2 to 4 hours before arrival of center. Small craft in unprotected anchorages break moorings.
Three	111–130 mph	Some structural damage to small residences and utility buildings, with a minor amount of curtainwall (an exterior wall having no structural function) failures. Mobile homes are destroyed. Flooding near the coast destroys smaller structures, and larger structures are damaged by floating debris. Terrain continuously lower than 5 feet above sea level (ASL) may be flooded inland 8 miles or more.
Four	131–155 mph	More extensive curtainwall failures, with some complete roof structure failure on small residences. Major erosion of beach. Major damage to lower floors of structures near the shore. Terrain continuously lower than 10 feet ASL may be flooded, requiring massive evacuation of residential areas inland as far as 6 miles.
Five	greater than 155 mph	Complete roof failure on many residences and industrial buildings. Some complete building failures, with small utility buildings blown over or away. Major damage to lower floors of all structures located less than 15 feet ASL and within 500 yards of the shoreline. Massive evacuation of residential areas on low ground within 5 to 10 miles of the shoreline may be required.

Once cut off from the warm ocean, the storm dies, starved for moisture and heat energy and dragged apart by friction as it moves over the land. Even though a hurricane weakens rapidly as it moves inland, the remnants of the storm can bring 6 to 12 inches or more of rain for hundreds of miles.

The breeding grounds of the hurricanes that affect the United States are in the Atlantic Ocean southeast of the Caribbean Sea. As hurricanes form, they move westward with the trade winds, usually making landfall along the Gulf and south Atlantic coasts. During the hurricane season, the area of their formation is constantly monitored by satellite. When a tropical storm is detected, radar-equipped airplanes, or "hurricane hunters," track the storm and make local measurements to help predict its path.

Like that for a tornado, the hurricane alerting system has two phases. A **hurricane watch** is issued for coastal areas when there is a threat of hurricane conditions within 24 to 36 hours. A **hurricane warning** indicates that hurricane conditions are expected within 24 hours (winds of 74 mi/h or greater, or dangerously high water and rough seas).

As you are probably aware, tropical storms and hurricanes are given names. How this is done is described in the chapter's second Highlight.

RELEVANCE QUESTION: *In what year was the latest tornado watch or warning issued for where you live? What should you do if a "watch" is issued? What should you do if a "warning" is issued?*

Check Your Understanding

The following sentences appear in the chapter. Circle the letter of the best meaning for each italicized word or phrase.

30. "It is *inadvisable* … to take shelter from a thunderstorm under a tree."
    a. Important
    b. Impossible
    c. Not recommended
    d. Unlucky

31. "When heard at a distance of 1 km (0.62 mi), from the discharge channel, thunder generally consists of a rumbling sound *punctuated* by several large claps."
    a. Followed
    b. Preceded
    c. Blended
    d. Interrupted

32. "The ice layer may build up to over half an inch in thickness, depending on the *magnitude* of the rainfall."
    a. Greatness in amount
    b. Temperature
    c. Magnetism
    d. Stickiness

33. "…damage to trees and power lines often *detracts from* the beauty."
    a. Takes away from
    b. Increases
    c. Destroys
    d. Makes possible

34. "Tornadoes occur around the world but are most *prevalent* in the United States and Australia."
    a. Scarce
    b. Common
    c. Violent
    d. Destructive

35. "Most tornadoes travel from southwest to northeast, but the direction of travel can be *erratic* and may change suddenly."
    a. Steady
    b. Circular
    c. Northward
    d. Irregular

36. "Once cut off from the warm ocean, the storm dies, starved for moisture and heat energy, and is dragged apart by *friction* as it moves over the land."
    a. High winds
    b. Warm temperatures
    c. The rubbing of one object against another
    d. The removal of obstacles

Circle the letter of the correct response.

37. Based on Table 20.2 in the preceding section of the physical science chapter, which of the following conclusions is accurate?
    a. A hurricane with maximum sustained wind speeds of 154 mph is classified as a Category 4 hurricane.
    b. A hurricane that produced an 11-foot storm surge would be a Category 2 hurricane.
    c. Terrain that is ten feet above sea level would probably be flooded during a Category 3 hurricane.
    d. A Category 4 hurricane is characterized by maximum sustained wind speeds in excess of 156 mph.

38. Based on Figure 20.7 in the preceding section of the physical science chapter, which of the following is an accurate conclusion?
    a. There are an average of 4.8 hurricanes in the Indian Ocean every year.
    b. In the eastern North Pacific Ocean, most cyclones and hurricanes occur in December.
    c. Australia gets an average of 20 typhoons per year.
    d. The region with the highest average of annual tropical cyclones is the central and western North Pacific Ocean.

For each of the following questions, either circle the letter of the correct response or write your answer in the blanks provided, as appropriate.

39. What is the critical alert for a tornado?
    a. Tornado alert
    b. Tornado warning
    c. Tornado watch
    d. Tornado prediction

40. The greatest number of hurricane casualties is caused by which of the following?
    a. High winds
    b. Low pressure
    c. Flying debris
    d. Storm surge

41. Where can lightning take place? That is, where can it begin and end? Describe what is meant by heat lightning and "a bolt from the blue."

    _____

    _____

    _____

42. What type of first aid should be given to someone suffering from the shock of lightning stroke?

    _____

    _____

    _____

43. An ice storm is likely to result along what type of front? Explain.

    _____

    _____

    _____

44. What is the most violent of storms and why?

    _____

    _____

    _____

45. A tornado is sighted close by. What should you do?

    _____

    _____

46. What is the major source of energy for a tropical storm? When does a tropical storm become a hurricane?

_____

_____

_____

47. Distinguish between a hurricane watch and a hurricane warning.

_____

_____

48. What months is the peak season for hurricanes? Tornadoes?

_____

_____

Discuss the following question with a partner or group, and then collaborate to write an answer on the blanks provided.

49. In what year was the latest tornado watch or warning issued for where you live? What should you do if a "watch" is issued? What should you do if a "warning" is issued?

_____

_____

_____

20.4 Atmospheric Pollution

LEARNING GOALS

▼ Identify the major atmospheric pollutants.

▼ Explain pollutant effects, such as smog and acid rain.

At the beginning of Chapter 19, a quote was presented from Shakespeare about the atmosphere: "... this most excellent canopy, the air. . . ." This was taken out of context, and there's more: "... this most excellent canopy, the air, look you, this brave o'erhanging firmament, this majestical roof fretted with golden fire, why, it appears no other thing to me but a foul and pestilent congregation of vapours" (Shakespeare, *Hamlet*).

Even Shakespeare in his day made reference to atmospheric pollution—an unfortunate topic of earth science. By pollution, we mean any atypical contributions to the environment resulting from the activities of human beings. Of course, gases and particulate matter are spewn into the air from volcanic eruptions and lightning-initiated forest fires, but these are natural phenomena over which we have little control.

Air pollution results primarily from the products of combustion and industrial processes that are released into the atmosphere. It has long been a common practice to vent these wastes, and the resulting problems are not new, particularly in areas of high human population.

Smoke and soot from the burning of coal plagued England over 700 years ago. London recorded air pollution problems in the late 1200s, and the use of particularly smoky types of coal was taxed and even banned. The problem was not alleviated, and in the middle 1600s, King Charles II was prompted to commission one of the outstanding scholars of the day, Sir John Evelyn, to make a study of the situation. The degree of London's air pollution at that time is described in the following passage from his report, *Fumifugium* (translated from the Latin as *On Dispelling of Smoke*).

... the inhabitants breathe nothing but impure thick mist, accompanied with a fuliginous and filthy vapor, corrupting the lungs. Coughs and consumption rage more in this one city (London) than in the whole world. When in all other places the aer is most serene and pure, it is here eclipsed with such a cloud ... as the sun itself is hardly able to penetrate. The traveler, at miles distance, sooner smells than sees the City.

However, the Industrial Revolution was about to begin, and Sir John's report was ignored and so gathered dust (and soot).

As a result of such air pollution, London has experienced several disasters involving the loss of life. Thick fogs are quite common in this island nation, and the combination of smoke and fog forms a particularly noxious mixture known as **smog**, a contraction of *smoke* and *fog*.

The presence of fog indicates that the temperature of the air near the ground is at the dew point, and with the release of latent heat, there is the possibility of a **temperature inversion**. As we saw in Chapter 19, the atmospheric temperature decreases with increasing altitude in the troposphere (with a lapse rate of about $6\frac{1}{2}$ C°/km). As a result, hot combustive gases generally rise. However, under certain conditions, such as rapid radiative cooling near the ground surface, the temperature may locally *increase* with increasing altitude. The lapse rate is then said to be *inverted*, giving rise to a temperature inversion (● Fig. 20.10).

Most common are radiation and subsidence inversions. *Radiation temperature inversions*, which are associated with the Earth's radiative heat loss, occur daily. The ground is heated by insolation during the day, and at night it cools by radiating heat back into the atmosphere (see Section 19.2). If it is a clear night, the land surface and the air near it cool quickly. The air some distance above the surface, however, remains relatively warm, thus giving rise to a temperature inversion. *Radiation fogs* provide common evidence of this cooling effect in valleys.

Subsidence temperature inversions occur when a high-pressure air mass moves over a region and becomes stationary. As the dense air settles, it becomes compressed and heated. If the temperature of the descending air exceeds that of the air below it, then the lapse rate is inverted, similar to that shown in Fig. 20.10.

With a temperature inversion, emitted gases and smoke do not rise and are held near the ground. Continued combustion causes the air to become polluted, creating particularly hazardous conditions for people with heart and lung ailments. Smog episodes in various parts of the world have contributed to numerous deaths (● Fig. 20.11).

538   Chapter 20 ATMOSPHERIC EFFECTS

highlight Naming Hurricanes

For several hundred years, many hurricanes in the West Indies were named after the saint's day on which they occurred. In 1953 the National Weather Service began to use women's names for tropical storms and hurricanes. This practice began in World War II when military personnel named typhoons in the western Pacific after their wives and girlfriends, using alphabetical order. The first hurricane of the season received a name beginning with A, the second one was given a name beginning with B, and so on.

The practice of naming hurricanes solely after women was changed in 1979 when men's names were included in the lists. A six-year list of names for Atlantic storms is given in Table 1. A similar list is available for Pacific storms. Names beginning with the letters Q, U, X, Y, and Z are excluded because of their scarcity. The lists are recycled. For example, the 2002 list will be used again in 2008.

In 1992 Hurricane Andrew was a very destructive storm. It made landfall in Florida, causing millions of dollars worth of damage. Note that Andrew is not in the 2004 list but has been replaced with Alex. If a hurricane is particularly destructive, its name is replaced so as not to cause confusion with another destructive storm of the same name in the next six-year cycle. Similarly, the 1989 Hurricane Hugo that hit the South Carolina coast had its name replaced.

More recently, Hurricane Mitch was particularly devastating, causing thousands of deaths and vast destruction in Central America in 1998. Mitch's name was replaced in the 2004 list.

What was the largest number of tropical storms ever to occur in one year? At the time of this writing, the busiest year was 1933, which holds the record with 21 tropical storms, 10 of which became hurricanes. Names for these storms would have consumed a year's list, but tropical storms were not named at the time, only numbered. The year for the largest number of hurricanes was 1969, with 12 hurricanes resulting from 18 tropical storms (third-busiest year). More recently, the second-busiest year was 1995 with 19 tropical storms, of which 11 became hurricanes.

TABLE 1 The Six-Year List of Names for Atlantic, Gulf of Mexico, Caribbean Sea Storms*

2002	2003	2004	2005	2006	2007
Arthur	Ana	Alex	Arlene	Alberto	Allison
Bertha	Bill	Bonnie	Bret	Beryl	Barry
Cristobal	Claudette	Charley	Cindy	Chris	Chantal
Dolly	Danny	Danielle	Dennis	Debby	Dean
Edouard	Erika	Earl	Emily	Ernesto	Erin
Fay	Fabian	Frances	Franklin	Florence	Felix
Gustav	Grace	Gaston	Gert	Gordon	Gabrielle
Hanna	Henri	Hermine	Harvey	Helene	Humberto
Isidore	Isabel	Ivan	Irene	Isaac	Iris
Josephine	Juan	Jeanne	Jose	Joyce	Jerry
Kyle	Kate	Karl	Katrina	Keith	Karen
Lili	Larry	Lisa	Lee	Leslie	Lorenzo
Marco	Mindy	Matthew	Maria	Michael	Michelle
Nana	Nicholas	Nicole	Nate	Nadine	Noel
Omar	Odette	Otto	Ophelia	Oscar	Olga
Paloma	Peter	Paula	Philippe	Patty	Pablo
Rene	Rose	Richard	Rita	Rafael	Rebekah
Sally	Sam	Shary	Stan	Sandy	Sebastien
Teddy	Teresa	Tomas	Tammy	Tony	Tanya
Vicky	Victor	Virginie	Vince	Valerie	Van
Wilfred	Wanda	Walter	Wilma	William	Wendy

*The 2008 names will be the same as the list for 2002, and so on.

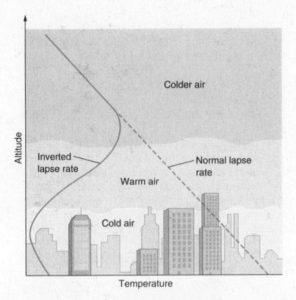

FIGURE 20.10 Temperature Inversion

Normally, the lapse rate near the Earth's surface decreases uniformly with increasing altitude. However, radiative cooling of the ground can cause the lapse rate to become inverted, and the temperature then increases with increasing altitude (usually below 1 mile). A similar condition may come about as a result of the subsidence of a high-pressure air mass.

The major source of air pollution is the combustion of *fossil fuels*—coal, gas, and oil. More accurately, air pollution results from the *incomplete* combustion of *impure* fuels. Technically, combustion (burning) is the chemical combination of certain substances with oxygen. Fossil fuels are the remains of plant and animal life and are composed chiefly of hydrocarbons (compounds of hydrogen and carbon).

If a fuel is pure and combustion is complete, the products, CO_2 and H_2O, are not usually considered pollutants, because they are a natural part of atmospheric cycles. For example, when carbon (as in coal) or methane, CH_4 (as in natural gas), is burned completely, the reactions are

$$C + O_2 \longrightarrow CO_2$$

$$CH_4 + 2\,O_2 \longrightarrow CO_2 + 2\,H_2O$$

However, if fuel combustion is incomplete, the products may include carbon (soot), various hydrocarbons, and carbon monoxide (CO). *Carbon monoxide* results from the incomplete combustion (oxidation) of carbon; that is,

$$2\,C + O_2 \longrightarrow 2\,CO$$

FIGURE 20.11 Smog Episode Waiting to Happen

Shown here is a picture of a 1940s steel mill on the Monongahela River near Pittsburgh, Pennsylvania. A similar scene in Donora, 20 miles down the river from Pittsburgh, gave rise to a 5-day smog episode in which hundreds of people became ill and at least 20 died.

540   Chapter 20   ATMOSPHERIC EFFECTS

But even increased concentrations of CO_2 can affect our environment. Carbon dioxide combines with water to form carbonic acid, a mild acid that many of us drink in the form of carbonated beverages (carbonated water):

$$CO_2 + H_2O \longrightarrow H_2CO_3$$

Carbonic acid is a natural agent of chemical weathering in geologic processes. But as a product of air pollution, increased concentrations may also exacerbate the corrosion of metals and react with certain materials, causing decomposition (● Fig. 20.12).

There is concern that an increase in the CO_2 content of the atmosphere may cause a change in global climate through the greenhouse effect. This concern will be considered later in the chapter.

Oddly enough, some by-products of complete combustion contribute to air pollution. For example, **nitrogen oxides (NO_x)** are formed when combustion temperatures are high enough to cause a reaction of the nitrogen and oxygen of the air. This reaction typically occurs when combustion is nearly complete, a condition that produces high temperatures, or when combustion takes place at high pressure—for example, in the cylinders of automobile engines.

These oxides, normally NO (nitric oxide) and NO_2 (nitrogen dioxide), can combine with water vapor in the air to form nitric acid (HNO_3), which is very corrosive. Also, this acid contributes to acid rain, which will be discussed shortly. Nitrogen dioxide (NO_2) has a pungent, sweet odor and is yellow-brown in color. During peak rush-hour traffic in some large cities, it is evident as a whiskey-brown haze.

Nitrogen oxides also can cause lung irritation and are key substances in the chemical reactions producing what is called *Los Angeles smog* because it was first identified in Los Angeles. This is not the classic London smoke-fog variety but a **photochemical smog** that results from the chemical reactions of hydrocarbons with oxygen in the air and other pollutants in the presence of sunlight. The sunlight supplies the energy for chemical reactions that take place in the air.

Over 15 million people live in the Los Angeles area, which has the form of a basin with the Pacific Ocean to the west and mountains to the east. This topography makes air pollution and temperature inversions a particularly hazardous combination. A temperature inversion essentially puts a "lid" on the city, which then becomes engulfed in its own fumes and exhaustive wastes.

FIGURE 20.12 Decomposition
The damage done to this statue in New York City by pollution and acid rain is evident (left). The statue looked quite different 60 years earlier (right).

FIGURE 20.13 Photochemical Smog in Los Angeles
Los Angeles has over 300 temperature inversions a year, giving rise to smog conditions.

Los Angeles has more than its share of temperature inversions, which may occur as frequently as 320 days per year. These inversions, a generous amount of air pollution, and an abundance of sunshine set the stage for the production of photochemical smog (●Fig. 20.13).

In comparison with the smoke-fogs of London, photochemical smog contains many more dangerous contaminants. These include organic compounds, some of which may be *carcinogens* (substances that cause cancer).

One of the best indicators of photochemical reactions, and a pollutant itself, is **ozone** (O_3), which is found in relatively large quantities in photochemically polluted air.

Fuel Impurities

Fuel impurities occur in a variety of forms. Probably the most common impurity in fossil fuels, and the most critical to air pollution, is *sulfur*. Sulfur is present in various fossil fuels in different concentrations. A low-sulfur fuel has less than 1% sulfur content, and a high-sulfur fuel greater than 2%. When fuels containing sulfur are burned, the sulfur combines with oxygen to form sulfur oxides (SO_x), the most common of which is **sulfur dioxide (SO_2)**:

$$S + O_2 \longrightarrow SO_2$$

A majority of SO_2 emissions come from the burning of coal and an appreciable amount from the burning of fuel oils. Coal and oil are the major fuels used in generating electricity. Almost half of the SO_2 pollution in the United States occurs in seven northeastern industrial states.

Sulfur dioxide in the presence of oxygen and water can react chemically to produce sulfurous and sulfuric acids. Sulfurous acid (H_2SO_3) is mildly corrosive and is used as an industrial bleaching agent. Sulfuric acid (H_2SO_4), a very corrosive acid, is a widely used industrial chemical. In the atmosphere, these sulfur compounds can cause considerable damage to practically all forms of life and property. Anyone familiar with sulfuric acid, the electrolyte used in car batteries, can appreciate its undesirability as an air pollutant.

The sulfur pollution problem has received considerable attention because of the occurrence of **acid rain**. Rain is normally slightly acidic as a result of carbon dioxide combining with water vapor to form carbonic acid. However, sulfur oxide and nitrogen oxide pollutants cause precipitation from contaminated clouds to be even more acidic, giving rise to acid rain (and also acid snow, sleet, fog, and hail; ● Fig. 20.14).

The problem is most serious in New York, New England, and Canada, where pollution emissions from the industrialized areas in the midwestern United States are carried by the general weather patterns. Other areas are not immune. Acid rain now occurs in the Southeast, and acid fogs are observed on the West Coast.

The government has imposed limits on the levels of sulfur emissions, and the effects of acid rain have

542   Chapter 20   ATMOSPHERIC EFFECTS

FIGURE 20.14 Formation of Acid Rain

(a) Sulfur dioxide and nitrogen oxide emissions react with water vapor in the atmosphere to form acid compounds. The acids are deposited in rain or snow and also may join dry airborne particles and fall to the Earth as dry deposition. (b) All rain is slightly acidic (slightly below 7.0 pH, because of natural CO_2 in the atmosphere). However, rain with a pH below 5.6 is considered acid rain. The map shows the pH values of acid rain at its peak in different parts of the country.

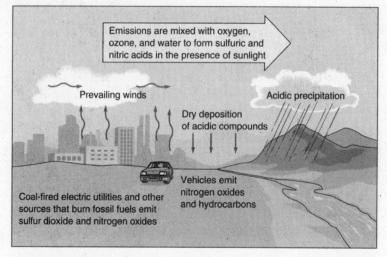

(a)

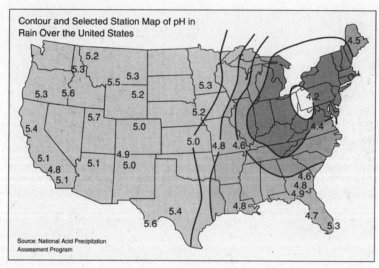

(b)

been reduced. However, before the regulations, rainfall with a pH of 1.4 had been recorded in the northeastern United States. This value surpasses the pH of lemon juice (pH 2.2). Canada had monthly rainfalls with an average pH of 3.5, which is as acidic as tomato juice (pH 3.5). The yearly average pH of the rain in these affected regions was about 4.2 to 4.4. Recall that a neutral solution has a pH of 7.0. (See Chapter 13 for a discussion of pH.)

In addition to acid rain, there are acid snows. Over the course of a winter, acid precipitations build up in snowpacks. During the spring thaw and resulting runoff, the sudden release of these acids gives an "acid shock" to streams and lakes.

Acid precipitations lower the pH of lakes, which threatens aquatic plant and animal life. Most fish species die at a pH of 4.5 to 5.0. As a result, many lakes in the northeastern United States and Canada

20.4 Atmospheric Pollution   **543**

are "dead" or in jeopardy. Natural buffers in area soils tend to neutralize the acidity, so waterways and lakes in an area don't necessarily match the pH of the rain. However, the neutralizing capability in some regions is being taxed, and the effects of acid rain still pose a problem.

Thus air pollution can be quite insidious and can consist of a great deal more than the common particulate matter (smoke, soot, and fly ash) that blackens the outside of buildings. Pollutants may be in the form of mists and aerosols. Some pollutants are metals, such as lead and arsenic. Approximately 100 atmospheric pollutants have been identified, 20 of which are metals that come primarily from industrial processes.

Figure 20.15 shows the sources and relative magnitudes of the various atmospheric pollutants. As can be seen, transportation is the major source of total air pollution. The United States is a mobile society, with over 130 million registered vehicles powered by internal combustion engines (● Fig. 20.16). The other major sources of air pollution are stationary sources and industrial processes. The term *stationary source* refers mainly to electrical generation facilities. These sources account for the majority of the sulfur oxide (SO_x) pollution, resulting primarily from the burning of coal, which always has some sulfur content.

Awareness of the problem of air pollution is readily evident today in the air quality reports in the media. How good the air is to breathe (or how polluted) is rated in many areas—in newspapers, on radio and TV, and on the Internet. The Environmental Protection Agency (EPA) now reports how good or bad the air is by rating it on a color-coded Air Quality Index (AQI), as shown in ● Fig. 20.17.

Note, in the reports shown in the figure, that ozone is the main pollutant. This is particularly true in the summer when photochemical processes give rise to an "ozone season." Many people check the AQI to determine whether they should jog or plan other outdoor activities. Elevated concentrations of ozone can reduce lung capacity, causing a shortness of breath; they can also cause headaches, nausea, and

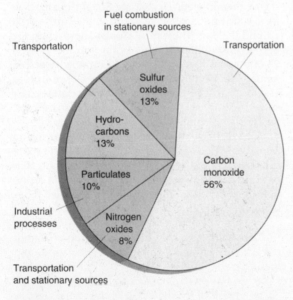

FIGURE 20.15 Air Pollutants and Their Major Sources

FIGURE 20.16 Transportation Air Pollution
Vast amounts of air pollution are generated by cars, trucks, and aircraft.

544   Chapter 20   ATMOSPHERIC EFFECTS

IN THE AIR
(today's forcast)

Air Quality Index (AGI)

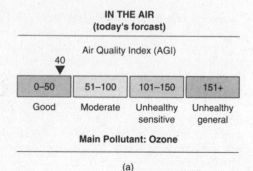

40 ▼			
0–50	51–100	101–150	151+
Good	Moderate	Unhealthy sensitive	Unhealthy general

Main Pollutant: Ozone

(a)

(b)

FIGURE 20.17 Pollution Reports

(a) A typical color-coded Air Quality Index as found in newspapers. This is a good day, with an index of 40. Note that the main pollutant is ozone. (b) A mobile board showing the AQI color report.

eye irritation. This is particularly true for the elderly and for people with asthma and other lung ailments. (Online ozone forecasts, data, and information may be found at the EPA's website **www.epa.gov/airnow** for many cities around the country.)

Yes, air pollution is here. But there are ways to make the air cleaner. As you might guess, this can be accomplished through the regulation of emissions from transportation, industry, and other pollution sources. And it works. During the 1990s, the air quality improved in more than 200 metropolitan areas. Los Angeles, for example, reports that smog has been reduced by 75% since 1985.

RELEVANCE QUESTION: Do you contribute to atmospheric pollution? Explain.

20.5 Pollution and Climate

LEARNING GOALS

▼ Define *climate*, and identify climatic changes.

▼ Explain the possible effects of atmospheric pollutants on climate.

It is generally believed that changes in the global climate are being, and will continue to be, brought about by atmospheric pollution. Climate is the name for the long-term average weather conditions of a region. Some regions are identified by their climates. For example, when someone mentions Florida or California, one usually thinks of a warm climate, and Arizona is known for its dryness and low humidity. Because of such favorable conditions, the climate of a region often attracts people to live there, and thus the distribution of population (and pollution) is affected.

Dramatic changes in climate have occurred throughout the Earth's history. Probably the most familiar of these changes are *ice ages*, when glacial ice sheets advanced southward over the world's northern continents. The most recent ice age ended some 10,000 years ago, after glaciers came as far south as the midwestern conterminous United States.

Evidence from ocean sediment cores supports the theory that dramatic changes in global climate result from subtle but regular variations in the Earth's orbit around the Sun. The Earth's closest approach to the Sun occurs at different times of the year in a cycle of 23,000 years. The Earth and Sun are now closest in January; in 10,000 years they will be closest in July. The result will be cooler summer temperatures, less snow melting, and a growth of the polar ice caps. Such a change could slowly lead to a new ice age.

Climatic fluctuations are continually occurring on a smaller scale also. For example, in the past several decades there has been a noticeable southward shift of world climate, which has produced drought conditions in some areas. The question being asked today is whether air pollution may be responsible for some of the observed climate variations.

There has been a shift in the frost and ice boundaries, a weakening of zonal wind circulation, and marked variations in the world's rainfall pattern. However, this pattern appears to be changing, possibly as a result of the depletion of the ozone layer, as will be discussed shortly.

Global climate is sensitive to atmospheric contributions that affect the radiation balance of the atmosphere. These contributions include the concentration of CO_2 and other "greenhouse" gases, the particulate concentration, and the extent of cloud cover, all of which affect the Earth's albedo (the fraction of insolation reflected back into space).

Air pollution and other human activities do contribute to changes in climatic conditions. Scientists are now trying to understand climate changes by using various models. These models of the workings of the Earth's atmosphere and oceans enable scientists to compare theories, using historical data on climate changes; however, specific data are scant.

Particulate pollution could contribute to changes in the Earth's thermal balance by decreasing the transparency of the atmosphere to insolation. We know this effect occurs from observing the results of volcanic eruptions; the particulate matter that is emitted causes changes in the albedo.

In 1991, Mount Pinatubo in the Philippines erupted. Debris was sent over 15 mi into the atmosphere, and over a foot of volcanic ash piled up in surrounding regions (● Fig. 20.18). Measurements indicate that Pinatubo was probably the largest volcanic eruption of the century, belching out tons of debris and sulfur dioxide (SO_2). The particulate matter caused beautiful sunrises and sunsets around the world during the following year. The sulfur dioxide gas reacts with oxygen and water to form tiny droplets, or aerosols, of sulfuric acid,

which may stay aloft for several years before falling back to the ground.

Computer models of atmospheric chemistry suggest that the acid aerosols could cause a thinning of the Earth's protective ozone layer, thus allowing more ultraviolet radiation to reach the ground. Other environmental concerns about the ozone layer are discussed in the chapter's third Highlight.

Supersonic transport (SST) aircraft operating in the lower stratosphere also have been a cause for concern because of particulate and gaseous emissions (● Fig. 20.19). In the troposphere, precipitation processes act to "wash" out particulate matter and gaseous pollutants, but there is no snow or rain washout mechanism in the stratosphere. Also, the stratosphere is a region of high chemical activity, and chemical pollutants, such as NO_x and hydrocarbons, could possibly give rise to climate-changing reactions.

Temperature increases may also cause pollution. Vast amounts of CO_2 are expelled into the atmosphere as a result of the combustion of fossil fuels. As discussed in Section 19.2, CO_2 and water vapor play important roles in the Earth's energy balance because of the greenhouse effect. An increase in the atmospheric concentration of CO_2 could alter the amount of radiation absorbed from the planet's surface and produce an increase in the Earth's average temperature.

During the nineteenth century, the atmospheric CO_2 content increased by about 10%, as determined from old records. During the twentieth century,

FIGURE 20.18 Volcanic Ash from Mount Pinatubo

Military personnel had to evacuate Clark Air Force Base in the Philippines when Mount Pinatubo erupted in June, 1991.

546   Chapter 20   ATMOSPHERIC EFFECTS

highlight   The Ozone Hole

In 1974, scientists in California warned that chlorofluorocarbon (CFC) gases might seriously damage the ozone layer through depletion. Observations generally supported this prediction, and in 1978 the United States banned the use of these gases as propellants in aerosol spray cans.

Even so, millions of tons of CFCs continue to leach into the atmosphere each year, primarily from refrigerants and spray propellants manufactured in other countries. The release of CFCs from car air conditioners is the single largest source of emissions. CFCs are also used in the manufacture of plastic foams.*

The major CFCs are CFC-11 ($CFCl_3$) and CFC-12 (CF_2Cl_2). When released, these gases slowly rise into the stratosphere, a process that takes 20 to 30 years. In the stratosphere the CFC molecules are broken apart by ultraviolet radiation, with the release of reactive chlorine atoms. These atoms in turn react with and destroy ozone molecules in the repeating cycle:

$$CFC \longrightarrow Cl$$

$$Cl + O_3 \longrightarrow ClO + O_2$$
$$\text{(ozone)}$$

---

*Other substances that cause ozone depletion are *halons*, a group of halogen compounds used as fire-extinguishing agents, and methyl bromide, which is used as a fumigation agent and also results from biomass burning.

$$ClO + O \longrightarrow Cl + O_2$$

Note that the chlorine atom is again available for reaction after the process. These atoms may remain in the atmosphere for a year or two. During this time, a single Cl atom may destroy as many as 100,000 ozone molecules.

Measurements indicate that the concentrations of CFCs in the atmosphere have more than doubled in the past 10 years. Worldwide ozone levels have declined an estimated 3% to 7% over the past few decades. Part of this decline is the result of normal fluctuations. But in 1985, scientists announced the discovery of an ozone "hole" over Antarctica (Fig. 1). Measurements have since revealed losses of greater than 50% in the total hole column and of greater than 95% at altitudes of 9 to 12 miles.

Investigations have shown that this polar hole in the ozone layer opens up annually during the southern springtime months of September and October. It is thought that the seasonal hole began forming in the late 1970s because of increasing concentrations of ozone-destroying chlorine pollutants in the stratosphere.

Ice crystals in high-altitude clouds in the lower stratosphere at the end of the polar winter are thought to provide surfaces on which chemical reactions take place. Such clouds and ozone holes are not evident at

lower altitudes. Satellite measurements taken in October 1991 showed that the atmospheric concentration of ozone over the South Pole had dwindled to a low level. These low levels were observed for another 2 years and probably were a result of the airborne aerosols from the 1991 Mt. Pinatubo eruption. The aerosols increase chlorine's effectiveness at destroying the ozone.

The worldwide depletion of the ultraviolet-absorbing ozone layer will have some significant effects. Experts estimate that the number of cases of skin cancer will increase by 60% and that there will be many additional cases of cataracts. In 1994, the National Weather Service began issuing a "UV index" forecast for many large cities. On a scale of 0 to 15, the index gives a relative indication of the amount of UV light that will be received at the Earth's surface at noontime the next day; the greater the number, the greater the amount of UV. The scale is based on upper-atmosphere ozone levels and clouds.

Crops and climate will also be affected. Sea levels may rise somewhere between 1 and 4 m (3 to 12 ft) by the year 2100 as a result of global warming and melting of the polar icecaps. Also, CFCs are greenhouse gases and can contribute to the warming in this manner.

International concern over ozone depletion prompted meetings and conventions, and in 1987, some 24 nations

FIGURE 20.19 Stratospheric Pollution

The supersonic transport produces a great deal of noise pollution during takeoff and landing. It also releases pollutants in the lower stratosphere where there are no weather conditions to wash them back to the ground.

20.5 Pollution and Climate **547**

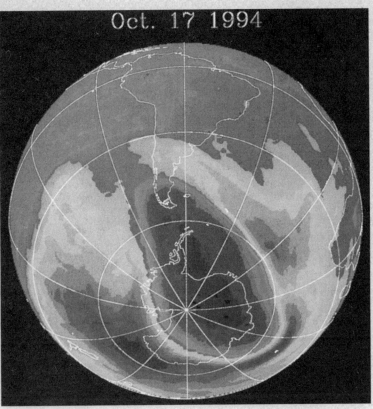

FIGURE 1 The Ozone Hole

A computer map of the South Pole region showing the total stratospheric ozone concentrations. The ozone hole, or region of minimal concentration, is shown in purple.

signed the *Montreal Protocol.* The agreement was to reduce the production of CFCs by half by 1998. The protocol was amended in 1990, and more than 90 nations agreed to phase out CFCs by the year 2000.

However, some new measurements showed worse damage to the ozone layer than was originally expected. Reacting to scientific assessments, the protocol parties decided to completely end production of halons by the beginning of 1994 and of CFCs by the beginning of 1996 in industrialized nations. (Developing countries would have a 10-year grace period.) Over 160 nations have now signed the treaty.

With only recycled and stockpiled CFCs available for use after January 1, 1996, considerable efforts were made to develop replacements. These are available and are used in new refrigerators and air conditioners. Such substitutes must be chemically nonreactive with ozone or must be destroyed by lower-atmosphere processes before reaching the ozone layer. Most of the substitutes are not as efficient as CFCs for refrigeration purposes, and as a result, there is a greater energy cost for the same cooling.

Even so, more efficient compounds will no doubt be developed, and this is a small price to pay to protect a life-sustaining part of our atmosphere.

because of larger populations and more combustion, the increase has been even greater. It appears that the Earth will be a warmer place in the twenty-first century, and climate changes will affect agriculture, water resources, and sea level. According to the U.S. Environmental Protection Agency (EPA) Global Warming site:

Global mean surface temperatures have increased 0.5–1.0 F°(0.3–0.6 C°) since the late nineteenth century. The twentieth century's ten warmest years all occurred in the last fifteen years of the century. Of these, 1998 was the warmest year on record. The snow cover in the Northern Hemisphere and floating ice in the Arctic Ocean have decreased. Globally, sea level has risen 4–8 inches over the past century. Worldwide precipitation over land has increased by about 1%. The frequency of extreme rainfall events has increased throughout much of the United States.

Increasing concentrations of greenhouse gases are likely to accelerate the rate of climatic change. Scientists expect that the average global surface temperature could rise

548   Chapter 20   ATMOSPHERIC EFFECTS

1–1.4 F° (0.6–2.5 C°) in the next fifty years, and 2.2–10 F° (1.4–5.8 C°) in the next century, with significant regional variation. Evaporation will increase as the climate warms, which will increase the average global precipitation. Soil moisture is likely to decline in many regions, and intense rainstorms are likely to become more frequent. Sea level is likely to rise two feet along most of the U.S. coast.

Calculations of climate changes for specific areas are much less reliable than global ones, and it is unclear whether regional climate will become more variable.

Time will tell. There are many unanswered questions about the effects of pollution, which has occurred over a relatively short time, on the natural interacting cycles of the atmosphere and biosphere, which have taken millions of years to become established.

RELEVANCE QUESTION: *How might you personally be affected by depletion of the ozone layer and by a stronger greenhouse effect? Give at least one answer for each.*

Important Terms

coalescence (20.1)	thunder	storm surge	nitrogen oxides (NO_x)
Bergeron process	ice storm	hurricane watch	photochemical smog
air mass (20.2)	tornado	hurricane warning	ozone
source region	tornado watch	pollution (20.4)	sulfur dioxide (SO_2)
front	tornado warning	smog	acid rain
lightning (20.3)	hurricane	temperature inversion	climate (20.5)

Review Questions

20.1 Condensation and Precipitation

1. When the temperature of the air is below the dew point without precipitation, the air is said to be what?
   (a) stable   (c) sublimed
   (b) supercooled   (d) coalesced

2. Which of the following is *not* essential to the Bergeron process?
   (a) silver iodide   (c) supercooled vapor
   (b) mixing   (d) ice crystals

3. Describe the three essentials of the Bergeron process and how they are related to methods of modern rainmaking.

4. (a) Is frost frozen dew? Explain.
   (b) How are large hailstones formed?

20.2 Air Masses

5. Which of the following air masses would be expected to be cold and dry?
   (a) cP   (c) cT
   (b) mA   (d) mE

6. What is a cold front advancing under a warm front called?
   (a) a warm front   (c) a cold front occlusion
   (b) a stationary front   (d) a warm front occlusion

7. How are air masses classified? Explain the relationship between air-mass characteristics and source regions.

8. Give the source region(s) of the air mass(es) that affect the weather in your area.

9. What is a front? List the meteorological symbols for four types of fronts.

10. Describe the weather associated with warm fronts and with cold fronts. What is the significance of the sharpness of their vertical boundaries?

20.3 Storms

11. What is the critical alert for a tornado?
    (a) tornado alert   (c) tornado watch
    (b) tornado warning   (d) tornado prediction

12. The greatest number of hurricane casualties is caused by which of the following?
    (a) high winds   (c) flying debris
    (b) low pressure   (d) storm surge

13. (a) Where can lightning take place? That is, where can it begin and end?
    (b) Describe what is meant by heat lightning and "a bolt from the blue."

14. What type of first aid should be given to someone suffering from the shock of a lightning stroke?

15. An ice storm is likely to result along what type of front? Explain.

16. What is the most violent of storms and why?

17. A tornado is sighted close by. What should you do?

18. What is the major source of energy for a tropical storm? When does a tropical storm become a hurricane?

19. Distinguish between a hurricane watch and a hurricane warning.

20. What months are the peak season for (a) hurricanes and (b) tornadoes?

20.4 Atmospheric Pollution

21. A subsidence temperature inversion is caused by which of the following?
    (a) a high-pressure air mass
    (b) acid rain
    (c) radiative cooling
    (d) subcritical air pressure

22. Which is a major source of air pollution?
    (a) nuclear electrical generation
    (b) incomplete combustion
    (c) temperature inversion
    (d) acid rain

23. Define the term *air pollution*.

24. Is air pollution a relatively new problem? Explain.

25. What are the two types of temperature inversions, and how does a temperature inversion affect atmospheric pollution in an area?

26. What are the products of complete combustion of hydrocarbons? What are the products of incomplete combustion?

27. How are nitrogen oxides (NO_x) formed and what role do they play in air pollution?

28. Distinguish between classical smog and photochemical smog. What is the prime indicator of the latter?

29. What is the major fossil-fuel impurity?

30. What are the causes and effects of acid rain? In which area is acid rain a major problem and why?

31. Name the major sources of the following pollutants.
    (a) carbon monoxide   (d) nitrogen oxides
    (b) sulfur dioxide   (e) ozone
    (c) particulate matter

20.5 Pollution and Climate

32. A change in the Earth's albedo could result from which of the following?
    (a) nitrogen oxides
    (b) acid rain
    (c) photochemical smog
    (d) particulate matter

33. Major concern about global warming arises from increased concentrations of which of the following?
    (a) sulfur oxides
    (b) nitrogen oxides
    (c) greenhouse gases
    (d) photochemical smog

34. Define climate.

35. What effect might each of the following have on the Earth's climate?
    (a) CO_2
    (b) particulate pollution
    (c) supersonic transports (SSTs)

36. What is a direct effect on humans that increases with atmospheric ozone depletion?

37. What effects could CFCs have on the Earth's climate?

38. What concern has been raised about air pollution in the stratosphere?

Applying Your Knowledge _____

1. Why do household barometers often have descriptive adjectives such as *rain* and *fair* on their faces, along with the direct pressure readings? (See Fig. 19.12.)

2. How could CO_2 pollution be decreased while our energy needs were still being met?

3. Assuming that the name has not been retired, what will be the name of the third Atlantic tropical storm in 2007?

550 Chapter 20 ATMOSPHERIC EFFECTS

Exercises

20.2 Air Masses

1. Locate the source regions for the following air masses that affect the conterminous United States:
   (a) cA   (d) mT
   (b) mP   (e) cP
   (c) cT

2. What would be the classifications of the air masses forming over the following source regions?
   (a) Sahara Desert   (d) Mid-Pacific Ocean
   (b) Antarctic Ocean   (e) Siberia
   (c) Greenland

3. On average, how far does (a) a cold front and (b) a warm front travel in 24 h?

4. How long does it take (a) a cold front and (b) a warm front to travel from west to east across your home state?

5. If thunder is heard 10 s after a lightning flash is observed, approximately how far away is the storm? Compute in kilometers and miles.

6. While picnicking on a summer day, you hear thunder 9 s after seeing a lightning flash from an approaching storm. Approximately how far away, in miles, is the storm?

Solution to Confidence Exercise

20.1 $d = \bar{v}t = \frac{1}{3}$ km/s $\times$ 3 s = 1 km
$ = \frac{1}{5}$ mi/s $\times$ 3 s = 0.6 mi

Answers to Multiple-Choice Review Questions

1. b	5. a	11. b	21. a	32. d
2. a	6. c	12. d	22. b	33. c

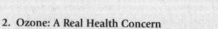

On the Web

1. **Stormy Weather**
   Go to **http://www.physicalscience.college/hmco.com/students** and follow the recommended links to learn more firsthand about El Niño and to answer the following questions. What is the role that El Niño plays in our weather patterns? What other theories are there to explain the causes of El Niño, and what is their common denominator? What is the Global Weather Machine? How accurate are weather forecasters?

2. **Ozone: A Real Health Concern**
   What exactly is the ozone hole? How did scientists first become aware of it? More basically, what is ozone and how is it formed? How is it destroyed? Why is it important? What is being done? What are TOMS Satellite Measurements? What steps might you take to reduce the risks posed by depletion of the ozone layer?

   Explore answers to these questions by following the recommended links at **http://www.physicalscience. college/hmco.com/students.**

Check Your Understanding

The following sentences appear in the chapter. Circle the letter of the BEST meaning for each italicized word.

50. "By pollution, we mean any *atypical* contributions to the environment resulting from the activities of human beings."
    a. Generous
    b. Foul
    c. Unusual
    d. Normal

51. "The problem was not *alleviated*, and in the middle 1600s, King Charles II was prompted to commission one of the outstanding scholars of the day, Sir John Evelyn, to make a study of the situation."
    a. Increased in size
    b. Made more bearable
    c. Understood
    d. Solved

52. "… the combination of smoke and fog forms a particularly *noxious* mixture known as smog, a contraction of smoke and fog."
    a. Dark
    b. Harmful
    c. Heavy
    d. Transparent

53. "Sulfuric acid, a very *corrosive* acid, is a widely used industrial chemical."
    a. Destructive
    b. Beneficial
    c. Inexpensive
    d. Lethal

54. "Thus air pollution can be quite *insidious* and can consist of a great deal more than the common particulate matter … that blackens the outside of buildings."
    a. Varied
    b. Harmful
    c. Effective
    d. Helpful

55. "The most recent ice age ended some 10,000 years ago, after glaciers came as far south as the Midwestern *conterminous* United States."
    a. Spread out
    b. Flat
    c. Sharing a boundary
    d. Similar in size

Circle the letter of the correct response.

56. Which of the following conclusions is accurately based upon the information in Figure 20.15 in the preceding section of the physical science chapter?
    a. Transportation pollutes the air with only carbon monoxide.
    b. Industrial processes are the major source of particulates.
    c. Nitrogen oxides come from transportation only.
    d. Hydrocarbons make up the majority of air pollutants.

For each of the following questions, either circle the letter of the correct response or write down your answer on the blanks provided, as appropriate.

57. A subsidence temperature inversion is caused by which of the following?
    a. A high-pressure air mass
    b. Acid rain
    c. Radiative cooling
    d. Subcritical air pressure

58. Which is a major source of air pollution?
    a. Nuclear electrical generation
    b. Incomplete combustion
    c. Temperature inversion
    d. Acid rain

59. Define the term *air pollution*.

_____

_____

60. Is air pollution a relatively new problem? Explain.

_____

_____

_____

61. What are the two types of temperature inversions, and how does a temperature inversion affect atmospheric pollution in an area?

_____

_____

_____

62. What are the products of complete combustion of hydrocarbons? What are the products of incomplete combustion?

_____

_____

_____

63. How are nitrogen oxides (NO_2) formed and what role do they play in air pollution?

_____

_____

_____

64. Distinguish between classical smog and photochemical smog. What is the prime indictor of the latter?

_____

_____

_____

65. What is the major fossil-fuel impurity?

_____

_____

66. What are the causes and effects of acid rain? In which area is acid rain a major problem and why?

_____

_____

_____

67. Name the major sources of the following pollutants.
    a. carbon monoxide _____
    b. sulfur dioxide _____
    c. particulate matter _____
    d. nitrogen oxides _____
    e. ozone _____

68. A change in the Earth's albedo could result from which of the following?
    a. Nitrogen oxides
    b. Acid rain
    c. Photochemical smog
    d. Particulate matter

69. Major concern about global warming arises from increased concentrations of which of the following?
    a. Sulfur oxides
    b. Nitrogen oxides
    c. Greenhouse gases
    d. Photochemical smog

70. Define *climate*.

_____

_____

_____

71. What effect might each of the following have on the Earth's climate?

    a. CO_2 _____

    _____

    b. particulate pollution _____

    _____

    c. supersonic transports (SSTs) _____

    _____

72. What is a direct effect on humans that increases with atmospheric ozone depletion?

_____

_____

_____

73. What effect could CFCs have on the Earth's climate?

_____

_____

_____

74. What concern has been raised about air pollution in the stratosphere?

_____

_____

_____

Discuss the following questions with a partner or group, and then collaborate to write an answer for each question on your own paper.

75. Do you contribute to atmospheric pollution? Explain.

76. How might you personally be affected by depletion of the ozone layer and by a stronger greenhouse effect? Give at least one answer for each.

77. Complete one of the two "On the Web" activities.

A People and a Nation (American History): "Transforming Fire: The Civil War, 1861–1865"

Applying the Reading Strategies

Write your response to the following question on your own paper.

1. Write at least one paragraph about what you already know about America's Civil War.

Previewing the Chapter

2. On what topic does this chapter focus?
   a. Wars in America
   b. Nineteenth-century America
   c. The Civil War
   d. Soldiers in the Civil War

3. Mark each feature in the list below that is included in this chapter.
   ____ Learning objectives or goals
   ____ Key terms highlighted within the text
   ____ Definitions of key terms
   ____ Chapter outline
   ____ Visual aids
   ____ Chapter summary
   ____ Review questions
   ____ Exercises

4. This chapter covers events during the years
   a. 1850–1865.
   b. 1861–1865.
   c. 1861–1862.
   d. 1864–1865.

5. True or False: The battle of Chancellorsville is discussed in this chapter.
   a. True
   b. False

6. This chapter is divided into how many major sections?
   a. Two
   b. Three
   c. Eight
   d. Sixteen

7. Most of the visual aids in this chapter are
   a. photographs and maps.
   b. maps and graphs.
   c. photographs and charts.
   d. cartoons and diagrams.

Reading the Chapter

Read the chapter entitled "Transforming Fire: The Civil War, 1861–1865" both actively and critically. Record in the margins of the text your reactions, observations, and other comments that reflect your critical reading of the information.

The three "Check Your Understanding" sections that appear throughout the excerpted chapter, "Transforming Fire: The Civil War 1861–1865," include questions that will help you check your comprehension of the information provided in the chapter. They encourage you to practice the reading strategies you have learned from this text supplement, so stop to complete them before you continue reading.

He was an ordinary twenty-seven-year-old store clerk from a New England town. But he went off, as though directed by a manly compass, to seek the extraordinary experiences of comradeship and war. In the spring of 1861, Charles Brewster, a member of a militia unit in Northampton, Massachusetts, left his mother and two sisters behind and joined Company C of the Tenth Massachusetts Volunteers. At that moment, Brewster had no idea of his capacity for leadership or his ability to uphold such values as courage and manliness. But the war released him from the boredom and failure of his life.

On April 18, only three days after the surrender of Fort Sumter, a mustering of Company C turned into a large public rally where forty new men enlisted. By April 24 seventy-five Northampton women committed their labor to sew uniforms for the company. Some women worked at home, while others sewed in the town hall. Local poets came to the armory to recite patriotic verses to the would-be soldiers. Yesterday farmers, clerks, and mechanics, today they were the heroes who would "whip secesh." By June 10, after weeks of drilling, Brewster's company attended a farewell ball, and four days later they strode down Main Street amid a cheering throng of spectators. Flags waved everywhere, several brass bands competed, and Brewster and his company boarded a train going south. En route the soldiers continued the joyous fervor of the day by singing "patriotic airs" to the accompaniment of a lone accordion.

Before their three-year enlistment ended, the Tenth Massachusetts participated in nearly every major battle fought by the Army of the Potomac from early 1862 to the summer of 1864. When the survivors of the Tenth were mustered out, only 220 of the nearly 1,000 in the original regiment were still on active duty. Their summer outing had transformed into the bloodiest war in history. They had seen thousands die of disease, practiced war upon civilians and the southern landscape, and loyally served the cause as variously defined, trying their best to fulfill their communities' expectations. In more than two hundred sometimes

War drastically altered the lives of millions of Americans. Many young men found in soldiering a combination of comradeship, devotion, boredom, and horror. Winslow Homer gave the ironic title *Home, Sweet, Home* to this painting of Union soldiers in camp about 1863. (Private Collection, photograph courtesy of Hirschl and Adler Galleries, New York)

15

TRANSFORMING FIRE: THE CIVIL WAR 1861–1865

387

388 Chapter 15 Transforming Fire: The Civil War, 1861–1865

lyrical letters to his mother and sisters, Brewster, who rose to lieutenant and adjutant of his regiment, left a trove of commentary on the meaning of war, the character of slavery and why it had to be destroyed, and especially the values of common, mid-nineteenth-century American men.

Brewster was as racist as many southerners in his perceptions of blacks. He was no "desperate hero" about battlefield courage, and he nearly died of dysentery more than once. He was personally eager for rank and recognition, and he eventually held only contempt for civilians who stayed at home. He was often miserably lonely and homesick, and he described battlefield carnage with an honest realism. The early romantic was transformed into a mature veteran by what he called the "terrible, terrible business" of war.

Most tellingly, Brewster grew in his attitudes about race. In 1862 he defied orders and took in a seventeen-year-old ex-slave as his personal servant, patronizingly clothing him with his own old pants sent from home. In 1864, after surviving some of the worst battles of the war in Virginia, which destroyed his regiment, and frightened of civilian life, Brewster reenlisted to be a recruiter of black troops. In this new role, Brewster worked from an office in Norfolk, Virginia, where his principal job was writing "love letters" for illiterate black women to their soldier husbands at the front. In imagining Brewster sitting at a table with a lonely freedwoman, swallowing his prejudices toward blacks and women, and repeatedly writing or reciting the phrases "give my love to . . ." and "your Husband untall Death," we can glimpse the enormous potential for human transformation at work in this war.

The Civil War brought astonishing, unexpected changes not only to Charles Brewster but everywhere in both North and South. Countless southern soldiers experienced similar transformations. But they, and their families, also experienced what few other groups of Americans have—utter defeat. For some Americans, wealth changed to poverty and hope to despair; for others, the suffering of war spelled opportunity. Contrasts abounded, between noble and crass motives and between individuals seeking different goals. Even the South's slaves, who hoped that they were witnessing God's "Holy War"—the "coming of the jubilee"—encountered unsympathetic liberators. When a Yankee soldier ransacked a slave woman's cabin, stealing her best quilts, she denounced him as a "nasty, stinkin' rascal" who had betrayed his cause of freedom. Angrily the soldier contradicted her, saying, "I'm fightin' for $14 a month and the Union."

Northern troops were not the only ones to feel anger over their sacrifices. Impoverished by the war, one southern farmer had endured inflation, taxes, and shortages to support the Confederacy. Then an impressment agent arrived to take still more from him—grain and meat, horses and mules, and wagons. In return, the agent offered only a certificate promising repayment sometime in the future. Bitter and disgusted, the farmer spoke for many by declaring, "The sooner this damned Government falls to pieces, the better it will be for us."

Many northern businessmen, however, viewed the economic effects of the war with optimistic anticipation. The conflict ensured vast government expenditures, a heavy demand for goods, and lucrative federal contracts. *Harper's Monthly* reported that an eminent financier expected a long war—the kind of war that would mean huge purchases, paper money, active speculation, and rising prices. "The battle of Bull Run," predicted the financier, "makes the fortune of every man in Wall Street who is not a natural idiot."

For millions, the Civil War was a life-changing event. It obliterated the normal patterns and circumstances of life. Millions of men were swept away into training camps and battle units. Armies numbering in the hundreds of thousands marched over the South, devastating once-peaceful countrysides. Families struggled to survive without their men; businesses tried to cope with the loss of workers. Women in both North and South took on extra responsibilities in the home and moved into new jobs in the work force. Many women joined the ranks of nurses and hospital workers. No sphere of life was untouched.

Change was most drastic in the South, where the leaders of the secession movement had launched a conservative revolution for their section's national independence. Born of states' rights doctrine, their break with the Union now had to be transformed into a centralized nation to fight a vast war. Never were men more mistaken: their revolutionary means were fundamentally incompatible with their conservative purpose. Southern whites had feared that a peacetime government of Republicans would interfere with slavery and upset the routine of plantation life. Instead their own actions led to a war that turned southern life upside down and imperiled the very existence of slavery. Jefferson Davis, president of the Confederate States of America, devised policies more objectionable to the elite than any proposed by President-elect Lincoln. Life in the Confederacy proved to be a shockingly unsouthern experience.

IMPORTANT EVENTS

1861 Battle of Bull Run
McClellan organizes Union Army
Union blockade begins
U.S. Congress passes first confiscation act
Trent affair
Some slaves admitted to Union lines as
"contraband" of war

1862 Union captures Fort Henry and
Fort Donelson
U.S. Navy captures New Orleans
Battle of Shiloh shows the war's
destructiveness
Confederacy enacts conscription
McClellan's Peninsula Campaign fails
to take Richmond
U.S. Congress passes second confiscation
act, initiating emancipation
Confederacy mounts offensive in Maryland
and Kentucky
Battle of Antietam ends Lee's drive into
Maryland in September
British intervention in the war on
Confederate side is averted by events
and northern diplomacy

1863 Emancipation Proclamation takes effect
U.S. Congress passes National Banking Act
Union enacts conscription
African American soldiers join Union Army
Food riots occur in southern cities

Battle of Chancellorsville ends in
Confederate victory but Jackson's death
Union wins key victories at Gettysburg
and Vicksburg
Draft riots take place in New York City
Battle of Chattanooga leaves South vulnerable
to Sherman's march into Georgia

1864 Battles of the Wilderness and Spotsylvania
produce heavy casualties on both sides in
the effort to capture and defend Richmond
Battle of Cold Harbor continues carnage in
Virginia
Lincoln requests Republican Party plank
abolishing slavery
Sherman captures Atlanta
Confederacy begins to collapse on the home
front, as southern hardship destroys morale
Lincoln wins reelection, eliminating any Con-
federate hopes for a negotiated end to war
Jefferson Davis proposes emancipation within
the Confederacy
Sherman marches through Georgia to the sea

1865 Sherman marches through Carolinas
U.S. Congress approves Thirteenth
Amendment
Lee abandons Richmond and Petersburg
Lee surrenders at Appomattox Court House
Lincoln assassinated
Death toll in war reaches 620,000

War altered the North as well, but less sharply. Because most of the fighting took place on southern soil, northern farms and factories remained virtually unscathed. The drafting of workers and the changing need for products slowed the pace of industrialization somewhat, but factories and businesses remained busy. Workers lost ground to inflation, but the economy hummed. A new pro-business atmosphere dominated Congress, where the seats of southern representatives were empty. To the alarm of many, the powers of the federal government and of the president increased during the war.

The war created social strains in both North and South. Disaffection was strongest in the Confederacy, where poverty and class resentment fed a lower-class antagonism to the war that threatened the Confederacy from within as federal armies assailed it from without. In the North, dissent also flourished, and antiwar sentiment occasionally erupted into violence.

Ultimately, the Civil War forced on the nation a social and political revolution regarding race. Its greatest effect was to compel leaders and citizens to deal directly with the issue they had struggled over but had been unable to resolve: slavery. This issue, in complex and indirect ways, had caused the war. Now the scope and demands of the war forced reluctant Americans to confront it. And blacks themselves embraced what was for them the most fundamental turning point in their experience as Americans. ■

America Goes to War, 1861–1862

 Few Americans understood what they were getting into when the war began. The onset of hostilities sparked patriotic sentiments, optimistic speeches, and joyous ceremonies in both North and South. Northern communities, large and small, raised companies of

390   Chapter 15   Transforming Fire: The Civil War, 1861–1865

In *Departure of the Seventh Regiment* (1861), flags and the spectacle of thousands of young men from New York marching off to battle give a deceptively gay appearance to the beginning of the Civil War.   (Museum of Fine Arts, Boston; M. and M. Karolik Collection)

volunteers eager to save the Union and sent them off with fanfare (a scene captured in the painting *Departure of the Seventh Regiment*). In the South, confident recruits boasted of whipping the Yankees and returning home at least before Christmas. Southern women sewed dashing uniforms for men who soon would be lucky to wear drab gray or butternut homespun. Americans went to war in 1861 with decidedly romantic notions of what they would experience.

Through the spring of 1861 both sides scrambled to organize and train their undisciplined armies. On

First Battle of Bull Run

July 21, 1861, the first battle took place outside Manassas Junction, Virginia, near a stream called Bull Run. General Irvin McDowell and 30,000 Union troops attacked General P. G. T. Beauregard's 22,000 southerners (see Map 15.1 on page 394). As raw recruits struggled amid the confusion of their first battle, federal forces began to gain ground. Then they ran into a line of Virginia troops under General Thomas Jackson. "There is Jackson standing like a stone wall," shouted one Confederate. "Stonewall" Jackson's line held, and the arrival of 9,000 Confederate reinforcements won the day for the South. Union troops fled back to Washington and shocked northern congressmen and spectators,

who had watched the battle from a point 2 miles away; a few of them were actually captured for their folly.

The unexpected rout at Bull Run gave northerners their first hint of the nature of the war to come. While the United States enjoyed an enormous advantage in resources, victory would not be easy. Pro-Union feeling was growing in western Virginia, and loyalties were divided in the four border slave states—Missouri, Kentucky, Maryland, and Delaware. But the rest of the Upper South, the states of North Carolina, Virginia, Tennessee, and Arkansas, had joined the Confederacy in the wake of the attack on Fort Sumter. Moved by an outpouring of regional loyalty, half a million southerners volunteered to fight, so many that the Confederate government could hardly arm them all. The United States therefore undertook a massive mobilization of troops around Washington, D.C.

Lincoln gave command of the army to General George B. McClellan, an officer who proved to be better at organization and training than at fighting. McClellan put his growing army into camp and devoted the fall and winter of 1861 to readying a formidable force of a quarter-million men whose mission would be to take Richmond, established as the Confederate capital by July 1861. "The vast preparation of the enemy," wrote one southern soldier, produced a "feeling of despondency" in the South for the first time. But southern morale remained high early in the war.

While McClellan prepared, the Union began to implement other parts of its overall strategy, which called for a blockade of southern ports and eventual capture of the Mississippi River. Like a constricting snake, this "Anaconda plan" would strangle the Confederacy (see Map 15.2 on page 412). At first the Union Navy had too few ships to patrol 3,550 miles of coastline and block the Confederacy's avenues of commerce and supply. Gradually, however, the navy increased the blockade's effectiveness, though it never stopped southern commerce completely.

Grand Strategy

Confederate strategy was essentially defensive. A defensive posture was not only consistent with the South's claim of independence, but acknowledged the North's advantage in resources (see Figure 15.1). Furthermore, communities all across the South demanded their defense. Jefferson Davis, however, wisely rejected a static or wholly defensive strategy. The South would pursue an "offensive defensive," taking advantage of opportunities to attack and using its interior lines of transportation to concentrate troops at crucial points. In its war aims, the Confederacy did not need to conquer the North; the Union effort, however, as time would tell, required conquest of the South.

Strategic thinking on both sides slighted the importance of "the West," that vast expanse of territory between Virginia and the Mississippi River. When the war began, both sides were unprepared for large-scale operations in the West, but before the end of the war they would prove to be decisive. Guerrilla warfare broke out in 1861 in the politically divided state of

Missouri, and key locations along the Mississippi and other major rivers in the West would prove to be crucial prizes in the North's eventual victory. In the Far West, beyond the Mississippi River, the Confederacy hoped to gain an advantage by negotiating treaties with the Creeks, Choctaws, Chickasaws, Cherokees, Seminoles, and smaller tribes of Plains Indians. Although early strategy evolved haphazardly, both sides would soon know they were in a war the scale of which few people had ever imagined.

The last half of 1861 brought no major land battles, but the North made gains by sea. Late in the summer Union naval forces captured Cape Hatteras and then seized Hilton Head, one of the Sea Islands off Port Royal, South Carolina. A few months later, similar operations secured vital coastal points in North Carolina, as well as Fort Pulaski, which defended Savannah. Federal naval operations established significant beachheads along the Confederate coastline (see Map 15.2).

Union Naval Campaign

The coastal victories off South Carolina foreshadowed a revolution in slave society. At the federal gunboats' approach, frightened planters abandoned their lands and fled. For a while, Confederate cavalry tried to round up slaves and move them to the interior as well. But thousands of slaves greeted what they hoped to be freedom with rejoicing and broke the hated cotton gins. Some entered their masters' homes and absconded with clothing and furniture, which they conspicuously displayed. Their jubilation and the growing stream of runaways who poured into the Union lines eliminated any doubt about which side slaves would support, given the opportunity. Unwilling at first to

Figure 15.1   Comparative Resources, Union and Confederate States, 1861   The North had vastly superior resources. Although the North's advantages in manpower and industrial capacity proved very important, the South still had to be conquered, its society and its will crushed. (Source: *The Times Atlas of World History*. Time Books, London, 1978. Used with permission.)

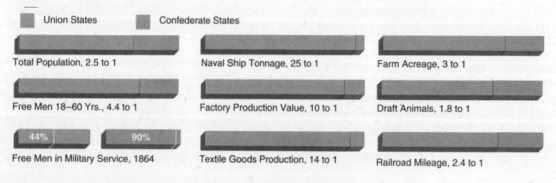

■ Union States   ■ Confederate States

Total Population, 2.5 to 1

Naval Ship Tonnage, 25 to 1

Farm Acreage, 3 to 1

Free Men 18–60 Yrs., 4.4 to 1

Factory Production Value, 10 to 1

Draft Animals, 1.8 to 1

44%   90%
Free Men in Military Service, 1864

Textile Goods Production, 14 to 1

Railroad Mileage, 2.4 to 1

392 Chapter 15 Transforming Fire: The Civil War, 1861–1865

wage a war against slavery, the federal government did not acknowledge the slaves' freedom—though it began to use their labor in the Union cause. This swelling tide of emancipated slaves, defined by many Union officers as "contraband" of war (confiscated enemy property), forced first a bitter and confused debate within the Union Army and government over how to treat the freedmen, and then a forthright attempt to harness their power.

The coastal incursions worried southerners, but the spring of 1862 brought even stronger evidence of the war's gravity. In March two ironclad ships—the *Monitor* (a Union warship) and the *Merrimack* (a Union ship recycled by the Confederacy)—fought each other for the first time; their battle, though indecisive, ushered in a new era in naval design. In April Union ships commanded by Admiral David Farragut smashed through log booms blocking the Mississippi River and fought their way upstream to capture New Orleans. Farther west three full Confederate regiments were organized, mostly of Cherokees, from Indian Territory, but a Union victory at Elkhorn Tavern, Arkansas, shattered southern control of Indian Territory. Thereafter, dissension within Native American groups and a Union victory the following year at Honey Springs, Arkansas, reduced Confederate operations in Indian Territory to guerrilla raids.

In February 1862 land and river forces in northern Tennessee won significant victories for the Union.

Grant's Tennessee Campaign and the Battle of Shiloh

A hard-drinking Union commander named Ulysses S. Grant saw the strategic importance of Fort Henry and Fort Donelson, the Confederate outposts guarding the Tennessee and Cumberland Rivers. If federal troops could capture these forts, Grant realized, they would open two prime routes into the heartland of the Confederacy. In just ten days he seized the forts, cutting off the Confederates so completely that he demanded unconditional surrender of Fort Donelson. A path into Tennessee, Alabama, and Mississippi now lay open before the Union Army. Grant's achievement of such a surrender from his former West Point roommate, Confederate commander Simon Bolivar Buckner, inspired northern public opinion that spring.

Grant moved on into southern Tennessee and the first of the war's shockingly bloody encounters, the Battle of Shiloh. On April 6 Confederate general Albert Sidney Johnston caught federal troops with their backs to the water awaiting reinforcements along the Tennessee River. The Confederates attacked early in the morning and inflicted heavy damage all day. Close to victory, General Johnston was shot from his horse and killed. Southern forces almost achieved a breakthrough, but Union reinforcements arrived that night. The next day the tide of battle turned, and after ten hours of terrible combat, Grant's men forced the Confederates to withdraw.

Neither side won a victory at Shiloh, yet the losses were staggering. Northern troops lost 13,000 men (killed, wounded, or captured) out of 63,000; southerners sacrificed 11,000 out of 40,000. Total casualties in this single battle exceeded those in all three of America's previous wars combined. Now both sides were beginning to sense the true nature of the war. "I saw an open field," Grant recalled, "over which Confederates had made repeated charges . . . , so covered with dead that it would have been possible to walk across the clearing, in any direction, stepping on dead bodies, without a foot touching the ground." Shiloh utterly changed Grant's thinking about the war. He had hoped that southerners soon would be "heartily tired" of the conflict. After Shiloh, "I gave up all idea of saving the Union except by complete conquest." Memories of Shiloh battlefield, and many others to come, would haunt the soldiers who survived for the rest of their lives. Herman Melville's "Shiloh, A Requiem" captures the pathos of that spring day when armies learned the truth about war.

> Skimming lightly, wheeling still,
>   The swallows fly low
> Over the field in clouded days,
>   The forest-field of Shiloh—
> Over the field where April rain
> Solaced the parched ones stretched in pain
> Through the pause of night
> That followed the Sunday fight
>   Around the church of Shiloh—
> The church so lone, the log-built one,
> That echoed to many a parting groan
>   And natural prayer
>   Of dying foemen mingled there—
> Foemen at morn, but friends at eve—
>   Fame or country least their care:
>   (What like a bullet can undeceive!)
>   But now they lie low,
> While over them the swallows skim,
>   And all is hushed at Shiloh.

Meanwhile, on the Virginia front, President Lincoln had a different problem. General McClellan was

Both armies experienced religious revivals during the war. This photograph shows members of a largely Irish regiment from New York celebrating Mass at the beginning of the war. Notice the presence of some female visitors in the left foreground. (Library of Congress)

McClellan and the Peninsula Campaign

slow to move. Only thirty-six, Mc-Clellan had already achieved notable success as an army officer and railroad president. Keenly aware of his historic role, he did not want to fail and insisted on having everything in order before he attacked. Habitually overestimating the size of enemy forces, McClellan called repeatedly for reinforcements and ignored Lincoln's directions to advance. McClellan advocated war of limited aims that would lead to a quick reunion. He intended no disruption of slavery, nor any war on noncombatants. McClellan's conservative vision of the war was practically outdated before he ever moved his army into Virginia. Finally he chose to move by a water route, sailing his troops down the Chesapeake, landing them on the peninsula between the York and James Rivers, and advancing on Richmond from the east (see Map 15.1).

After a bloody but indecisive battle at Fair Oaks on May 31–June 1, the federal armies moved to within 7 miles of the Confederate capital. They could see the spires on Richmond churches. The Confederate commanding general, Joseph E. Johnston, was badly wounded at Fair Oaks, and President Jefferson Davis placed his chief military adviser, Robert E. Lee, in command. The fifty-five-year-old Lee was an aristocratic Virginian, a life-long military officer, and a veteran of distinction from the War with Mexico. Although he opposed secession and found slavery distasteful, Lee loyally gave his allegiance to his state. He soon foiled McClellan's legions.

First, he sent Stonewall Jackson's corps of 17,000 northwest into the Shenandoah valley behind Union forces, where they threatened Washington, D.C., and with rapid-strike mobility drew some federal troops away from Richmond to protect their own capital. Further, in mid-June, in an extraordinary four-day ride around the entire Union Army, Confederate cavalry under J. E. B. Stuart, a self-styled Virginia cavalier, with red cape and plumed hat, confirmed the exposed position of a major portion of McClellan's army north of the rain-swollen Chickahominy River. Then, in a series of engagements known as the Seven Days Battles, June 26–July 1, Lee struck at McClellan's army. Lee never managed to close his pincers around the retreating Union forces, but the daring move of taking the majority of his army northeast and attacking the Union right flank, while leaving only a small force to

394 Chapter 15 Transforming Fire: The Civil War, 1861–1865

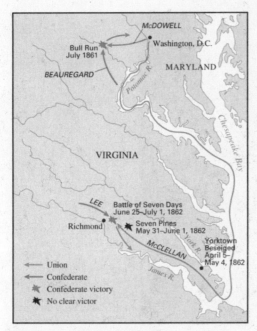

Map 15.1 McClellan's Campaign The water route chosen by McClellan to threaten Richmond during the peninsular campaign.

defend Richmond, forced McClellan (always believing he was outnumbered) to retreat toward the James River.

During the sustained fighting of the Seven Days, the Union forces suffered 20,614 casualties, and the Confederates 15,849. After repeated rebel assaults against entrenched positions on high ground at Malvern Hill, an officer concluded: "It was not war, it was murder." By August 3 McClellan withdrew his army back to the Potomac and the environs of Washington. Richmond remained safe for almost two more years.

Buoyed by these results, Jefferson Davis conceived an ambitious plan to turn the tide of the war and gain recognition of the Confederacy by European nations. He ordered a general offensive, sending Lee north into Maryland and Generals Kirby Smith and Braxton Bragg into Kentucky. Calling on residents of Maryland and Kentucky to make a separate peace with his government, Davis also invited northwestern states like Indiana, which sent much of their trade down the Mississippi to New Orleans, to leave the

Confederate Offensive in Maryland and Kentucky

Union. This was a coordinated effort to take the war to the North, to contest the allegiance of the border states, and to try to force a decisive turning point.

The plan was promising, but every part of the offensive failed. In the bloodiest day of the entire war, September 17, 1862, McClellan turned Lee back from Sharpsburg, Maryland. In the Battle of Antietam 5,000 men died (3,500 had died at Shiloh), and another 18,000 were wounded. Lee was lucky to escape destruction, for McClellan had intercepted a lost battle order, wrapped around cigars for each Confederate corps commander and inadvertently dropped by a courier. But McClellan moved slowly, failed to use his larger forces in simultaneous attacks all along the line, and allowed Lee's stricken army to retreat to safety across the Potomac. In the wake of Antietam, Lincoln removed McClellan from command.

In Kentucky Generals Smith and Bragg secured Lexington and Frankfort, but their effort to force the Yankees back to the Ohio River was stopped at the Battle of Perryville on October 8. Bragg's army retreated back into Tennessee where, on December 31, 1862, to January 2, 1863, they fought an indecisive but much bloodier battle at Murfreesboro. Casualties exceeded even those of Shiloh and many lives were sacrificed on a bitter winter landscape.

Confederate leaders had marshaled all their strength for a breakthrough but had failed. Outnumbered and disadvantaged in resources, the South could not continue the offensive. Profoundly disappointed, Davis admitted to a committee of Confederate representatives that southerners were entering "the darkest and most dangerous period we have yet had." Tenacious defense and stoic endurance now seemed the South's only long-range hope.

But 1862 also brought painful lessons to the North. Confederate general J. E. B. Stuart executed a daring cavalry raid into Pennsylvania in October. Then on December 13 Union general Ambrose Burnside, now in command of the Army of the Potomac, unwisely ordered his soldiers to attack Lee's army, which held fortified positions on high ground at Fredericksburg, Virginia. Lee's men performed so coolly and controlled the engagement so thoroughly that Lee was moved to say, "It is well that war is so terrible. We should grow too fond of it." Burnside's repeated assaults up Marye's Heights shocked even the opponents. "The Federals had fallen like the steady dripping of rain from the eaves of a house," remarked Confederate general James Longstreet. And a Union officer observed the carnage of 1,300 dead and 9,600

395

In October 1862 in New York City, photographer Mathew Brady opened an exhibition of photographs from the Battle of Antietam. Although few knew it, Brady's vision was very poor, and this photograph of Confederate dead was actually made by his assistants, Alexander Gardner and James F. Gibson.   (Library of Congress)

wounded Union soldiers: "The whole plain was covered with men, prostrate and dropping. . . . I had never before seen fighting like that—nothing approaching it in terrible uproar and destruction . . . the next brigade coming up in succession would do its duty, and melt like snow coming down on warm ground."

The rebellion was far from being suppressed. Both sides were learning that they would have to pay a terrible price. And people on both home fronts had now to decide just what they would endure to win a war of one society against the other.

War Transforms the South

 The war caused tremendous disruptions in civilian life and altered southern society beyond all expectations. One of the first traditions to fall was the southern preference for local and limited government. States' rights had been a formative ideology for the Confederacy, but state governments were weak and sketchy operations. The average citizen, on whom the hand of gov-

ernment had rested lightly, probably knew county authorities best. To withstand the massive power of the North, however, the South needed to centralize; like the colonial revolutionaries, southerners faced a choice of join together or die separately. No one saw the necessity of centralization more clearly than Jefferson Davis. If the states of the Confederacy insisted on fighting separately, said Davis, "we had better make terms as soon as we can."

Promptly Davis moved to bring all arms, supplies, and troops under his control. But by early 1862 the

The Confederacy and Centralization of Power

scope and duration of the conflict required something more. Tens of thousands of Confederate soldiers had volunteered for just one year's service, planning to return home in the spring to plant their crops. To keep southern armies in the field, the War Department encouraged reenlistments and called for new volunteers. However, as one official admitted, "the spirit of volunteering had died out." Three states threatened or instituted a draft. Finally, faced with a critical shortage of troops, in April

396 Chapter 15 Transforming Fire: The Civil War, 1861–1865

This Confederate soldier, like thousands of his comrades, took advantage of an opportunity to pose with his wife and brother. As the death toll mounted and suffering increased, southern women grew less willing to urge their men into battle. (Collection of Larry Williford)

1862 the Confederate government enacted the first national conscription (draft) law in American history. Thus the war forced unprecedented change on states that had seceded out of fear of change.

Jefferson Davis was a strong chief executive. He adopted a firm leadership role toward the Confederate Congress, which raised taxes and later passed a tax-in-kind—paid in farm products. Almost three thousand agents dispersed to collect the tax, assisted by almost fifteen hundred appraisers. Where opposition arose, the government suspended the writ of habeas corpus (which prevented individuals from being held without trial) and imposed martial law. In the face of political opposition that cherished states' rights, Davis proved unyielding. This tax system, however, proved inadequate to the South's war effort.

To replace the food that men in uniform would have grown, Davis exhorted farmers to switch from cash crops to food crops; he encouraged the states to require them to do so. But the army remained short of food and labor. In emergencies the War Department resorted to impressing slaves to work on fortifications, and after 1861 the government relied heavily on con-

fiscation of food to feed the troops. Officers swooped down on farms in the line of march and carted away grain, meat, wagons, and draft animals.

Soon the Confederate administration in Richmond gained virtually complete control over the southern economy. Because it controlled the supply of labor through conscription, the administration could compel industry to work on government contracts and supply the military's needs. The Confederate Congress also gave the central government almost complete control of the railroads. New statutes even limited corporate profits and dividends. A large bureaucracy sprang up to administer these operations: over seventy thousand civilians staffed the Confederate administration. By the war's end, the southern bureaucracy was larger in proportion to population than its northern counterpart. Early in the war, Davis hoped that such centralization would inspire a new national loyalty across the South.

Clerks and subordinate officials crowded the towns and cities where Confederate departments set up their offices. The sudden population booms that resulted overwhelmed the housing supply and stimulated new construction. The pressure was especially great in Richmond, whose population increased 250 percent. Mobile's population jumped from 29,000 to 41,000; Atlanta began to grow; and 10,000 people poured into war-related industries in little Selma, Alabama.

Wartime Southern Cities and Industry

As the Union blockade disrupted imports of manufactured products, the traditionally agricultural South forged industries. Many planters shared Davis's hope that industrialization would bring "deliverance, full and unrestricted, from all commercial dependence" on the North or the world. Indeed, beginning almost from scratch, the Confederacy achieved tremendous feats of industrial development. Chief of Ordnance Josiah Gorgas increased the capacity of Richmond's Tredegar Iron Works and other factories to the point that by 1865 his Ordnance Bureau was supplying all Confederate small arms and ammunition. Meanwhile, the government constructed new railroad lines to improve the efficiency of the South's transportation system. Much of the labor on railroads and ironworks consisted of slaves relocated from farms and plantations.

White women, restricted to narrow roles in antebellum society, gained substantial new responsibilities in wartime. The wives and mothers of soldiers now headed households and performed men's work, including raising crops and tending animals. Women in non-

Changing Roles of Women

slaveowning families cultivated fields themselves, while wealthier women suddenly had to manage field hands unaccustomed to female overseers. In the cities, white women—who had been virtually excluded from the labor force—found a limited number of respectable new paying jobs. Clerks had always been males, but the war changed that, too. "Government girls" staffed the Confederate bureaucracy, and female schoolteachers appeared in the South for the first time.

Some women gained confidence from their new responsibilities. Among these was Janie Smith, a young North Carolinian. Raised in a rural area by prosperous parents, she now faced grim realities as the war reached her farm and troops turned her home into a hospital. "It makes me shudder when I think of the awful sights I witnessed that morning," she wrote to a friend. "Ambulance after ambulance drove up with our wounded. . . . Under every shed and tree, the tables were carried for amputating the limbs. . . . The blood lay in puddles in the grove; the groans of the dying and complaints of those undergoing amputation were horrible." But Janie Smith learned to cope with crisis. She ended her account with the proud words, "I can dress amputated limbs now and do most anything in the way of nursing wounded soldiers."

Patriotic sacrifice appealed to some women, but others resented their new burdens. Many among the wealthy found their war-imposed tasks difficult and their changed situation distasteful. A Texas woman who had struggled to discipline slaves pronounced herself "sick of trying to do a man's business." Others grew angry over shortages and resented cooking and unfamiliar contact with lower-class women. Some women grew scornful of the war and demanded that their men return to help provide for families.

For millions of ordinary southerners change brought privation and suffering. Mass poverty descended for the first time on a large minority of the white population.

Human Suffering, Hoarding, and Inflation

Many yeoman families had lost their breadwinners to the army. As a South Carolina newspaper put it, "The duties of war have called away from home the sole supports of many, many families. . . . Help must be given, or the poor will suffer." The poor sought help from relatives, neighbors, friends, anyone. Sometimes they pleaded their cases to the Confederate government. "In the name of humanity," begged one woman, "discharge my husband he is not able to do your government much good and he might do his children some good . . . my poor children have no home nor no Father." To the extent that the South eventually lost the will to fight in the face of defeat, women played a key role in bringing the war to an end.

Other factors aggravated the effect of the labor shortage. The South was in many places so sparsely populated that the conscription of one skilled craftsman could work a hardship on the people of an entire county. Often they begged in unison for the exemption or discharge of the local miller or the neighborhood tanner, wheelwright, or potter. Physicians also were in short supply. Most serious, however, was the loss of a blacksmith. As a petition from Alabama explained, "Our Section of County [is] left entirely Destitute of any man that is able to keep in order any kind of Farming Tules."

The blockade of Confederate shipping created shortages of common but important items—salt, sugar, coffee, nails—and speculation and hoarding made the shortages worse. Greedy businessmen cornered the supply of some commodities; prosperous citizens stocked up on food. The *Richmond Enquirer* criticized a planter who purchased so many wagonloads of supplies that his "lawn and paths looked like a wharf covered with a ship's loads." "This disposition to speculate upon the yeomanry of the country," lamented the *Richmond Examiner*, "is the most mortifying feature of the war." North Carolina's Governor Zebulon Vance worried about "the cry of distress . . . from the poor wives and children of our soldiers. . . . What will become of them?"

Inflation raged out of control, fueled by the Confederate government's heavy borrowing and inadequate taxes, until prices had increased almost 7,000 percent. Inflation particularly imperiled urban dwellers without their own sources of food. As early as 1861 and 1862, newspapers reported that "want and starvation are staring thousands in the face," and troubled officials predicted that "women and children are bound to come to suffering if not starvation." Some families came to the aid of their neighbors, and "free markets," which disbursed goods as charity, sprang up in various cities. But other people would not cooperate: "It is folly for a poor mother to call on the rich people about here," raged one woman. "Their hearts are of steel they would sooner throw what they have to spare to the dogs than give it to a starving child." Private charity, as well as a rudimentary relief program organized by the Confederacy, failed to meet the need.

398   Chapter 15   Transforming Fire: The Civil War, 1861–1865

As their fortunes declined, people of once-modest means looked around and found abundant evidence that all classes were not sacrificing equally. And they noted that the Confederate government enacted policies that favored the upper class.

Inequities of the Confederate Draft

Until the last year of the war, for example, prosperous southerners could avoid military service by hiring substitutes. Prices for substitutes skyrocketed until it cost a man $5,000 or $6,000 to send someone to the front in his place. Well over 50,000 upper-class southerners purchased such substitutes. Mary Boykin Chesnut knew of one young aristocrat who "spent a fortune in substitutes. . . . He is at the end of his row now, for all able-bodied men are ordered to the front. I hear he is going as some general's courier." The rich traded on their social connections to avoid danger. "It is a notorious fact," complained an angry Georgian, that "if a man has influential friends—or a little money to spare—he will never be enrolled." A Confederate senator from Mississippi, James Phelan, informed Jefferson Davis that apparently "nine tenths of the youngsters of the land whose relatives are conspicuous in society, wealthy, or influential obtain some safe perch where they can doze with their heads under their wings."

Anger at such discrimination exploded in October 1862 when the Confederate Congress exempted from military duty anyone who was supervising at least twenty slaves. "Never did a law meet with more universal odium," observed one representative. "Its influence upon the poor is most calamitous." Protests poured in from every corner of the Confederacy, and North Carolina's legislators formally condemned the law. Its defenders argued, however, that the exemption preserved order and aided food production, and the statute remained on the books. The twenty-slave law is indicative of the racial fears many Confederates felt as the war threatened to overturn southern society.

Dissension spread and alert politicians and newspaper editors warned of class warfare. The bitterness of letters to Confederate officials suggests the depth of the people's anger. "If I and my little children suffer [and] die while there Father is in service," threatened one woman, "I invoke God Almighty that our blood rest upon the South." Another woman swore to the secretary of war that unless help was provided to poverty-stricken wives and mothers "an allwise god . . . will send down his fury and judgment in a very grate manar . . . [on] those that are in power." War magnified existing social tensions in the Confederacy, and created a few new ones.

Wartime Northern Economy and Society

 With the onset of war, a tidal wave of change rolled over the North as well. Factories and citizens' associations geared up to support the war, and the federal government and its executive branch gained new powers. The energies of an industrializing, capitalist society were harnessed to serve the cause of the Union. Idealism and greed flourished together, and the northern economy proved its awesome productivity. Northern factories ran overtime, and unemployment was low. Northern farms and factories came through the war unharmed, whereas most of the South suffered extensive damage. To Union soldiers on the battlefield, sacrifice was a grim reality, but northern civilians experienced the bustle and energy of wartime production.

At first the war was a shock to business. Northern firms lost their southern markets, and many companies had to change their products and find new customers in order to remain open. Southern debts became uncollectible, jeopardizing not only northern merchants but also many western banks. In farming regions, families struggled with an aggravated shortage of labor. A few enterprises never pulled out of the tailspin caused by the war. Cotton mills lacked cotton; construction declined; shoe manufacturers sold few of the cheap shoes that planters had bought for their slaves.

Northern Business, Industry, and Agriculture

But certain entrepreneurs, such as wool producers, benefited from shortages of competing products, and soaring demand for war-related goods swept some businesses to new success. To feed the hungry war machine, the federal government pumped unprecedented sums into the economy. The Treasury issued $3.2 billion in bonds and paper money called greenbacks, and the War Department spent over $360 million in revenues from new taxes, including a broad excise tax and the nation's first income tax. Government contracts soon totaled more than $1 billion.

Secretary of War Edwin M. Stanton's list of the supplies needed by the Ordnance Department indicates the scope of government demand: "7,892 cannon, 11,787 artillery carriages, 4,022,130 small-arms, . . . 1,022,176,474 cartridges for small-arms, 1,220,555,435 percussion caps, . . . 26,440,054 pounds of gunpowder, 6,395,152 pounds of niter, and 90,416,295 pounds of lead." Stanton's list covered only

Check Your Understanding

The following sentences appear in the chapter. Circle the letter of the BEST meaning for each italicized word.

8. "On April 18, only three days after the surrender of Fort Sumter, a *mustering* of Company C turned into a large public rally…."
   a. Parade
   b. Transformation
   c. Disappearance
   d. Gathering

9. "He was often miserably lonely and homesick, and he described battlefield *carnage* with an honest realism."
   a. Action
   b. Slaughter
   c. Terrain
   d. Noise

10. "[The Civil War] *obliterated* the normal patterns and circumstances of life."
   a. Contributed to
   b. Wiped out
   c. Interrupted
   d. Produced

11. "Because most of the fighting took place on southern soil, northern farms and factories remained virtually *unscathed*."
   a. Unharmed
   b. Not productive
   c. Uncultivated
   d. Nonfunctional

12. *Guerilla* warfare broke out in 1861 in the politically divided state of Missouri…."
   a. Traditional
   b. Involving soldiers with guns and ammunition
   c. Related to a small, irregular military unit
   d. Brutal

13. "States' rights had been a formative *ideology* for the Confederacy, but state governments were weak and sketchy operations."
   a. Set of beliefs
   b. Motto
   c. Goal
   d. Religion

14. For millions of ordinary southerners change brought *privation* and suffering."
   a. Prosperity
   b. Loneliness
   c. Great wealth
   d. Lack of basic necessities

Circle the letter of the correct response.

15. Based upon Map 15.1 in the preceding section of the history chapter, which of the following conclusions is accurate?
   a. The Battle of Bull Run had no clear victor.
   b. The Battle of Seven Days was the first battle of the Civil War.
   c. The Battle of Seven Pines occurred after the siege of Yorktown.
   d. Confederate forces moved south to encounter the Union forces at the Battle of Bull Run.

16.–20. On your own paper, write five review questions that would help you focus on material in this section and that would be likely to appear on a test. Also, write your answer to each of these questions.

Discuss the following question with a partner or group, and then collaborate to write an answer to the question on your own paper.

21. Defend the contention that the revolutionary means chosen by secession leaders were incompatible with their conservative purpose.

398   Chapter 15   Transforming Fire: The Civil War, 1861–1865

As their fortunes declined, people of once-modest means looked around and found abundant evidence that all classes were not sacrificing equally. And they noted that the Confederate government enacted policies that favored the upper class. Until the last year of the war, for example, prosperous southerners could avoid military service by hiring substitutes. Prices for substitutes skyrocketed until it cost a man $5,000 or $6,000 to send someone to the front in his place. Well over 50,000 upper-class southerners purchased such substitutes. Mary Boykin Chesnut knew of one young aristocrat who "spent a fortune in substitutes. . . . He is at the end of his row now, for all able-bodied men are ordered to the front. I hear he is going as some general's courier." The rich traded on their social connections to avoid danger. "It is a notorious fact," complained an angry Georgian, that "if a man has influential friends—or a little money to spare—he will never be enrolled." A Confederate senator from Mississippi, James Phelan, informed Jefferson Davis that apparently "nine tenths of the youngsters of the land whose relatives are conspicuous in society, wealthy, or influential obtain some safe perch where they can doze with their heads under their wings."

Inequities of the Confederate Draft

Anger at such discrimination exploded in October 1862 when the Confederate Congress exempted from military duty anyone who was supervising at least twenty slaves. "Never did a law meet with more universal odium," observed one representative. "Its influence upon the poor is most calamitous." Protests poured in from every corner of the Confederacy, and North Carolina's legislators formally condemned the law. Its defenders argued, however, that the exemption preserved order and aided food production, and the statute remained on the books. The twenty-slave law is indicative of the racial fears many Confederates felt as the war threatened to overturn southern society.

Dissension spread and alert politicians and newspaper editors warned of class warfare. The bitterness of letters to Confederate officials suggests the depth of the people's anger. "If I and my little children suffer [and] die while there Father is in service," threatened one woman, "I invoke God Almighty that our blood rest upon the South." Another woman swore to the secretary of war that unless help was provided to poverty-stricken wives and mothers "an allwise god . . . will send down his fury and judgment in a very grate manar . . . [on] those that are in power." War magnified existing social tensions in the Confederacy, and created a few new ones.

Wartime Northern Economy and Society

 With the onset of war, a tidal wave of change rolled over the North as well. Factories and citizens' associations geared up to support the war, and the federal government and its executive branch gained new powers. The energies of an industrializing, capitalist society were harnessed to serve the cause of the Union. Idealism and greed flourished together, and the northern economy proved its awesome productivity. Northern factories ran overtime, and unemployment was low. Northern farms and factories came through the war unharmed, whereas most of the South suffered extensive damage. To Union soldiers on the battlefield, sacrifice was a grim reality, but northern civilians experienced the bustle and energy of wartime production.

At first the war was a shock to business. Northern firms lost their southern markets, and many companies had to change their products and find new customers in order to remain open. Southern debts became uncollectible, jeopardizing not only northern merchants but also many western banks. In farming regions, families struggled with an aggravated shortage of labor. A few enterprises never pulled out of the tailspin caused by the war. Cotton mills lacked cotton; construction declined; shoe manufacturers sold few of the cheap shoes that planters had bought for their slaves.

Northern Business, Industry, and Agriculture

But certain entrepreneurs, such as wool producers, benefited from shortages of competing products, and soaring demand for war-related goods swept some businesses to new success. To feed the hungry war machine, the federal government pumped unprecedented sums into the economy. The Treasury issued $3.2 billion in bonds and paper money called greenbacks, and the War Department spent over $360 million in revenues from new taxes, including a broad excise tax and the nation's first income tax. Government contracts soon totaled more than $1 billion.

Secretary of War Edwin M. Stanton's list of the supplies needed by the Ordnance Department indicates the scope of government demand: "7,892 cannon, 11,787 artillery carriages, 4,022,130 small-arms, . . . 1,022,176,474 cartridges for small-arms, 1,220,555,435 percussion caps, . . . 26,440,054 pounds of gunpowder, 6,395,152 pounds of niter, and 90,416,295 pounds of lead." Stanton's list covered only weapons; the government also purchased huge quantities of uniforms, boots, food, camp equipment, saddles, ships, and other necessities. War-related spending revived business in many northern states. In 1863 a merchants' magazine examined the effects of the war in Massachusetts: "Seldom, if ever, has the business of Massachusetts been more active or profitable than during the past year. . . . In every department of labor the government has been, directly or indirectly, the chief employer and paymaster." Government contracts saved Massachusetts shoe manufacturers from ruin.

Nothing illustrated the wartime partnership between business and government better than the work of Jay Cooke, a wealthy New York financier. Cooke threw himself into the marketing of government bonds to finance the war effort. With imagination and energy, he convinced both large investors and ordinary citizens to invest enormous sums, in the process earning hefty commissions for himself. But the financier's profit served the Union cause, as the interests of capitalism and government, finance and patriotism, merged. The booming economy, the Republican alliance with business, and the frantic wartime activity combined to create a new pro-business atmosphere in Washington.

War aided some heavy industries in the North, especially iron and steel production. Although new railroad construction slowed, repairs helped the manufacture of rails to increase. Of considerable significance for the future was the railroad industry's adoption of a standard gauge (width) for track, which eliminated the unloading and reloading of boxcars and created a unified transportation system.

The northern economy also grew because of a complementary relationship between agriculture and industry. Mechanization of agriculture had begun before the war. Wartime recruitment and conscription, however, gave western farmers an added incentive to purchase labor-saving machinery. The shift from human labor to machines created new markets for industry and expanded the food supply for the urban industrial work force. The boom in the sale of agricultural tools was tremendous. Cyrus and William McCormick built an industrial empire in Chicago from the sale of their reapers. Between 1862 and 1864 the manufacture of mowers and reapers doubled to 70,000 yearly; even so, manufacturers could not satisfy the demand. By the end of the war, 375,000 reapers were in use, triple the number in 1861. Large-scale commercial agriculture had become a reality. As a result, northern farm families whose breadwinners went to

Despite initial problems, the task of supplying a vast war machine kept the northern economy humming. This photograph shows businesses on the west side of Hudson Street in New York City in 1865.   (© Collection of The New-York Historical Society)

400   Chapter 15   Transforming Fire: The Civil War, 1861–1865

war did not suffer as much as their counterparts did in the South. "We have seen," one magazine observed, "a stout matron whose sons are in the army, cutting hay with her team . . . and she cut seven acres with ease in a day, riding leisurely upon her cutter."

Northern industrial and urban workers did not fare as well. After the initial slump, jobs became plentiful, but inflation ate up much of a worker's paycheck. The price of coffee had tripled; rice and sugar had doubled; and clothing, fuel, and rent had all climbed. Between 1860 and 1864 consumer prices rose at least 76 percent, while daily wages rose only 42 percent. Workers' families consequently suffered a substantial decline in their standards of living.

New Militancy Among Northern Workers

As their real wages shrank, industrial workers lost job security. To increase production, some employers were replacing workers with labor-saving machines. Other employers urged the government to promote immigration to secure cheap labor. Workers responded by forming unions and sometimes by striking. Skilled craftsmen organized to combat the loss of their jobs and status to machines; women and unskilled workers, who were excluded by the craftsmen, formed their own unions. In recognition of the increasingly national scope of business activity, thirteen occupational groups—including tailors, coal miners, and railway engineers—formed national unions during the Civil War, and the number of strikes climbed steadily.

Employers reacted with hostility to this new labor independence. Manufacturers viewed labor activism as a threat to their freedom of action and accordingly formed statewide or craft-based associations to cooperate and pool information. These employers shared blacklists of union members and required new workers to sign "yellow dog" contracts (promises not to join a union). To put down strikes, they hired strikebreakers from among blacks, immigrants, and women, and sometimes used federal troops to break the will of unions.

Despite the unions' emerging presence, they did not prevent employers from making profits, nor from profiteering on government contracts. Unscrupulous businessmen took advantage of the suddenly immense demand for army supplies by selling clothing and blankets made of "shoddy"—wool fibers reclaimed from rags or worn cloth. Shoddy goods often came apart in the rain; most of the shoes purchased in the early months of the war were worthless. Contractors sold inferior guns for double the usual price and passed off tainted meat as good. Corruption was so widespread that it led to a year-long investigation by the House of Representatives. A group of contractors who had demanded $50 million for their products dropped their claims to $17 million as a result of the findings of the investigation. Those who romanticize the Civil War era rarely learn of these historical realities.

Legitimate enterprises also made healthy profits. The output of woolen mills increased so dramatically that dividends in the industry nearly tripled. Some cotton mills made record profits on what they sold, even though they reduced their output. Brokerage houses worked until midnight and earned unheard-of commissions. Railroads carried immense quantities of freight and passengers, increasing their business to the point that railroad stocks doubled and tripled in value. The price of Erie Railroad stock rose from $17 to $126 a share during the war.

Government and Business Partnership

Railroads also were a leading beneficiary of government largesse. With the South absent from Congress, the northern, rather than southern, route of the transcontinental railroad quickly prevailed. In 1862 and 1864 Congress chartered two corporations, the Union Pacific Railroad and the Central Pacific Railroad, and assisted them financially in connecting Omaha, Nebraska, with Sacramento, California. For each mile of track laid, the railroads received a loan of from $16,000 to $48,000 in government bonds plus 20 square miles of land along a free 400-foot-wide right of way. Overall, the two corporations gained approximately 20 million acres of land and nearly $60 million in loans.

Other businessmen benefited handsomely from the Morrill Land Grant Act (1862). To promote public education in agriculture, engineering, and military science, Congress granted each state 30,000 acres of federal land for each of its congressional districts. The states could sell the land, as long as they used the income for the purposes Congress had intended. The law eventually fostered sixty-nine colleges and universities, but one of its immediate effects was to enrich a few prominent speculators. Hard-pressed to meet wartime expenses, some states sold their land cheaply to wealthy entrepreneurs. At the same time, the Homestead Act of 1862 offered cheap, and sometimes free, land to people who would settle the West and improve their property.

Economic Nationalism

Before the war, there was no national banking, taxation, or currency. Banks operating under state charters issued no fewer than seven thousand different kinds of notes, which were difficult to distinguish from forgeries. During the war, Congress and the Treasury Department established a national banking system empowered to issue national bank notes. At the close of the war in 1865, Congress forced most state banks to join the national system by means of a prohibitive tax. This process created sounder currency, but also inflexibility in the money supply and an eastern-oriented financial structure that, later in the century, pushed farmers in need of credit and cash to revolt.

In response to the war, the Republicans created an activist federal government. They converted the sale of war bonds into a crusade, affirming that the country could absorb any level of debt or expense for the cause of union. Indeed, with agricultural legislation, the land grant colleges, higher tariffs, and railroad subsidies, the federal government entered the economy forever. Moreover, Republican economic policies bonded people to the nation as never before. As freeing the slaves became a fundamental war aim, this economic nationalism would loom important as a buttress for a controversial cause.

The powers of the federal government and the president grew steadily during the crisis. Abraham Lincoln, like Jefferson Davis, found

**Expansion of
Presidential
Power**

that war required active presidential leadership. At the beginning of the conflict, Lincoln launched a major shipbuilding program without waiting for Congress to assemble. The lawmakers later approved his decision, and Lincoln continued to act in advance of Congress when he deemed such action necessary. In one striking exercise of executive power, Lincoln suspended the writ of habeas corpus for everyone living between Washington, D.C., and Philadelphia. There was scant legal justification for this act, but the president's motive was practical: to ensure the loyalty of Maryland, which surrounded the capital on three sides. Later in the war, with congressional approval, Lincoln repeatedly suspended habeas corpus and invoked martial law, mainly in the border states but elsewhere as well. Between fifteen and twenty thousand U.S. citizens were arrested on suspicion of disloyal acts. These measures have led some to claim that Lincoln achieved "dictatorial" powers as a wartime president.

On occasion Lincoln used his wartime authority to bolster his own political fortunes. He and his gener-

als proved adept at furloughing soldiers so they could vote in close elections; those whom Lincoln furloughed, of course, usually voted Republican. He also came to the aid of other officeholders in his party. When the Republican governor of Indiana, who was battling Democrats in his legislature who sought a negotiated end to the war, ran short of funds, Lincoln had the War Department supply $250,000. This procedure lacked constitutional sanction, but it advanced the Union cause.

In thousands of self-governing towns and communities, northern citizens felt a personal connection to

**The Union
Cause**

representative government. Secession threatened to destroy their system, and northerners rallied to its defense. Secular and church leaders supported the cause, and even ministers who preferred to separate politics and pulpit denounced "the iniquity of causeless rebellion." In the first two years of the war, northern morale remained remarkably high for a cause that today may seem abstract—the Union—but at the time meant the preservation of a social and political order that people cherished.

But social attitudes on the northern home front evolved in directions that would have shocked the soldiers in the field. In the excitement of moneymaking, an eagerness to display one's wealth flourished in the largest cities. *Harper's Monthly* reported that "the suddenly enriched contractors, speculators, and stock-jobbers . . . are spending money with a profusion never before witnessed in our country, at no time remarkable for its frugality. . . . The men button their waistcoats with diamonds . . . and the women powder their hair with gold and silver dust." The *New York Herald* summarized that city's atmosphere: "Not to keep a carriage, not to wear diamonds, . . . is now equivalent to being a nobody. This war has entirely changed the American character. . . . The individual who makes the most money—no matter how—and spends the most—no matter for what—is considered the greatest man."

Yet idealism coexisted with ostentation. Many churches endorsed the Union cause as God's cause. One Methodist newspaper described the war as a contest between "equalizing, humanizing Christianity" and "disunion, war, selfishness, [and] slavery." Abolitionists campaigned to turn the war into a crusade against slavery. Free black communities and churches both black and white responded to the needs of slaves who flocked to the Union lines, sending clothing, ministers, and teachers to aid the freedpeople. Indeed,

402   Chapter 15   Transforming Fire: The Civil War, 1861–1865

northern blacks gave wholehearted support to the war, volunteering by the thousands at first and drilling their own militia units in spite of the initial rejection they received from the Lincoln administration.

Northern women, like their southern counterparts, took on new roles. Those who stayed home or-

Northern Women

ganized over ten thousand soldiers' aid societies, rolled bandages, and raised $3 million to aid injured troops. Women were instrumental in pressing for the first trained ambulance corps in the Union armies, and they formed the backbone of the U.S. Sanitary Commission, a civilian agency officially recognized by the War Department in 1861. The Sanitary Commission provided crucial nutritional and medical aid to soldiers. Although most of its officers were men, the bulk of its volunteers who ran its seven thousand auxiliaries were women. Women organized elaborate "Sanitary Fairs" all across the North to raise money and awareness for soldiers' health and hygiene.

Approximately 3,200 women also served as nurses in frontline hospitals, where they pressed for better care of the wounded. Yet women were only about one-quarter of all nurses, and they had to fight for a chance to serve at all. The professionalization of medicine

Walt Whitman, now America's most celebrated wartime poet. His *Drum Taps* series, part of his evolving masterpiece *Leaves of Grass*, left some of the most haunting and moving poetic images of both the death and new life wrought by the war.   (National Portrait Gallery, Smithsonian Institution, Washington, D.C.)

since the Revolution had created a medical system dominated by men, and many male physicians did not want women's aid. Even Clara Barton, famous for her persistence in working in the worst hospitals at the front, was ousted from her post in 1863. But with Barton, women such as the stern Dorothea Dix (see page 277), well-known for her efforts to reform asylums for the insane, and an Illinois widow, Mary Ann Bickerdyke, who served tirelessly in Sherman's army in the West, established a heroic tradition for Civil War nurses. They also advanced the professionalization of nursing as several schools of nursing were established in northern cities during or after the war.

The poet Walt Whitman left a record of his experiences as a volunteer nurse in Washington, D.C. As

Walt Whitman's War

he dressed wounds and tried to comfort suffering and lonely men, Whitman found "the marrow of the tragedy concentrated in those Army Hospitals." But despite "indescribably horrid wounds," he also found inspiration in such suffering and a deepening faith in American democracy. Whitman celebrated the "incredible dauntlessness" and sacrifice of the common soldier who fought for the Union. As he had written in the preface to his great work *Leaves of Grass* (1855), "The genius of the United States is not best or most in its executives or legislatures, but always most in the common people." Whitman worked this idealization of the common man into his poetry, which also explored homoerotic themes and rejected the lofty meter and rhyme of European verse to strive for a "genuineness" that would appeal to the masses.

In "The Wound Dresser," Whitman meditated unforgettably on the deaths he witnessed on both sides:

On, on I go, (open doors of time! open hospital doors!)
The crush'd head I dress, (poor crazed hand tear not
    the bandage away,)
The neck of the cavalry-man with the bullet through
    and through I examine,
Hard the breathing rattles, quite glazed already the eye,
    yet life struggled hard,
(Come sweet death! be persuaded O beautiful death!
    In mercy come quickly.)

Whitman mused for millions in the war who suffered the death of a husband, brother, father, or friend. Indeed, the scale of death in this war shocked many Americans into believing that this conflict had to be for purposes larger than themselves.

Thus northern society embraced strangely contradictory tendencies. Materialism and greed flourished alongside idealism, religious conviction, and self-sacrifice. While some soldiers risked their lives willingly out of a desire to preserve the Union or extend freedom, many others openly sought to avoid service. Under the law, a draftee could stay at home by providing a substitute or paying a $300 commutation fee. Many wealthy men chose these options, and in response to popular demand, clubs, cities, and states provided the money for others to escape conscription. In all, 118,000 substitutes were provided and 87,000 commutations paid before Congress ended the commutation system in 1864. Naturally, in decades to come Americans would commemorate and build monuments to soldiers' sacrifice and idealism, not to opportunism.

The Advent of Emancipation

 Despite the sense of loyalty to cause that animated soldiers and civilians on both sides, the governments of the United States and the Confederacy lacked clarity about the purpose of the war. Throughout the first several months of the struggle, both Davis and Lincoln studiously avoided references to slavery. Davis realized that emphasis on the issue could increase class conflict in the South. To avoid identifying the Confederacy only with the interests of slaveholders, he articulated a broader, traditional ideology. Davis told southerners that they were fighting for constitutional liberty: northerners had betrayed the founders' legacy, and southerners had seceded to preserve it. As long as Lincoln also avoided making slavery an issue, Davis's line seemed to work.

Lincoln had his own reasons for not mentioning slavery. It was crucial at first not to antagonize the Union's border slave states, whose loyalty was tenuous. Also for many months Lincoln hoped that a pro-Union majority would assert itself in the South. It might be possible, he thought, to coax the South back into the Union and stop the fighting, short of what he later called "the result so fundamental and astounding"—emancipation. Raising the slavery issue would severely undermine both goals. Powerful political considerations also dictated Lincoln's reticence. The Republican Party was a young and unwieldy coalition. Some Republicans burned with moral outrage over slavery; others were frankly racist, dedicated to protecting free whites from the Slave Power and the competition of cheap slave labor. A forthright stand by Lincoln on the subject of slavery could split the party, gratifying some groups and alienating others. No

northern consensus on what to do about slavery existed early in the war.

The president's hesitancy ran counter to some of his personal feelings. Lincoln was a compassionate man whose humility and moral anguish during the war were evident in his speeches and writings. But as a politician, Lincoln distinguished between his own moral convictions and his official acts. His political positions were studied and complex, calculated for maximum advantage.

Lincoln, the Gradual Emancipator

Many blacks furiously attacked Lincoln during the first year of the war for his refusal to convert the struggle into an "abolition war." When Lincoln countermanded General John C. Frémont's order of liberation for slaves owned by disloyal masters in Missouri in September 1861, the *Anglo-African* declared that the president, by his actions, "hurls back into the hell of slavery thousands . . . rightfully set free." As late as July 1862, Frederick Douglass condemned Lincoln as a "miserable tool of traitors and rebels," and characterized administration policy as reconstruction of "the old union on the old and corrupting basis of compromise, by which slavery shall retain all the power that it ever had." Douglass wanted the old union destroyed and a new one created in the crucible of a war that would destroy slavery and rewrite the Constitution in the name of human equality. To his own amazement, within a year, just such a profound result began to take place.

Lincoln first broached the subject of slavery in a substantive way in March 1862, when he proposed that the states consider emancipation on their own. He asked Congress to promise aid to any state that decided to emancipate, appealing especially to border state representatives. What Lincoln proposed was gradual emancipation, with compensation for slaveholders and colonization of the freed slaves outside the United States. To a delegation of free blacks he explained that "it is better for us both . . . to be separated."

Until well into 1864 Lincoln's administration promoted a wholly impractical scheme to colonize blacks in Central America or the Caribbean. Lincoln saw colonization as one option among others in dealing with the impending freedom of America's 4.2 million slaves. As yet, he was unconvinced that America had any prospect as a truly biracial society, and he desperately feared that white northerners might not support a war for black freedom. Led by Frederick Douglass, black abolitionists vehemently opposed these machinations by the Lincoln administration.

404   Chapter 15   Transforming Fire: The Civil War, 1861–1865

Other politicians had much greater plans for a struggle against slavery. A group of Republicans in Congress, known as the Radicals and led by men such as George Julian, Charles Sumner, and Thaddeus Stevens, dedicated themselves to a war for emancipation. They were instrumental in creating a special House-Senate committee on the conduct of the war, which investigated Union reverses, sought to make the war effort more efficient, and prodded the president to take stronger measures. Early in the war these Radicals, with widening support, turned their attention to slavery.

In August 1861, at the Radicals' instigation, Congress passed its first confiscation act. Designed to punish the Confederates, the law confiscated all property used for "insurrectionary purposes." Thus if the South used slaves in a hostile action, those slaves were declared seized and liberated as contraband of war. A second confiscation act (July 1862) went much further: it confiscated the property of anyone who supported the rebellion, even those who merely resided in the South and paid Confederate taxes. Their slaves were declared "forever free of their servitude." The logic behind these acts was that the insurrection—as Lincoln termed it— required strong measures to stop it. Let the government use its full powers, free the slaves, and crush the insurrection, urged the Radicals.

Confiscation Acts

Lincoln refused to adopt that view in the summer of 1862. He stood by his proposal of voluntary gradual emancipation by the states and made no effort to enforce the second confiscation act. His stance provoked a public protest from Horace Greeley, editor of the powerful *New York Tribune*. In an open letter to the president entitled "The Prayer of Twenty Millions," Greeley pleaded with Lincoln to "execute the laws" and declared, "On the face of this wide earth, Mr. President, there is not one disinterested, determined, intelligent champion of the Union cause who does not feel that all attempts to put down the Rebellion and at the same time uphold its inciting cause are preposterous and futile." Lincoln's reply was an explicit statement of his calculated approach to the question. He disagreed, he said, with all those who would make the maintenance or destruction of slavery the paramount issue of the war. "I would save the Union," announced Lincoln. "If I could save the Union without freeing any slave I would do it, and if I could save it by freeing all the slaves I would do it; and if I could save it by freeing some and leaving others alone I would also do that.

What I do about slavery, and the colored race, I do because I believe it helps to save the Union." Lincoln closed with a personal disclaimer: "I have here stated my purpose according to my view of official duty; and I intend no modification of my oft-expressed personal wish that all men everywhere could be free."

When he wrote those words, Lincoln had already decided to boldly issue a presidential Emancipation Proclamation. He was waiting, however, for a Union victory so that it would not appear to be an act of desperation. Yet the letter to Greeley was not simply an effort to stall; it was an integral part of Lincoln's approach to the future of slavery, as the text of the Emancipation Proclamation would show. Lincoln was concerned to condition public opinion as best he could for the coming social revolution.

On September 22, 1862, shortly after Union success at the Battle of Antietam, Lincoln issued the first part of his two-part proclamation. Invoking his powers as commander-in-chief of the armed forces, he announced that on January 1, 1863, he would emancipate the slaves in the states "in rebellion against the United States." Lincoln made plain that he would judge a state to be in rebellion in January if it lacked bona fide representatives in the U.S. Congress. Thus his September proclamation was less a declaration of the right of slaves to be free than a threat to southerners: unless they put down their arms and returned to Congress, they would lose their slaves. "Knowing the value that was set on the slaves by the rebels," said Garrison Frazier, a black Georgia minister, "the President thought that his proclamation would stimulate them to lay down their arms . . . and their not doing so has now made the freedom of the slaves a part of the war." Lincoln had little expectation that southerners would give up their effort, but he was careful to offer them the option, thus trying to put the onus of emancipation on them.

Emancipation Proclamations

In the fateful January 1 proclamation, Lincoln excepted (as areas in rebellion) every Confederate county or city that had fallen under Union control. Those areas, he declared, "are, for the present, left precisely as if this proclamation were not issued." Nor did Lincoln liberate slaves in the border slave states that remained in the Union. "The President has purposely made the proclamation inoperative in all places where . . . the slaves [are] accessible," charged the anti-administration *New York World*. "He has proclaimed emancipation only where he has notoriously no power to execute it." Partisanship aside, even Secretary of

State Seward, a moderate Republican, said sarcastically, "We show our sympathy with slavery by emancipating slaves where we cannot reach them and holding them in bondage where we can set them free." A British official, Lord Russell, commented on the "very strange nature" of the document, noting that it did not declare "a principle adverse to slavery." Russell may have missed the point.

Lincoln was worried about the constitutionality of his acts. Making the liberation of the slaves "a fit and necessary war measure" raised a variety of legal questions. How long did a war measure remain in force? Did it expire with the suppression of a rebellion? The proclamation did little to clarify the status or citizenship of the freed slaves, although it did open the possibility of military service for blacks. How indeed would this change the character and purpose of the war?

Thus the Emancipation Proclamation was an ambiguous document that said less than it seemed to say. But if as a legal document it was wanting, as a moral and political document it had great meaning. Because the proclamation defined the war as a war against slav-

ery, radicals could applaud it, even if the president had not gone as far as Congress. Yet at the same time it protected Lincoln's position with conservatives, leaving him room to retreat if he chose and forcing no immediate changes on the border slave states. It was a delicate balancing act, but one from which there was no real turning back.

Most important, though, thousands of slaves had already reached Union lines in various sections of the South. They had "voted with their feet" for emancipation, as many said, well before the proclamation. And now, every advance of federal forces into slave society was a liberating step. This Lincoln knew in taking his own initially tentative, and then forthright, steps toward emancipation.

Across the North and in Union-occupied sections of the South, blacks and their white allies celebrated the Emancipation Proclamation with unprecedented fervor. Full of praise songs, these celebrations demonstrated that whatever the fine print of the proclamation, black folks knew that they had lived to see a new day. At a large "contraband camp" in Washington,

A group of "contrabands" (liberated slaves), photographed at Cumberland Landing, Virginia, May 14, 1862, at a sensitive point in the war when their legal status was still not fully determined. The faces and generations of the women, men, and children represent the human drama of emancipation. (Library of Congress)

406   Chapter 15   Transforming Fire: The Civil War, 1861–1865

D.C., some six hundred black men, women, and children gathered at the superintendent's headquarters on New Year's Eve and sang through the night. In chorus after chorus of "Go Down, Moses," they announced the magnitude of their painful but beautiful exodus. One newly supplied verse concluded with "Go down, Abraham, away down in Dixie's land, tell Jeff Davis to let my people go!"

The need for men soon convinced the administration to recruit northern and southern blacks for the Union Army. By the spring of 1863, African American troops were answering the call of a dozen or more black recruiters barnstorming the cities and towns of the North. Lincoln came to see black soldiers as "the great available and yet unavailed of force for restoring the Union." African American leaders hoped that military service would secure equal rights for their people. Once the black soldier had fought for the Union, wrote Frederick Douglass, "there is no power on earth which can deny that he has earned the right of citizenship in the United States." If black soldiers turned the tide, asked another man, "would the nation refuse us our rights?"

In June 1864 Lincoln gave his support to a constitutional ban on slavery. Reformers such as Elizabeth Cady Stanton and Susan B. Anthony were pressing for an amendment that would write emancipation into the Constitution. On the eve of the Republican national convention, Lincoln called the party's chairman to the White House and instructed him to have the party "put into the platform as the keystone, the amendment of the Constitution abolishing and prohibiting slavery forever." The party promptly called for the Thirteenth Amendment. Republican delegates probably would have adopted such a plank without his urging, but Lincoln demonstrated his commitment by lobbying Congress for quick approval of the measure. The proposed amendment passed in early 1865 and was sent to the states for ratification. The war to save the Union had also become the war to free the slaves.

It has long been debated whether Abraham Lincoln deserved the label (one he never claimed for himself) of "Great Emancipator." Was

Who Freed the Slaves?

Lincoln ultimately a reluctant emancipator, following rather than leading Congress and public opinion? Or did Lincoln give essential presidential leadership to the most transformative and sensitive aspect of the war by going slow on emancipation, but once moving, never backpedaling on the main issue— black freedom. Once he had realized the total character of the war and decided to prosecute it to the

unconditional surrender of the Confederates, Lincoln made the destruction of slavery central to the war's purpose.

Others have argued, however, that the slaves themselves are the central story in the achievement of their own freedom. When they were in proximity to the war zones, or had opportunities as traveling laborers, slaves fled for their freedom by the thousands. Some worked as camp laborers for the Union armies, and eventually more than 180,000 black men served in the Union Army and Navy. Sometimes freedom came as a combination of confusion, fear, and joy in the rural hinterlands of the South. Some found freedom as individuals in 1861, and some not until 1865 as members of trains of refugees. Some slaves remained supportive of their masters' welfare until the war was over. Some freedmen traversed great distances to reach contraband camps.

However freedom came to individuals, emancipation was a historical confluence of two essential forces: one, a policy directed by and dependent on the military authority of the president in his effort to win the war; and two, the will and courage necessary for acts of self-emancipation. In his annual message in December 1862, Lincoln asserted that "in *giving* freedom to the slave, we *assure* freedom to the free." Likewise, most blacks understood the long-term meaning in those words—in the midst of total war they comprehended their freedom as both given and taken.

Before the war was over, the Confederacy, too, addressed the issue of emancipation. Jefferson Davis himself offered a proposal for black freedom of a kind. He was dedicated to independence, but late in the war he was willing to sacrifice slavery to achieve that goal. Davis concluded late in 1864 that the military situation of the Confederacy was so desperate that independence with emancipation was preferable to defeat with emancipation. He proposed that the Confederate government purchase forty thousand slaves to work for the army as laborers, with a promise of freedom at the end of their service. Soon Davis upgraded the idea, calling for the recruitment and arming of slaves as soldiers, who likewise would gain their freedom at war's end. The wives and children of these soldiers, he made plain, must also receive freedom from the states. Davis and his advisers envisioned an "intermediate" status for ex-slaves of "serfage or peonage." Thus at the bitter end, a few southerners were willing to sacrifice some of the racial, if not class, destiny for which they had launched their revolution.

A Confederate Plan of Emancipation

ℋow do historians know...

that ex-slaves fully embraced their new freedom? Jourdon Anderson was a former slave from Tennessee. Residing in Dayton, Ohio, with his family in August 1865, four months after the war ended, Anderson received a letter from his former owner, Colonel P. H. Anderson, asking him to return to the old place. "I have often felt uneasy about you," Anderson told his old master. As for the "good chance . . . you propose," Anderson said to the former slaveholder, "we have concluded to test your sincerity by asking you to send us our wages for the time we served you." With remarkable wit and irony, Anderson described the dignity with which he and his family lived in freedom (his children were in school and his wife was called "Mrs. Anderson"). Published in the *Cincinnati Commercial* and the *New York Tribune*, this astonishing letter, dictated by Anderson, demonstrates that freedom meant everything to the freedpeople: a free public identity, choice, education, and, not least, the "justice" represented by wages. (Photo: *New York Daily Tribune*, August 22, 1865)

Dayton, Ohio, August 7, 1865

To My Old Master, Colonel P. H. Anderson,
Big Spring, Tennessee

Sir: I got your letter and was glad to find you had not forgotten Jourdon, and that you wanted me to come back and live with you again, promising to do better for me than anybody else can. I have often felt uneasy about you. I thought the Yankees would have hung you long before this for harboring Rebs they found at your house. . . . Although you shot at me twice before I left you, I did not want to hear of your being hurt, and am glad you are still living. It would do me good to go back to the dear old home again and see Miss Mary and Miss Martha and Allen, Esther, Green, and Lee. Give my love to them all, and tell them I hope we will meet in the better world, if not in this. . . .

I want to know particularly what the good chance is you propose to give me. I am doing tolerably well here; I get $25 a month, with victuals and clothing; have a comfortable home for Mandy (the folks here call her Mrs. Anderson), and the children, Milly, Jane and Grundy, go to school and are learning well; the teacher says Grundy has a head for a preacher. . . . Now, if you will write and say what wages you will give me, I will be better able to decide whether it would be to my advantage to move back again.

As to my freedom, which you say I can have, there is nothing to be gained on that score, as I got my free-papers in 1864. . . . Mandy says she would be afraid to go back without some proof that you are sincerely disposed to treat us justly and kindly—and we have concluded to test your sincerity by asking you to send us our wages for the time we served you. This will make us forget and forgive old scores, and rely on your justice and friendship in the future. I served you faithfully for thirty-two years and Mandy twenty years. At $25 a month for me, and $2 a week for Mandy, our earnings would amount to $11,680. Add to this the interest for the time our wages has been kept back and deduct what you paid for our clothing and three doctor's visits to me, and pulling a tooth for Mandy, and the balance will show what we are in justice entitled to. Please send the money by Adams Express, in care of V. Winters, esq, Dayton, Ohio. If you fail to pay us for faithful labors in the past we can have little faith in your promises in the future. We trust the good Maker has opened your eyes to the wrongs which you and your fathers have done to me and my fathers, in making us toil for you for generations without recompense. Here I draw my wages every Saturday night, but in Tennessee there was never any pay day for the negroes any more than for the horses and cows. . . .

In answering this letter please state if there would be any safety for my Milly and Jane, who are now grown up and both good-looking girls. You know how it was with poor Matilda and Catherine. I would rather stay here and starve and die if it comes to that than have my girls brought to shame by the violence and wickedness of their young masters. You will also please state if there has been any schools opened for the colored children in your neighborhood, the great desire of my life now is to give my children an education, and have them form virtuous habits.

P.S.—Say howdy to George Carter, and thank him for taking the pistol from you when you were shooting at me.

From your old servant,
Jourdon Anderson

408   Chapter 15   Transforming Fire: The Civil War, 1861–1865

Bitter debate over Davis's plan resounded through the Confederacy. When the Confederate Congress approved slave enlistments without the promise of freedom in March 1865, Davis insisted on more. He issued an executive order to guarantee that owners would emancipate slave soldiers, and his allies in the states started to work for emancipation of the soldiers' families.

The war ended before much could come of these desperate policy initiatives on the part of the Confederacy. By contrast, Lincoln's Emancipation Proclamation stimulated a vital infusion of forces into the Union armies. Before the war was over, 134,000 slaves (and 52,000 free African Americans) had fought for freedom and the Union. Their participation aided northern victory while it discouraged recognition of the Confederacy by foreign governments, especially Great Britain, which had freed the slaves in its empire thirty years earlier. As both policy and process, emancipation had profound practical and moral implications for the new nation to be born out of the war.

The Soldiers' War

The intricacies of policymaking and social revolutions were far from the minds of most ordinary soldiers. Military service completely altered their lives. Enlistment took young men from their homes and submerged them in large organizations whose military discipline ignored their individuality. Army life meant tedium, physical hardship, and separation from loved ones. Yet the military experience had powerful attractions as well. It molded men on both sides so thoroughly that they came to resemble one another far more than they resembled civilians back home. Many soldiers forged amid war a bond with their fellows and a connection to a noble purpose that they cherished for years afterward.

Union soldiers may have sensed most clearly the massive scale of modern war. Most were young; the average soldier was between eighteen and twenty-one. Many went straight from small towns and farms into large armies supplied by extensive bureaucracies. By late 1861 there were 640,000 volunteers in arms, a stupendous increase over the regular army of 20,000 men. Many soldiers found adapting to camp life and military discipline daunting.

Soldiers benefited from certain new products, such as canned condensed milk, but blankets, clothing, and arms were often of poor quality. Vermin abounded. Hospitals were badly managed at first.

Hospitals and Camp Life

Rules of hygiene in large camps were scarcely enforced; latrines were poorly made or carelessly used. One investigation turned up "an area of over three acres, encircling the camp as a broad belt, on which is deposited an almost perfect layer of human excrement." Water supplies were unsafe and typhoid epidemics common. About 57,000 men died from dysentery and diarrhea; in fact, 224,000 Union troops died from disease or accidents, far more than the 140,000 who died as a result of battle. Confederate troops were less well supplied, especially in the latter part of the war, and they had no sanitary commission. Still, an extensive network of hospitals, aided by many white female volunteers and black women slaves, sprang up to aid the sick and wounded.

On both sides troops quickly learned that soldiering was far from glorious. "The dirt of a camp life knocks all its poetry into a cocked hat," wrote a North Carolina volunteer in 1862. One year later he marveled at his earlier innocence. Fighting had taught him "the realities of a soldier's life. We had no tents after the 6th of August, but slept on the ground, in the woods or open fields, without regard to the weather. . . . I learned to eat fat bacon raw, and to like it. . . . Without time to wash our clothes or our persons, and sleeping on the ground all huddled together, the whole army became lousy more or less with body lice." Union troops "skirmished" against lice by boiling their clothes or holding them over a hot fire, but, reported one soldier, "I find some on me in spite of all I can do."

Few had seen violent death before, but war soon exposed them to the blasted bodies of their friends and comrades. "Any one who goes over a battlefield after a battle," wrote one Confederate, "never cares to go over another. . . . It is a sad sight to see the dead and if possible more sad to see the wounded—shot in every possible way you can imagine." Many men died gallantly; there were innumerable striking displays of courage. But far more often soldiers gave up their lives in mass sacrifice, in tactics that made little sense.

Advances in technology made the Civil War particularly deadly. By far the most important were the rifle and the "minie ball." Bullets fired from a smoothbore musket tumbled and wobbled as they flew through the air and thus were not accurate at distances over 80 yards. Cutting spiraled grooves inside the barrel gave the projectile a spin and much greater accuracy, but rifles remained

The Rifled Musket

Union soldiers in camp, posing for a photograph, with black servants. The drudgery of camp life never prohibited soldiers from displaying their individuality.   (National Archives)

difficult to load and use until the Frenchman Claude Minie and the American James Burton developed a new kind of bullet. Civil War bullets were sizable lead slugs with a cavity at the bottom that expanded upon firing so that the bullet "took" the rifling and flew accurately. With these bullets, rifles were accurate at 400 yards and useful up to 1,000 yards.

This meant, of course, that soldiers assaulting a position defended by riflemen were in greater peril than ever before. Even though Civil War rifles were cumbersome to load (relatively few of the new, untried, breechloading and repeating rifles were ordered), the defense gained a significant advantage. While artillery now fired from a safe distance, there was no substitute for the infantry assault or the popular turning movements aimed at an enemy's flank. Thus advancing soldiers had to expose themselves repeatedly to accurate rifle fire. Because medical knowledge was rudimentary, even minor wounds often led to amputation, and to death through infection. Never before in Europe or America had such massive forces pummeled each other with weapons of such destructive power. As losses mounted, many citizens wondered at what Union soldier (and future Supreme Court justice) Oliver Wendell Holmes, Jr., called "the butcher's bill."

Still, Civil War soldiers developed deep commitments to each other and to their task. As campaigns dragged on, fighting and dying with their comrades became their reality, and most soldiers who did not desert grew determined to see the struggle through. "We now, like true Soldiers go determined not to yield one inch," wrote a New York corporal. When at last the war was over, "it seemed like breaking up a family to separate," one man observed. Another admitted, "We shook hands all around, and laughed and seemed to make merry, while our hearts were heavy and our eyes ready to shed tears."

The bonding may have been most dramatic among officers and men in the northern black regiments, for there white and black troops took their first steps toward bridging a deep racial divide. Racism in the Union Army was strong. Most white soldiers wanted nothing to do with black people and regarded them as inferior. "I never came out here for to free the black devils," wrote one soldier, and another objected to fighting beside African Americans because, "We are a too superior race for that." For many, acceptance of black troops grew only because they could do heavy labor and "stop Bullets as well as white people." A

The Black Soldier's Fight for Manhood

410   Chapter 15   Transforming Fire: The Civil War, 1861–1865

popular song celebrated "Sambo's Right to Be Kilt" as the only justification for black enlistments.

But among some a change occurred. While recruiting black troops in Virginia in late 1864, Charles Brewster sometimes denigrated the very men he sought to enlist. But he was delighted at the sight of a black cavalry unit because it made the local "secesh" furious, and he praised black soldiers who "fought nobly" and filled hospitals with "their wounded and mangled bodies." White officers who volunteered to lead black units only to gain promotion found that experience altered their opinions. After just one month with black troops, a white captain informed his wife, "I have a more elevated opinion of their abilities than I ever had before. I know that many of them are vastly the superiors of those . . . who would condemn them all to a life of brutal degradation." One general reported that his "colored regiments" possessed "remarkable aptitude for military training," and another observer said, "They fight like fiends."

Black troops created this change through their own dedication. They had a mission to destroy slavery and demonstrate their equality. "When Rebellion is crushed," wrote a black volunteer from Connecticut, "who will be more proud than I to say, 'I was one of the first of the despised race to leave the free North with a rifle on my shoulder, and give the lie to the old story that the black man will not fight.'" Corporal James Henry Gooding of Massachusetts's black Fifty-fourth Regiment explained that his unit intended "to live down all prejudice against its color, by a determination to do well in any position it is put." After an engagement he was proud that "a regiment of white men gave us three cheers as we were passing them," because "it shows that we did our duty as men should."

Through such experience under fire the blacks and whites of the Fifty-fourth Massachusetts forged deep bonds. Just before the regiment launched its costly assault on Fort Wagner in Charleston harbor, in July 1863, a black soldier called out to abolitionist Colonel Robert Gould Shaw, who would perish that day, "Colonel, I will stay by you till I die." "And he kept his word," noted a survivor of the attack. "He has never been seen since." Indeed, the heroic assault on Fort Wagner was celebrated for demonstrating the valor of black men. This bloody chapter in the history of American racism proved many things, not least of which was that black men had to die in battle to be acknowledged as men.

Such valor emerged despite persistent discrimination. Off-duty black soldiers were sometimes attacked by northern mobs; on duty, they did most of the "fa-

Company E, 4th U.S. Colored Infantry, photographed at Fort Lincoln, Virginia, in 1864. Nothing so symbolized the new manhood and citizenship among African Americans in the midst of the war as such young black men in blue.   (Chicago Historical Society)

tigue duty," or heavy labor. The Union government, moreover, paid white privates $13 per month plus a clothing allowance of $3.50, whereas black privates earned only $10 per month less $3 for clothing. Outraged by this injustice, several regiments refused to accept any pay whatsoever, and Congress eventually remedied the inequity. In this instance, at least, the majority of legislators agreed with a white private that black troops had "proved their title to manhood on many a bloody field fighting freedom's battles."

1863: The Tide of Battle Turns

The fighting in the spring and summer of 1863 did not settle the war, but it began to suggest the outcome. The campaigns began in a deceptively positive way for Confederates, as their Army of Northern Virginia performed brilliantly in the Battle of Chancellorsville.

For once, a large Civil War army was not slow and cumbersome but executed tactics with speed and precision. On May 2 and 3, west of Fredericksburg, Virginia, some 130,000 members of the Union Army of the Potomac bore down on fewer than 60,000 Confederates. Boldly, as if they enjoyed being outnumbered, Lee and Stonewall Jackson divided their forces, ordering 30,000 men under Jackson on a day-long march westward to gain position for a flank attack. This classic turning movement was boldly carried out in the face of great numerical disadvantage. Arriving at their position late in the afternoon, Jackson's seasoned "foot cavalry" found unprepared Union troops laughing, smoking, and playing cards. The Union soldiers had no idea they were under attack until frightened deer and rabbits bounded out of the forest, followed by gray-clad troops. The Confederate attack drove the entire right side of the Union Army back in confusion. Eager to press his advantage, Jackson rode forward with a few officers to study the ground. As they returned at twilight, southern troops mistook them for federals and fired, fatally wounding their commander. The next day Union forces left in defeat. Chancellorsville was a remarkable southern victory but costly because of the loss of Stonewall Jackson.

Battle of Chancellorsville

July brought crushing defeats for the Confederacy in two critical battles—Vicksburg and Gettysburg—that severely damaged Confederate hopes for independence. Vicksburg was a vital western citadel, the last major fortification on the Mississippi River in

Siege of Vicksburg

southern hands (see Map 15.2). After months of searching through swamps and bayous, General Ulysses S. Grant found an advantageous approach to the city. He laid siege to Vicksburg in May, bottling up the defending army of General John Pemberton. If Vicksburg fell, Union forces would control the river, cutting the Confederacy in two and gaining an open path into its interior. To stave off such a result, Jefferson Davis gave command of all other forces in the area to General Joseph E. Johnston and beseeched him to go to Pemberton's aid. Meanwhile, at a council of war in Richmond, General Robert E. Lee proposed a Confederate invasion of the North. Although such an offensive would not relieve Vicksburg directly, it could stun and dismay the North and, if successful, possibly even lead to peace. By invading the North a second time, Lee hoped to take the war out of war-weary Virginia, garner civilian support in Maryland, win a major victory on northern soil, threaten major cities, and thereby force a Union capitulation on his terms.

Lee's troops streamed through western Maryland and into Pennsylvania, threatening both Washington and Baltimore. As his emboldened army advanced, the possibility of a major battle near the Union capital became more and more likely. Confederate prospects along the Mississippi, however, darkened. Davis repeatedly wired General Johnston, urging him to concentrate his forces and attack Grant's army. Johnston, however, did little, telegraphing back, "I consider saving Vicksburg hopeless." Grant's men, meanwhile, were supplying themselves from the abundant crops of the Mississippi River valley and could continue their siege indefinitely. Their rich meat-and-vegetables diet became so tiresome, in fact, that one day, as Grant rode by, a private looked up and muttered, "Hardtack," referring to the dry biscuits that were the usual staple of soldiers' diets. Soon a line of soldiers was shouting "Hardtack! Hardtack!" demanding respite from turkey and sweet potatoes.

In such circumstances the fall of Vicksburg was inevitable, and on July 4, 1863, its commander surrendered. The same day a battle that had been raging for three days concluded at Gettysburg, Pennsylvania (see Map 15.3). On July 1 Confederate forces hunting for a supply of shoes had collided with part of the Union Army. Heavy fighting on the second day over two steep hills left federal forces in possession of high ground along

Battle of Gettysburg

412   Chapter 15   Transforming Fire: The Civil War, 1861–1865

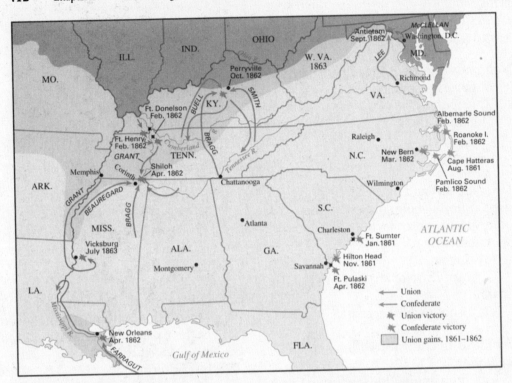

Map 15.2   War in the West, 1861–1863   Here is an overview of the Union's successful campaigns in the west and its seizure of key points on the Mississippi River, as well as along the Atlantic coast in 1862 and 1863. These actions were decisive in paving the way for ultimate northern victory.

Cemetery Ridge, running more than a mile south of the town. There they enjoyed the protection of a stone wall and a clear view of their foe across almost a mile of open field.

Undaunted, Lee believed his reinforced troops could break the Union line, and on July 3 he ordered a direct assault. Full of foreboding, General James Longstreet warned Lee that "no 15,000 men ever arrayed for battle can take that position." But Lee stuck to his plan. Virginians under General George E. Pickett and North Carolinians under General James Pettigrew methodically marched up the slope in a doomed assault known as Pickett's Charge. For a moment a few hundred Confederates breached the enemy's line, but most fell in heavy slaughter. On July 4 Lee had to withdraw, having suffered almost 4,000 dead and about 24,000 missing and wounded. The Confederate general reported to President Davis that "I am alone to blame" and offered to resign. Davis replied that to find a more capable commander was "an impossibility."

The Confederacy had reached what many consider its "high water mark" on that ridge at Gettysburg.

Southern troops displayed unforgettable courage and dedication at Gettysburg, and the Union Army, which suffered 23,000 casualties (nearly one-quarter of the force), under General George G. Meade exhibited the same bravery in stopping the Confederate invasion. But the results there and at Vicksburg were disastrous for the South. The Confederacy was split in two; west of the Mississippi General E. Kirby Smith had to operate on his own, virtually independent of Richmond. Moreover, the heartland of Louisiana, Tennessee, and Mississippi lay exposed to invasion, and Lee's defeat spelled the end of major southern offensive actions. Too weak to prevail in attack, the Confederacy henceforth would have to conserve its limited resources and rely on a prolonged defense. By refusing to be beaten, and wearing down northern morale, the South might yet win, but its prospects were darker than ever before.

Check Your Understanding

The following sentences appear in the chapter. Circle the letter of the BEST meaning for each italicized word.

22. "Railroads also were a leading beneficiary of government *largesse*."
    a. Restrictions
    b. Organization
    c. Passengers
    d. Generosity

23. "He [Lincoln] and his generals proved adept at *furloughing* soldiers so they could vote in close elections."
    a. Assembling
    b. Pressuring
    c. Giving a leave of absence or vacation
    d. Furnishing with necessities

24. "Yet idealism coexisted with *ostentation*."
    a. Careful planning for the future
    b. Showy display of wealth
    c. Hope and optimism
    d. Arrogance

25. "In the first two years of the war, northern *morale* remained remarkably high for a cause that today may seem abstract...."
    a. Opinion
    b. Fears and anxieties
    c. Wealth
    d. Confidence and cheerfulness

26. "Led by Frederick Douglass, black abolitionists vehemently opposed these *machinations* by the Lincoln administration."
    a. Schemes
    b. Attitudes
    c. Taxes
    d. Laws

27. "Let the government use its full powers, free the slaves, and crush the *insurrection*, urged the Radicals."
    a. Enemy
    b. Criminal activity
    c. Revolt
    d. Freedom

28. "...the Emancipation Proclamation was an *ambiguous* document that said less than it seemed to say."
    a. Illegal
    b. Wordy and confusing
    c. Open to more than one interpretation
    d. Upsetting

29. "In chorus after chorus of 'Go Down, Moses,' they announced the magnitude of their painful but beautiful *exodus*."
    a. Departure
    b. Suffering
    c. Triumph
    d. Faith

30. "Because medical knowledge was *rudimentary*, even minor wounds often led to amputation and to death through infection."
    a. Extensive
    b. Basic and undeveloped
    c. Non-existent
    d. Totally worthless

31. "Vicksburg was a vital western *citadel*, the last major fortification on the Mississippi River in southern hands."
    a. Military stronghold
    b. City
    c. Tourist destination
    d. Model

32.–36. On your own paper, write five review questions that would help you focus on material in this section and that would be likely to appear on a test. Also, write your answers to each of these questions.

Discuss the following questions with a partner or group, and then collaborate to write answers to the questions on your paper.

37. Discuss the impact of the Civil War on women in northern and southern societies.

38. Discuss Lincoln's issuance of the Emancipation Proclamation. Why is it said that "as a legal document it was wanting, as a moral and political document it had great meaning…"? What was its impact on the war?

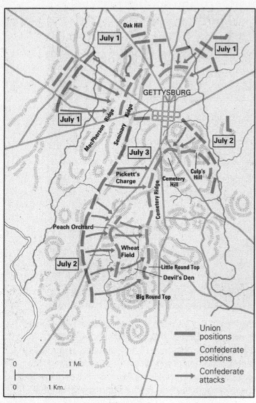

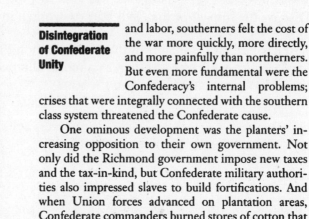

Map 15.3 Battle of Gettysburg In the war's greatest battle, fought around a small market town in southern Pennsylvania, Lee's invasion of the North was repulsed. Union forces had the advantage of high ground, shorter lines, and superior numbers. The casualties for the two armies—dead, wounded, and missing—exceeded 50,000 men.

Disunity, South and North

 Both northern and southern governments waged the final two years of the war in the face of increasing opposition at home. Dissatisfactions that had surfaced earlier grew more intense and sometimes violent. The gigantic costs of a *civil* war that neither side seemed able to win fed the unrest. But protest also arose from fundamental stresses in the social structures of North and South.

The Confederacy's problems were both more serious and more deeply rooted than the North's. Vastly disadvantaged in industrial capacity, natural resources,

Disintegration of Confederate Unity

and labor, southerners felt the cost of the war more quickly, more directly, and more painfully than northerners. But even more fundamental were the Confederacy's internal problems; crises that were integrally connected with the southern class system threatened the Confederate cause.

One ominous development was the planters' increasing opposition to their own government. Not only did the Richmond government impose new taxes and the tax-in-kind, but Confederate military authorities also impressed slaves to build fortifications. And when Union forces advanced on plantation areas, Confederate commanders burned stores of cotton that lay in the enemy's path. Such interference with plantation routines and financial interests was not what planters had expected of their government, and they complained bitterly.

Nor were the centralizing policies of the Davis administration popular. The increasing size and power of the Richmond government startled and alarmed planters who had condemned federal usurpations. In fact, the Confederate constitution had granted substantial powers to the central government, especially in time of war. But many planters assumed with R. B. Rhett, editor of the *Charleston Mercury*, that the Confederate constitution "leaves the States untouched in their Sovereignty, and commits to the Confederate Government only a few simple objects, and a few simple powers to enforce them." Governor Joseph E. Brown of Georgia took a similarly inflated view of the importance of the states. During the brief interval between Georgia's secession from the Union and its admission to the Confederacy, Brown sent an ambassador to Europe to seek recognition for the sovereign republic of Georgia from Queen Victoria, Napoleon III, and the king of Belgium.

Years of opposition to the federal government within the Union had frozen southerners in a defensive posture. Now they erected the barrier of states' rights as a defense against change, hiding behind it while their capacity for creative statesmanship atrophied. Planters sought, above all, a guarantee that their plantations and their lives would remain untouched; many were not deeply committed either to building a southern nation or to winning independence. If the Confederacy had been allowed to depart from the Union in peace and continue as a semideveloped cotton-growing region, they would have been content. When secession revolutionized their world, they could not or would not adjust.

414 Chapter 15 Transforming Fire: The Civil War, 1861–1865

These "children of the battlefield" aroused great interest in the North after a burial detail at Gettysburg found this ambrotype clutched in the hand of a fallen Union soldier. After thousands of copies of the picture were circulated, the wife of Sergeant Amos Humiston of the 154th New York Infantry *(above)* recognized her children and knew that she was a widow.   (The C. Craig Caba Gettysburg Collection, from *Gettysburg.* Larry Sherer © 1991 Time-Life Books, Inc.)

Confused and embittered planters struck out at Jefferson Davis. Conscription, thundered Governor Brown, was "subversive of [Georgia's] sovereignty, and at war with all the principles for the support of which Georgia entered into this revolution." Searching for ways to frustrate the law, Brown bickered over draft exemptions and ordered local enrollment officials not to cooperate with the Confederacy. The *Charleston Mercury* told readers that "conscription . . . is . . . the very embodiment of Lincolnism, which our gallant armies are today fighting." In a gesture of stubborn selfishness, Robert Toombs of Georgia, a former U.S. senator, refused to switch from cotton to food crops, defying the wishes of the government, the newspapers, and his neighbors' petitions. His action bespoke the inflexibility of the southern elite at a crucial point in the Confederacy's struggle to survive.

The southern courts ultimately upheld Davis's power to conscript. Despite his cold formality and inability to disarm critics, Davis possessed two important virtues: iron determination and total dedication to

independence. These qualities kept the Confederacy afloat. But his actions earned him the hatred of most influential and elite citizens.

Meanwhile, for ordinary southerners, the dire predictions of hunger and suffering were becoming a reality. Food riots occurred in the spring of 1863 in Atlanta, Macon, Columbus, and Augusta, Georgia, and in Salisbury and High Point, North Carolina. On April 2 a crowd assembled in Richmond to demand relief. A passerby, noticing the excitement, asked a young girl, "Is there some celebration?" "We celebrate our right to live," replied the girl. "We are starving. As soon as enough of us get together we are going to the bakeries and each of us will take a loaf of bread." Soon they did just that, sparking a riot that Davis himself had to quell at gunpoint.

Throughout the rural South, ordinary people resisted more quietly—by refusing to cooperate with conscription, tax collection, and impressments of food. "In all the States impressments are evaded by every

Food Riots in Southern Cities

means which ingenuity can suggest, and in some openly resisted," wrote a high-ranking commissary officer. Farmers who did provide food for the army refused to accept payment in certificates of credit or government bonds, as required by law. Conscription officers increasingly found no one to draft—men of draft age were hiding out in the forests. "The disposition to avoid military service is general," observed one of Georgia's senators in 1864. In some areas tax agents were killed in the line of duty.

Jefferson Davis was ill equipped to deal with such discontent. Austere and private by nature, he failed to communicate with the masses. Often he buried himself in military affairs or administrative details. His class perspective also distanced him from the sufferings of the common people. While his social circle in Richmond dined on duck and oysters, ordinary southerners recovered salt from the drippings on their smokehouse floors and went hungry. State governors who responded to people's needs won the public's loyalty, but Davis failed to reach out to the plain folk and thus lost their support.

Such discontent was certain to affect the Confederate armies. "What man is there that would stay in the army and no that his family is

Desertions from the Confederate Army

sufring at home?" an angry citizen wrote anonymously to the secretary of war. Worried about their loved ones and resentful of what they saw as a rich man's war, large numbers of men did indeed leave the armies. Their friends and neighbors gave them support. Mary Boykin Chesnut observed a man being dragged back to the army as his wife looked on. "Desert agin, Jake!" she cried openly. "You desert agin, quick as you kin. Come back to your wife and children."

Desertion did not become a serious problem for the Confederacy until mid-1862, and stiffer policing solved the problem that year. But from 1863 on, the number of men on duty fell rapidly as desertions soared. By mid-1863, John A. Campbell, the South's assistant secretary of war, wondered whether "so general a habit" as desertion could be considered a crime. Campbell estimated that 40,000 to 50,000 troops were absent without leave and that 100,000 were evading duty in some way. Furloughs, amnesty proclamations, and appeals to return had little effect; by November 1863 Secretary of War James Seddon admitted that one-third of the army could not be accounted for. The situation would worsen.

The defeats at Gettysburg and Vicksburg dealt a heavy blow to Confederate morale. When the news

The impoverishment of nonslaveholding white families was a critical problem for the Confederacy. The sale of this sheet music was intended not only to boost morale but also to raise money that could be used to aid the hungry and needy. This effort and larger government initiatives, however, failed to solve the problem.   (Chicago Historical Society)

reached Josiah Gorgas, the genius of Confederate ordnance operations, he confided to his diary, "Today absolute ruin seems our portion. The Confederacy totters to its destruction." In desperation President Davis and several state governors resorted to threats and racial scare tactics to drive southern whites to further sacrifice. Defeat, Davis warned, would mean "extermination of yourselves, your wives, and children." Governor Charles Clark of Mississippi predicted "elevation of the black race to a position of equality—aye, of superiority, that will make them your masters and rulers."

From this point on, the internal disintegration of the Confederacy quickened. A few newspapers began to call openly for peace. "We are for peace," admitted the *Raleigh* (North Carolina) *Daily Progress*, "because there has been enough of blood and carnage, enough of widows and orphans." A neighboring journal, the *North Carolina Standard*, tacitly admitted that defeat was inevitable and called for negotiations. Similar proposals were made in several state legislatures, though they were presented as plans for independence on

416 Chapter 15 Transforming Fire: The Civil War, 1861–1865

honorable terms. Confederate leaders began to realize that they were losing the support of the common people. Governor Zebulon Vance of North Carolina wrote privately that victory would require more "blood and misery . . . and our people will not pay this price I am satisfied for their independence."

In North Carolina a peace movement grew under the leadership of William W. Holden, a popular Democratic politician and editor. Over

Southern Peace Movements

one hundred public meetings took place in the summer of 1863 in support of peace negotiations, and many seasoned political observers believed that Holden had the majority of the people behind him. In Georgia early in 1864, Governor Brown and Alexander H. Stephens, vice president of the Confederacy, led a similar effort. Ultimately, however, these movements came to naught. The lack of a two-party system threw into question the legitimacy of any criticism of the government; even Holden and Brown could not entirely escape the taint of dishonor and disloyalty. That the movement existed at all demonstrates deep disaffection.

The results of the 1863 congressional elections strengthened dissent in the Confederacy. Everywhere secessionists and supporters of the administration lost seats to men not identified with the government. Many of the new representatives were former Whigs who opposed the Davis administration or publicly favored peace. In the last years of the war, Davis's support in the Confederate Congress dwindled. Davis used the government bureaucracy and the army to enforce his unpopular policies. A few editors and a core of courageous, determined soldiers kept the Confederacy alive in spite of disintegrating popular support.

By 1864 much of the opposition to the war had moved entirely outside the political sphere. Southerners were simply giving up the struggle and withdrawing their cooperation from the government. Deserters dominated whole towns and counties. Secret societies favoring reunion, such as the Heroes of America and the Red Strings, sprang up. Active dissent was particularly common in upland and mountain regions. "The condition of things in the mountain districts of North Carolina, South Carolina, Georgia, and Alabama," admitted Assistant Secretary of War Campbell, "menaces the existence of the Confederacy as fatally as either of the armies of the United States." The government was losing the support of its citizens.

In the North opposition to the war was similar but less severe. Alarm intensified over the growing cen-

Antiwar Sentiment in the North

tralization of government, and by 1863 war-weariness was widespread. Resentment of the draft sparked protest, especially among poor citizens, and the Union Army struggled with a desertion rate as high as the Confederates'. But the Union was so much richer than the South in human resources that none of these problems ever threatened the effectiveness of the government. Fresh recruits were always available, especially after black enlistments began, and there were no shortages of food and other necessities.

Also, Lincoln possessed a talent that Davis lacked: he knew how to stay in touch with the ordinary citizen. Through letters to newspapers and to soldiers' families, he reached the common people and demonstrated that he had not forgotten them. The daily carnage, the tortuous political problems, and the ceaseless criticism weighed heavily on him. But this president—a self-educated man of humble origins—was able to communicate his suffering. His moving words helped to contain northern discontent, though they could not remove it.

Much of the wartime protest in the North was political in origin. The Democratic Party fought to

Peace Democrats

regain power by blaming Lincoln for the war's death toll, the expansion of federal powers, inflation and the high tariff, and the emancipation of blacks. Appealing to tradition, its leaders called for an end to the war and reunion on the basis of "the Constitution as it is and the Union as it was." The Democrats denounced conscription and martial law and defended states' rights and the interests of agriculture. They charged repeatedly that Republican policies were designed to flood the North with blacks, depriving white males of their status, their jobs, and their women. These claims appealed to southerners who had settled north of the Ohio River, to conservatives, to many poor people, and to some eastern merchants who had lost profitable southern trade. In the 1862 congressional elections, the Democrats made a strong comeback, and peace Democrats—who would go much further than others in their party to end the war—had influence in New York State and majorities in the legislatures of Illinois and Indiana.

Led by outspoken men like Representative Clement L. Vallandigham of Ohio, the peace Democrats made themselves highly visible. Vallandigham criticized Lincoln as a dictator who had suspended the writ of habeas corpus without congressional authority and had arrested thousands of innocent citizens. Like other Democrats, he condemned both conscription and emancipation and urged voters to use their power at the polls to depose "King Abraham." Vallandigham stayed carefully within legal bounds, but his attacks seemed so damaging to the war effort that military authorities arrested him for treason after Lincoln suspended habeas corpus. Lincoln wisely decided against punishment—and martyr's status—for the Ohioan and exiled him to the Confederacy. (Eventually Vallandigham returned to the North through Canada.)

Lincoln believed that antiwar Democrats were linked to secret organizations that harbored traitorous ideas. These societies, he feared, encouraged draft resistance, discouraged enlistment, sabotaged communications, and plotted to aid the Confederacy. Likening such groups to a poisonous snake, Republicans sometimes branded them—and by extension the peace Democrats—as "Copperheads." Though Democrats were connected with these organizations, most engaged in politics rather than treason. And though some saboteurs and Confederate agents were active in the North and Canada, they never genuinely threatened the Union war effort.

More violent opposition to the government arose from ordinary citizens facing the draft, which became

New York City Draft Riots

law in 1863. The urban poor and immigrants in strongly Democratic areas were especially hostile to conscription. Federal enrolling officers made up the lists of eligibles, a procedure open to personal favoritism and prejudice. Many men, including some of modest means, managed to avoid the army by hiring a substitute or paying commutation, but the poor viewed the commutation fee as discriminatory, and many immigrants suspected (wrongly, on the whole) that they were called in disproportionate numbers. (Approximately 200,000 men born in Germany and 150,000 born in Ireland served in the Union Army.)

As a result, there were scores of disturbances and melees. Enrolling officers received rough treatment in many parts of the North, and riots occurred in New Jersey, Ohio, Indiana, Pennsylvania, Illinois, and Wisconsin. By far the most serious outbreak of violence occurred in New York City in July 1863. The war was unpopular in that Democratic stronghold, and racial, ethnic, and class tensions ran high. Shippers had recently broken a longshoremen's strike by hiring black strikebreakers to work under police protection.

Mobs in the New York City draft riots directed much of their anger at African Americans. Rioters burned an orphanage for black children and killed scores of blacks. This wood engraving, which appeared in the *Illustrated London News* on August 8, 1863, depicts a lynching in Clarkson Street.   (Chicago Historical Society)

Working-class New Yorkers feared an inflow of black labor from the South and regarded blacks as the cause of the war. Poor Irish workers resented being forced to serve in the place of others who could afford to avoid the draft.

Military police officers came under attack first, and then mobs crying "Down with the rich" looted wealthy homes and stores. But blacks became the special target. Those who happened to be in the rioters' path were beaten; soon the mob rampaged through African American neighborhoods, destroying an orphan asylum. At least seventy-four people died in the violence, which raged out of control for three days. Only the dispatch of army units fresh from Gettysburg ended the episode.

Discouragement and war-weariness reached a peak in the summer of 1864, when the Democratic Party nominated the popular General George B. McClellan for president and inserted a peace plank into its platform. The plank, written by Vallandigham, condemned "four years of failure to restore the Union by the experiment of war," called for an armistice, and spoke vaguely about preserving the Union. Lincoln, running with Tennessee's Andrew Johnson on a "National Union" ticket, concluded that it was "exceedingly probable that this Administration will not be

418　Chapter 15　Transforming Fire: The Civil War, 1861–1865

reelected." During a publicized interchange with Confederate officials sent to Canada, Lincoln insisted that the terms for peace include reunion and "the abandonment of slavery." A wave of protest arose in the North from voters who were weary of war and dedicated only to reunion. Lincoln quickly backtracked, denying that his offer meant "that nothing *else* or *less* would be considered, if offered." He would insist on freedom only for those slaves (about 134,000) who had joined the Union Army under his promise of emancipation. Lincoln's action showed his political weakness, but the fortunes of war soon changed the electoral situation.

1864–1865: The Final Test of Wills

 During the final year of the war, the Confederates could still have won their version of victory if military stalemate and northern antiwar sentiment had forced a negotiated settlement to end the war. But events, northern determination, and Lincoln's insistence on the unconditional surrender of Confederate forces prevailed as Americans endured the bloodiest nightmare in their history.

The North's long-term diplomatic strategy succeeded in 1864. From the outset, the North had pursued one paramount goal: to prevent recognition of the Confederacy by European nations. Foreign recognition would belie Lincoln's claim that the United States was fighting an illegal rebellion and would open the way to the financial and military aid that could ensure Confederate independence. The British elite, however, felt considerable sympathy for southern planters, whose aristocratic values were similar to their own. And both England and France stood to benefit from a divided and weakened America. Thus to achieve their goal, Lincoln and Secretary of State Seward needed to avoid both serious military defeats and controversies with the European powers.

Northern Diplomatic Strategy

Aware that the textile industry employed one-fifth of the British population directly or indirectly, southerners banked on British recognition of the Confederacy. But at the beginning of the war, British mills had a 50 percent surplus of cotton on hand; later on, new sources of supply in India, Egypt, and Brazil helped to meet Britain's needs. And throughout the war, some southern cotton continued to reach Europe, despite the Confederacy's embargo on cotton production, an ill-fated policy initiative aimed at securing British sup-

port. Refusing to be stampeded into recognition of the Confederacy, the British government kept its eye on the battlefield. France, though sympathetic to the South, was unwilling to act independently of Britain. Confederate agents managed to purchase valuable arms and supplies in Europe and obtained loans from European financiers, but they never achieved a diplomatic breakthrough.

More than once the Union strategy nearly broke down. An acute crisis occurred in 1861 when the overzealous commander of an American frigate stopped the British steamer *Trent* and removed two Confederate ambassadors, James Mason and John Slidell, sailing to Britain. They were imprisoned in Boston after being brought ashore. This action was cheered in the North, but the British interpreted it as a violation of freedom of the seas and demanded the prisoners' release. Lincoln and Seward waited until northern public opinion cooled and then released the two southerners. Soon forgotten, the incident nevertheless strained U.S.-British relations at a sensitive early stage in the war.

Then the sale to the Confederacy of warships constructed in England sparked vigorous protest from U.S. ambassador Charles Francis Adams. A few English-built ships, notably the *Alabama*, reached open water to serve the South. Over a period of twenty-two months, without entering a southern port (because of the Union blockade), the *Alabama* destroyed or captured more than sixty U.S. ships. But the British government, as a neutral power, soon barred delivery of warships such as the Laird rams (built by a private company), formidable vessels whose pointed prows were designed to end the blockade by battering the Union ships.

On the battlefield, the northern victory was far from won in 1864. General Nathaniel Banks's Red River campaign, designed to capture more of Louisiana and Texas, quickly fell apart, and the capture of Mobile Bay in August did not cause the fall of Mobile. Union general William Tecumseh Sherman commented that the North had to "keep the war South until they are not only ruined, exhausted, but humbled in pride and spirit." Sherman soon brought total war to the southern heartland. On the eastern front during the winter of 1863–1864, the two armies in Virginia settled into a stalemate awaiting yet another spring offensive by the North.

Battlefield Stalemate and a Union Strategy for Victory

Military authorities throughout history have agreed that deep invasion is very risky: the farther an

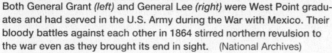
Both General Grant *(left)* and General Lee *(right)* were West Point graduates and had served in the U.S. Army during the War with Mexico. Their bloody battles against each other in 1864 stirred northern revulsion to the war even as they brought its end in sight.   (National Archives)

army penetrates enemy territory, the more vulnerable its own communications and supply lines. Moreover, observed the Prussian expert Karl von Clausewitz, if the invader encountered a "truly national" resistance, his troops would be "everywhere exposed to attacks by an insurgent population." Thus if southerners mounted such a "truly national" resistance, their defiance and the South's vast size could make a northern victory improbable.

General Grant, by now in command of all the federal armies, decided to test these conditions—and southern will—with a strategic innovation of his own: raids on a massive scale. Grant, less tied to tradition and maneuver by the book than most other Union commanders, proposed to use whole armies, not just cavalry, to destroy Confederate railroads, thus ruining the enemy's transportation and damaging the South's economy. Abandoning their lines of support, Union troops would live off the land while laying to waste all resources useful to the military and to the civilian population of the Confederacy. After General George H. Thomas's troops won the Battle of Chattanooga in

November 1863 by ignoring orders and charging up Missionary Ridge, the heartland of Georgia lay open. Moving to Virginia, Grant entrusted General Sherman with 100,000 men for an invasion deep into the South, toward the rail center of Atlanta.

Jefferson Davis countered by positioning the army of General Joseph E. Johnston in Sherman's path.

Atlanta

Davis's entire political strategy for 1864 was based on demonstrating Confederate military strength and successfully defending Atlanta. The U.S. presidential election of 1864 was approaching, and Davis hoped that southern resolve would lead to the defeat of Lincoln and the election of a president who would sue for peace. When General Johnston slowly but steadily fell back toward Atlanta, Davis grew anxious and sought assurances that Atlanta would be held. From a purely military point of view, Johnston maneuvered skillfully, but the president of the Confederacy could not take a purely military point of view. When Johnston provided no information and continued to retreat, Davis replaced him with the one-legged

420   Chapter 15   Transforming Fire: The Civil War, 1861–1865

General John Hood, who knew his job was to fight. "Our all depends on that army at Atlanta," wrote Mary Boykin Chesnut. "If that fails us, the game is up."

For southern morale, the game was up. Hood attacked but was beaten, and Sherman's army occupied Atlanta on September 2, 1864. The victory buoyed northern spirits and ensured Lincoln's reelection. "There is no hope," Mary Chesnut acknowledged; and a government clerk in Richmond wrote, "Our fondly-cherished visions of peace have vanished like a mirage of the desert." Davis exhorted southerners to fight on and win new victories before the federal elections, but he had to admit that "two-thirds of our men are absent . . . most of them absent without leave." In a desperate diversion, Hood's army marched north to cut Sherman's supply lines and force him to withdraw, but Sherman began to march sixty thousand of his men straight to the sea, planning to live off the land and destroying Confederate resources as he went (see Map 15.4).

Sherman's army was an unusually formidable force, composed almost entirely of battle-tested veterans and officers who had risen through the ranks from

Sherman's March to the Sea

the midwestern states. Before the march began, army doctors weeded out any men who were weak or sick. Tanned, bearded, tough, and unkempt, the remaining veterans were determined, as one put it, "to Conquer this Rebelien or Die." They believed "the South are to blame for this war" and were ready to make the South pay. Although many harbored racist attitudes, most had come to support emancipation because, as one said, "Slavery stands in the way of putting down the rebellion." Confederate General Johnston later commented, "There has been no such army since the days of Julius Caesar."

As Sherman's men moved across Georgia, they cut a path 50 to 60 miles wide and more than 200 miles long. The totality of the destruction they caused was awesome. A Georgia woman described the "Burnt Country" this way: "The fields were trampled down and the road was lined with carcasses of horses, hogs, and cattle that the invaders, unable either to consume or to carry with them, had wantonly shot down to starve our people and prevent them from making their crops. The stench in some places was unbearable."

Map 15.4 Sherman's March to the Sea   The West proved a decisive theater at the end of the war. From Chattanooga, Union forces drove into Georgia, capturing Atlanta. Then General Sherman embarked on his march of destruction through Georgia to the coast and then northward through the Carolinas.

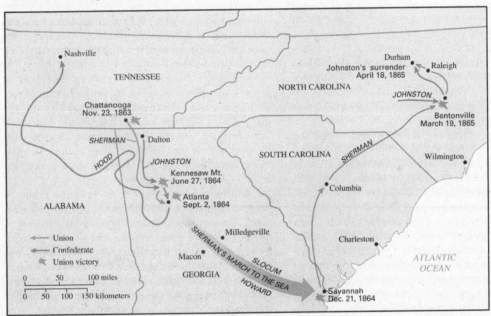

Such devastation diminished the South's material re-sources and sapped its will to resist.

After reaching Savannah in December, Sherman marched his armies north into the Carolinas. To his soldiers, South Carolina was "the root of secession." They burned and destroyed as they moved through, encountering little resistance. The opposing army of General Johnston was small, but Sherman's men should have been prime targets for guerrilla raids and harassing attacks by local defense units. The absence of both led South Carolina's James Chesnut, Jr. (a politician and the husband of Mary Chesnut), to write that his state "was shamefully and unnecessarily lost. . . . We had time, opportunity and means to de-stroy him. But there was wholly wanting the energy and ability required by the occasion." The South put up no "truly national" resistance; its people had lost the will to continue the struggle.

Sherman's march drew additional human re-sources to the Union cause. In Georgia alone as many as nineteen thousand slaves gladly took the opportu-nity to escape bondage and join the Union troops as they passed through the countryside. Others remained on the plantations to await the end of the war, either from an ingrained wariness of whites or negative expe-riences with federal soldiers. The destruction of food harmed slaves as well as white rebels, and many blacks lost livestock, clothing, crops, and other valuables to their liberators. In fact, the brutality of Sherman's troops shocked these veterans of the whip. "I've seen them cut the hams off of a live pig or ox and go off leavin' the animal groanin'," recalled one man. "The master had 'em kilt then, but it was awful."

It was awful, too, in Virginia, where the path to victory proved protracted and ghastly. Throughout the spring and summer of 1864, in-tent on capturing Richmond, Grant hurled his troops at Lee's army in Virginia and suffered appalling losses: almost 18,000 casualties in the Battle of the Wilderness, where skeletons poked out of the shallow graves dug one year before; more than 8,000 at Spotsylvania; and 12,000 in the space of a few hours at Cold Harbor (see Map 15.5).

Virginia's Bloody Soil

Before the assault at Cold Harbor (which Grant later admitted was a grave mistake), Union troops pinned scraps of paper bearing their names and ad-dresses to their backs, certain they would be mowed down as they rushed Lee's trenches. In four weeks in May and June, Grant lost as many men as were en-rolled in Lee's entire army. From early May until July,

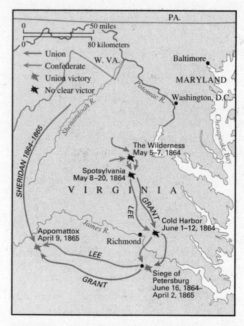

Map 15.5 The War in Virginia, 1864–1865 At great cost, Grant hammered away at Lee's army until the weakened southern forces finally surren-dered at Appomattox Court House.

when Union forces had marched and fought all the way from forests west of Fredericksburg to Peters-burg, south of Richmond, which they besieged, the two armies engaged each other nearly every day, often in full-scale battles. The war had reached a horrible modern scale. Wagon trains carrying thousands of Union wounded crawled back toward Washington. "It was as if war," wrote historian Bruce Catton, "the great clumsy machine for maiming people, had at last been perfected. Instead of turning out its grist spas-modically, with long waits between each delivery, it was at last able to produce every day, without any gaps at all."

Undaunted, Grant kept up the pressure, saying, "I propose to fight it out along this line if it takes all sum-mer." Though costly, and testing northern morale to its limits, these battles prepared the way for eventual victory: Lee's army shrank until offensive action was no longer possible, while Grant's army kept replenish-ing its forces with new recruits. The siege of Peters-burg, with the armies facing each other in miles of trenches, lasted throughout the winter of 1864–1865.

422   Chapter 15   Transforming Fire: The Civil War, 1861–1865

At the war's end, the U.S. flag flew over the state capitol in Richmond, Virginia, which bore many marks of destruction.   (National Archives)

The end finally came in the spring of 1865. Grant kept battering Lee, who tried but failed to break through the Union line. With the numerical superiority of Grant's army now greater than two to one, Confederate defeat was inevitable. On April 2 Lee abandoned Richmond and Petersburg. On April 9, hemmed in by Union troops, short of rations, and with fewer than thirty thousand men left, Lee surrendered at Appomattox Court House. Grant treated his rival with respect and paroled the defeated troops, allowing cavalrymen to keep their horses and take them home. The war was over at last. Within weeks, Confederate forces under Johnston surrendered and Davis, who had fled Richmond but wanted the war to continue, was captured in Georgia. The North rejoiced, and most southerners fell into despair, expecting waves of punishment. In the profound relief and stillness of the surrender field at Appomattox, no one could know the tasks of healing and justice that lay ahead.

Surrender at Appomattox

With Lee's surrender, Lincoln knew that the Union had been preserved, yet he lived to see but a few days of war's aftermath. On the evening of Good Friday, April 14, he accompanied his wife to Ford's Theatre in Washington to enjoy a popular comedy. There John Wilkes Booth, an embittered southern sympathizer, shot the president in the head at point-blank range. Lincoln died the next day. Twelve days later, troops tracked down and killed Booth. The Union had lost its wartime leader, and millions publicly mourned the martyred chief executive along the route of the funeral train that took his body home to Illinois. Relief at the war's end mingled hauntingly with a renewed sense of loss and anxiety about the future. Millions never forgot where they were and how they felt at the news of Lincoln's assassination.

Property damage and financial costs were enormous, though difficult to tally. U.S. loans and taxes during the conflict totaled almost $3 billion, and interest on the war debt was $2.8 billion. The Confederacy borrowed over $2 billion but lost far more in the destruction of homes, crops, livestock, and other property. As an example of the wreckage that attended four years of conflict on southern soil, the number of hogs in South Carolina plummeted from 965,000 in 1860 to approximately 150,000 in 1865, leaving many families without their primary source of meat.

Financial Tally

In southern war zones the landscape was desolated. Over wide regions fences and crops were destroyed; houses, barns, and bridges burned; and fields abandoned and left to erode. Union troops had looted factories and put two-thirds of the South's railroad system out of service. Visitors to the countryside were struck by how empty and impoverished it looked.

Estimates of the total cost of the war exceed $20 billion—five times the total expenditures of the federal government from its creation to 1861. The northern government increased its spending by 700 percent in the first full year of the war; by the last year its spending had soared to twenty times the prewar level. By 1865 the federal government accounted for over 26 percent of the gross national product.

Many of these changes were more or less permanent. In the 1880s, interest on the war debt still accounted for approximately 40 percent of the federal budget and Union soldiers' pensions for as much as 20 percent. The federal government had used its power to support manufacturing and business interests by means of tariffs, loans, and subsidies, and wartime measures left the government more deeply involved in the banking and transportation systems. If southerners had hoped to remove government from the economy, the war had now irrepressibly bound them together.

The human costs of the Civil War were especially staggering. The total number of military casualties on

Death Toll

both sides exceeded 1 million—a frightful toll for a nation of 31 million people. Approximately 360,000 Union soldiers died, 110,000 of them from wounds suffered in battle. Another 275,175 Union soldiers were wounded but survived. On the Confederate side, an estimated 260,000 lost their lives, and almost as many suffered wounds. More men died in the Civil War than in all other American wars combined until Vietnam. Of an estimated 194,743 northerners in southern prisons, 30,218 died, compared with 25,976 of 214,865 southerners who died in northern prisons. The prison story from the war is one in

which neither side could claim pride, although it caused embittered debate in war memory for decades.

These unprecedented losses flowed from fundamental strife over the nature of the Union and the liberty of black people. Both sides saw vital interests in the struggle. As Julia Ward Howe wrote in her famous "Battle Hymn," they had heard "the trumpet that shall never call retreat." And so the war took its horrifying course. The first great legacy of the war in the lives of its survivors was, therefore, death itself. Although precise figures on enlistments are impossible to obtain, it appears that 700,000 to 800,000 men served in the Confederate armies. Far more, possibly 2.3 million, served in the Union armies. All these men were taken from home, family, and personal goals; their lives, if they survived at all, were disrupted in ways that were never repaired.

Summary

The Civil War altered American society forever. During the war, in both North and South, women had taken on new roles. Industrialization and large economic enterprises grew in power. Ordinary citizens found that their futures were increasingly tied to huge organizations. The character and extent of government power changed markedly. Under Republican leadership, the federal government had expanded its

The death of President Lincoln caused a vast outpouring of grief in the North. As this Currier and Ives print shows, on its way to Illinois, his funeral train stopped at several cities to allow local services to be held.   (Anne S. K. Brown Military Collection, John Hay Library, Brown University)

424   Chapter 15   Transforming Fire: The Civil War, 1861–1865

power not only to preserve the Union but also to extend freedom. A social revolution and government authority emancipated the slaves, and Lincoln had called for "a new birth of freedom" in America. A republic desperately divided against itself had survived, yet in new constitutional forms yet to take shape under tremendous political strife during Reconstruction.

It was unclear, however, how or whether the nation would use its power to protect the rights of the former slaves. Secession was dead, but whether Americans would continue to embrace a centralized nationalism remained to be seen. How would white southerners, embittered and impoverished, respond to efforts to reconstruct the nation? How long would military occupation last in the South, and who would rule its civil society? How would the country care for the maimed, the orphans, the farming women without men to work their land, and all the dead who had to be properly found and buried? And of central importance: what would be the place of black men and women in American life? Black veterans and former slaves eagerly sought an answer. They would find it during Reconstruction.

In the Civil War Americans had undergone an epic of destruction and survival. White southerners had experienced defeat as few other Americans have ever faced. Blacks were walking proudly but anxiously from slavery to freedom. White northerners were, by and large, self-conscious victors in a massive war for the nation's existence and for new definitions of what freedom meant in America. The war, including all its drama, sacrifice, and social and political changes, left a compelling memory in American hearts and minds for generations.

LEGACY FOR A PEOPLE AND A NATION
The Confederate Battle Flag

The most widespread and controversial symbol to emerge from the Civil War era is the Confederate flag. Rather than the official flag of the Confederacy, it was a battle flag that soldiers carried to mark the center of a unit's position in the confusion of combat. Over time, this flag has taken on powerful emotional meanings.

At Confederate veterans' reunions and parades from the 1870s well into the twentieth century, the flag was an emblem of the South's Lost Cause. After extended controversy, many captured Confederate flags were returned by the federal government to southern states in 1905 as a gesture of reconciliation. Increasingly, Confederate remembrance merged with white supremacy at the turn of the twentieth century and African Americans resented the flag's appearance.

In the late 1940s the flag became a fixture of popular culture with heightened racial meanings. In 1948 it was a symbol of the States' Rights ("Dixiecrat") Party. By the 1950s waving the Confederate flag became a demonstration of defiance among southern whites against the civil rights revolution. With the spread of American popular culture abroad, the Confederate flag can now be found all over the world.

What does this flag mean as a symbol? Some southern whites argue that it is merely a marker of regional pride and identity. Some stress the flag's countercultural value as a symbol of rebellion against the establishment, or "political correctness." But to most blacks and to many whites, it expresses racism. The flag is loaded with coded meanings that can be interpreted in opposite ways. Some claim it represents the "nobility" of southern military tradition; others conclude that it stands for the hatred embodied in the history of the Ku Klux Klan.

In recent times, the Confederate flag has been the center of legal and political controversy. Disputes have emanated from city councils, high schools, and universities over public and private uses of the flag. Most visible of all have been the debates in the states of Georgia, South Carolina, and Alabama over whether to cease flying the Confederate flag at official sites. The debate over the meaning and legacy of the Confederate flag may never end. At issue are important questions and traditions: free speech, equal protection under law, perception versus reality, official government endorsement of collective symbols, the significance of race and racism in our national memory, and the meaning of the Civil War itself.

For Further Reading, see page A-18 of the Appendix. For Web resources, go to http://college.hmco.com.

Check Your Understanding

The following sentences appear in the chapter. Circle the letter of the BEST meaning for each italicized word.

39. "One *ominous* development was the planters' increasing opposition to their own government."
    a. Odd
    b. Threatening
    c. Fortunate
    d. Unexpected

40. "The increasing size and power of the Richmond government startled and alarmed planters who had condemned federal *usurpations*."
    a. Seizures
    b. Loans
    c. Taxation
    d. Announcements

41. "Furloughs, *amnesty* proclamations, and appeals to return had little effect…."
    a. Threat of punishment
    b. Government pardon
    c. Pleading
    d. Emancipation

42. "…though some *saboteurs* and Confederate agents were active in the North and Canada, they never genuinely threatened the Union war effort."
    a. Soldiers
    b. Anti-war protestors
    c. Enemy agents
    d. Military leaders

43. "As a result, there were scores of disturbances and *melees*."
    a. Protests
    b. Speeches
    c. Violent riots
    d. Crimes

44. "[Sherman's brutality] was awful, too, in Virginia, where the path to victory proved *protracted* and ghastly."
    a. Long and drawn-out
    b. Expensive
    c. Unpredictable
    d. Savage and inhumane

Circle the letter of the correct response.

45. Based on Map 15.3 in the preceding section of the history chapter, which of the following conclusions is accurate?
    a. Union forces were on Oak Hill in July 1.
    b. On July 2, Confederate forces attacked Union forces in a peach orchard and wheat field.
    c. Most of the Battle of Gettysburg occurred within the town of Gettysburg.
    d. On July 2, Confederate forces had Union troops completely surrounded.

46.–50. On your own paper, write five review questions that would help you focus on material in this section and that would be likely to appear on a test. Also, write your answers to each of these questions.

Discuss the following questions with a partner or group, and then collaborate to write answers to the questions on your paper.

51. Discuss the strengths and weaknesses of the North and the South during the Civil War, and explain why the North won.

52. From reading this chapter, what did you learn about the Civil War that surprised you?

53. What did you learn that contradicted your previous knowledge about the Civil War?

Answer Key

Part 1
Features of College Textbooks

Exercise 1: Using Learning Goals

1. b
2. c
3. c
4. d

Exercise 2: Using Key Terms

Circled terms: assertive communication, assertiveness, nonassertive behavior, aggressive behavior, direct aggression, passive aggression

Definitions:

assertive communication: communication that occurs when a person stands up for his or her personal rights without damaging others' rights

assertiveness: honest and direct communication that allows you to take charge of yourself and your world

nonassertive behavior: behavior designed to avoid conflict

aggressive behavior: domineering behavior designed to get your own way, even if it alienates others

direct aggression: the outward expression of dominating or humiliating communication

passive aggression: behavior that attacks or embarrasses people in a manipulative way

Exercise 3: Using a Chapter Outline

1. c
2. b
3. a
4. b

Exercise 4: Using Headings to Understand Organization

1. b
2. a
3. d
4. d

Exercise 5: Using Visual Aids

Answers will vary. One possible answer: The use of certain words in leading questions can effect how witnesses remember something they have seen. Therefore, eyewitness testimony is not always completely accurate.

Exercise 6: Using a Chapter Summary

Answers will vary.

Exercise 7: Using Review Questions, Discussion Questions, and Exercises

1. c
2. b
3. b
4. c
5. b

Exercise 8: Using a Study Guide

1. c
2. d
3. a
4. c

Part 2
Strategies for Reading College Textbooks

Exercise 9: Describing Your Own Reading Environment

Answers will vary.

Exercise 10: Determining Your Best Reading Time

Answers will vary.

Exercise 11: Combating External Distractions

Answers will vary.

Exercise 12: Clearing Your Mind Before Reading

Answers will vary.

Exercise 13: Applying the Time Management Guidelines

Answers will vary.

Exercise 14: Previewing a Textbook Chapter

1. b
2. d
3. a

4. a

Exercise 15: Thinking Before Reading

Answers will vary.

Exercise 16: Turning Headings Into Questions

Answers will vary. Some possible answers include:

What has been discovered in the search for leadership traits?

What are leadership behaviors?

What did the Michigan studies reveal?

What did the Ohio State studies reveal?

What is the Managerial Grid?

What are the situational approaches to leadership?

Exercise 17: Reading Actively

Answers will vary.

Exercise 18: Defining Unfamiliar Words

Answers will vary.

Exercise 19: Reviewing a Reading Selection

Answers will vary.

Exercise 20: Writing Marginal Notations

Answers will vary.

Exercise 21: Outlining Textbook Information

Answers will vary. One possible answer might be:

3. Differences between retarded people and others
   a. Perform mental operations more slowly
   b. Know fewer facts
   c. Not very good at using mental strategies for learning and problem solving
4. Reasons for deficiencies
   a. Deficiencies in metamemory
   b. Deficiencies in metacognition
5. Improving intellectual abilities of mentally retarded people
   a. Program emphasizing parent-child communication
   b. Mainstreaming in regular classrooms

C. Learning disabilities
   1. Kinds of learning disabilities
      a. Dyslexia
      b. Dysphasia
      c. Dysgraphia
      d. Dyscalculia
   2. Debate about causes of learning disabilities
      a. Dysfunction in brain
      b. Dysfunctional information processing
   3. Steps in diagnosing learning disabilities
      a. Look for weakness in skills
      b. Compare actual ability to ability that was predicted by IQ score
      c. Test for brain damage
      d. Test all senses
      e. Review factors like poverty, family conflicts, inadequate instruction
      f. Eliminate alternative diagnoses

Exercise 22: Diagramming Textbook Information

Answers will vary. One possible answer:

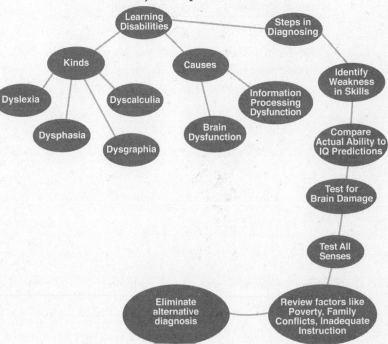

Exercise 23: Considering Reading Speed

Answers will vary.

Exercise 24: Reading Critically

Answers will vary.

Exercise 25: Writing to Learn

Answers will vary.

Part 3: Using Textbook Features and the Reading Strategies: Practice Exercises

Exercise 1: Economics: "Demand"

1. c
2. c
3. b
4. d
5. b
6. a
7. As the price rises, the quantity demanded by consumers goes down.
8. The law of demand says that the higher the price, the lower the quantity demanded in the market.
9. *Answers will vary.* One possible answer: computers
10. b

Exercise 2: Psychology: "Stress and Stressors"

1. a
2. *Answers will vary. Possible answers:* What are stress and stressors? What is the relationship between stress and stressors?
3. *Answers will vary.*
4. b
5. d
6. c
7. b
8. b
9. c
10. d

Exercise 3: Communication: "Kinesics: Body Communication"

1. *Answers will vary.*
2. c
3. b
4. c
5. b
6. d
7. b
8. a
9. b

10. c

Exercise 4: Chemistry: "The Scientific Method"

1. **scientific method:** the process that lies at the center of scientific inquiry

    hypothesis: a possible explanation for an observation

    theory: a set of test hypotheses that gives an overall explanation of some natural phenomenon

    model: a set of tested hypotheses that gives an overall explanation of some phenomenon; another word for *theory*

    natural law: a statement about some generally observed behavior

    law of conservation of mass: observation that the total mass of materials is not affected by a chemical change in those materials

2. b
3. a
4. d
5. a
6. b
7. First, make quantitative or qualitative observations. Second, formulate a hypothesis to explain the observations. Third, perform experiments to test whether the hypothesis is valid.
8. A law summarizes what happens; a theory is an attempt to explain why it happens.
9. No, it is useful whenever a systematic approach of observation and hypothesis testing can be used.
10. *Answers will vary.*

Exercise 5: Humanities: "Impressionism"

1. *Answers will vary.*
2. c
3. d
4. c
5. Impressionism tried to understand the permutations of light and color and capture the moment when the eye perceives light on surfaces.
6. Both were preoccupied with light and color, and both depicted ordinary experiences and everyday life. However,

Impressionists painted light while Realists painted objects, and Impressionists' subjects were the middle-class at leisure while the Realists' subjects were lower-class, rural workers.

7. Impressionists broke with Renaissance tradition by painting light rather than the scenes themselves and by violating Renaissance traditions of perspective and three-dimensional space.

8. The term *Impressionism* originated from Claude Monet's painting entitled *Impression—Sunrise.*

9. Impressionism emerged as a logical extension of <u>Realism</u>. However, while Realists focused on <u>objects</u> themselves, the Impressionists attended to the effects of <u>light</u> and <u>shade</u> on surfaces, thus breaking significantly with the <u>Renaissance</u> tradition. Further, although the Impressionists shared the Realists' interest in <u>everyday life</u>, they generally depicted <u>middle-class leisure</u> rather than <u>working-class toil</u>.

10. *Answers will vary.*

Part 4: College Textbook Chapters with Exercises

Business: "Exploring the World of Business"

1. *Answers will vary.*
2. *Answers will vary.*
3. d
4. b
5. c
6. a
7. b
8. d
9. a
10. c
11. a
12. a
13. **free enterprise:** the system of business in which individuals are free to decide what to produce, how to produce it, and at what price to sell it

    e-business: the organized effort of individuals to produce and sell, for a profit, the products and services that satisfy society's needs through the facilities available on the Internet

    business: the organized effort of individuals to produce and sell, for a profit, the goods and services that satisfy society's needs

    consumers: individuals who purchase goods or services for their own personal use

    profit: what remains after all business expenses have been deducted from sales revenue

14. There are four compelling reasons for studying business described in this chapter:
    1) To become a better-informed consumer and investor
    2) For help in choosing a career
    3) To be a successful employee
    4) To start your own business

15. Deciding what kind of career you want to devote your life to can be both daunting and puzzling, especially when you don't know what all the possibilities are. Choices range from small, local businesses owned by one individual to large corporations with offices and facilities in countries around the globe. There are also employment opportunities with federal, state, county, and local governments and with not-for-profit organizations. One thing to remember when choosing a career is that a person's choice of a career is ultimately a reflection of what he or she values and holds most important. What you choose to do with your life will be based on what you feel is most important.

16. The four resources are (1) material resources, which include raw materials used in the manufacturing process as well as buildings and machinery; (2) human resources, the people who furnish their labor in return for wages; (3) financial resources, which is money used to pay employees, purchase materials, and keep the business operating; and (4) information, which tells the managers of the business how effectively the other resources are being used. Economists refer to the factors of production as natural resources, labor, capital, and entrepreneurship.

17. Consumers purchase goods and services for their own personal use rather than to resell them to others.

18. The greatest rewards go to the greatest risk takers. The business that is able to successfully satisfy customers' needs is said to be the business that will realize the greatest profit potential.

19. d

20. c

21. b

22. a

23. b

24. b

25. The four basic economic questions are (1) what and how much to produce, (2) how to produce, (3) for whom to produce, and (4) who owns and controls the factors of production. In a capitalist economy, the first question is answered by consumers as they spend their money. The second question is answered by producers as they compete for sales and profits. The third question is answered by those who have the money to buy the product. The fourth question is answered by who provides the natural resources, labor, capital, and/or entrepreneurship. The distribution of goods and services, therefore, depends on the current prices of economic resources, goods, and services, and who can afford to buy them.

26. The four main ingredients of laissez-faire capitalism are:
   1) Private ownership of property, which includes land, labor, and capital.
   2) Economic freedom (for owners, the right to rent, sell, or invest their resources to produce any product and offer it for sale at the price they choose).
   3) Competitive markets (the interaction of buyers and sellers of a particular type of product or resource).
   4) Limited role of government. (The government should be limited to providing defense against foreign enemies, ensuring internal order, and furnishing public works and education.

27. Our economy is a mixed economy because it exhibits elements of both capitalism and socialism.

28. See Figure 1.3. In the circular flow that characterizes our business system, households and businesses exchange resources for goods and services, using money as the medium of exchange. Government collects taxes from businesses and households and uses tax revenues to purchase the resources and products with which to provide its services of protecting and promoting the public welfare.

29. Capitalism is a market economy (sometimes referred to as a free market economy). The basic economic questions are answered by private business owners who control the factors of production. Socialism and communism, on the other hand, are controlled by government planning and government ownership. Decisions are made by government planners and, in many cases, the wants and needs of the government are more important than those of consumers.

30. *Gross domestic product (GDP)* is the total dollar value of all goods and services produced by citizens *physically* located within a country. GDP excludes production amounts for U.S. citizens working abroad in foreign countries. GDP as an economic measure is important because it is a measure of a nation's economic output.

31. While student answers will vary, on the term they choose, you may want to review the material in Table 1.1. Each of the following seven terms are defined: balance of trade, consumer price index, inflation rate, prime interest rate, producer price index, productivity rate, and unemployment rate.

32. The four forms of competition are pure competition, monopolistic competition, oligopoly, and monopoly.

Under pure competition, there are many buyers and sellers of a product, and no single buyer or seller is powerful enough to affect the price of that product. Under monopolistic competition, there are many buyers and relatively many sellers who differentiate their products from the products of competitors. An oligopoly is a market situation in which there are few sellers, so each seller has considerable control over price. A monopoly is a market with only one producer.

33. Under pure competition, the market price of any product is the price at which the quantity demanded is exactly equal to the quantity supplied.

34. *Answers will vary.* Yes, each individual votes in the competitive marketplace with his or her dollars.

35. *Answers will vary.*

The government is involved in answering the four basic economic questions with regard to public welfare. The question of what goods and services will be produced is answered when government provides goods and services that would not be produced by private enterprise or that would otherwise be too expensive for the average citizen. The question of how these goods will be produced is answered by government through taxation that is necessary to pay for goods and services society needs. The question of who will receive these goods and services is answered by government through programs such as Social Security and national defense. The question of who owns the major factors of production is answered by government ensuring that all factors of production are available and shared by businesses involved in a capitalistic society.

Student answers will vary on whether government participates or interferes in the system.

36. b

37. c

38. a

39. In the beginning, the colonists produced what they needed to survive. Then they started to produce more than they could consume themselves. Ownership took the form of a sole proprietorship. Soon a domestic system was formed in which an entrepreneur distributed raw materials to various homes, where families finished the products. Trade with England and other countries became important. The factory system was started, wherein all materials, machinery, and workers required to manufacture a product were assembled in one place. Specialization brought the separation of the manufacturing process into distinct tasks and the assignment of different tasks to different individuals. The period from 1870 to 1900 witnessed a second revolution with many of the characteristics of our modern business system. The United States shifted from a farm economy to a manufacturing economy because of the developing oil industry, labor furnished by immigration, and new means of communication. Ownership began to switch from private to corporate shareholders.

40. *Student answers will vary.* While discussing this question, you want to refer to the list of issues that will challenge American business in the section entitled, "The Challenges Ahead."

41. *Answers will vary.* The shrinking size of the globe, the intervention of foreign competition, the Great Depression, World Wars I and II, and the ever-increasing age of our population (among other factors) have contributed to our mixed economic system.

42. *Answers will vary.* Currently, gross domestic product is the measure used by the nations of the world. A system that measures only those goods and services that contribute *directly* to an individual citizen's standard of living might be better.

43. *Answers will vary.* If there are several products of the same type, the consumer will purchase the products of better quality. Businesses are thus forced to improve their products constantly to maintain or enlarge their share of the market.

44. *Answers will vary.*

An Introduction to Physical Science: "Atmospheric Effects"

1. *Answers will vary.*
2. b
3. c
4. d
5. b
6. d
7. c
8. c
9. a
10. d
11. b
12. c
13. a
14. a
15. b
16. b
17. a
18. b
19. a
20. Bergeron process essentials: (1) ice crystals, (2) supercooled water vapor, and (3) mixing. Silver iodide crystals are substituted for ice crystals, and dry ice is used to cool vapor and form ice crystals.
21. No. Frost is the deposition of water vapor. Hailstones are formed from successive cycles and condensation in cumulus clouds.
22. a
23. c
24. Air masses are classified according to the surface and the latitude of their source regions.

    If the source region is a water surface and at low latitude, the air mass would be warm and moist. Similarly, land areas at high latitudes provide cold and dry air-mass characteristics.
25. See Table 20.1 and Figure 20.3.
26. The boundary air masses

    Warm

    Cold

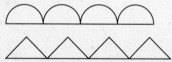

Stationary

Occluded

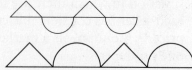

27. See Section 20.2 for descriptions. The sharpness of a front's vertical boundary gives an indication of the rate of change of the weather. In general, cold fronts have sharper vertical boundaries than warm fronts, and hence lead to more sudden weather changes.
28. Dew evaporates when the air temperature rises above the dew point.
29. *Answers will vary.*
30. c
31. d
32. a
33. a
34. b
35. d
36. c
37. a
38. d
39. b
40. d

    Lightning can take place entirely within a cloud (intracloud or cloud discharges), between two clouds (cloud-to-cloud discharges), between a cloud and the Earth (cloud-to-ground or ground discharges), or between a cloud and the surrounding air (air discharges). Lightning has reportedly even occurred in clear air, apparently giving rise to the expression "a bolt from the blue." When lightning occurs below the horizon or behind clouds, it often illuminates the clouds with flickering flashes. This commonly occurs on a still summer night and is known as heat lightning.
41. Resuscitate and keep warm. (Have someone call 911, or you do so as soon as possible after resuscitating.)
42. Warm front. A warm front advances over colder air. If the temperature of the cold air and Earth's surface is below freezing, precipitation falling may be cool and freeze on contact, producing an ice storm.

43. The tornado. Although the hurricane has more energy, the energy of a tornado is concentrated in a small region, giving a greater energy density. The larger hurricane, however, is usually more destructive on making landfall.

44. Seek shelter fast.

45. Latent heat. When the wind speed reaches 74 mi/h (118 km/h).

46. A hurricane watch is issued for coastal areas when there is a threat of a hurricane within 24 to 36 hours. A hurricane warning indicates that hurricane conditions are expected within 24 hours.

47. Hurricanes: August – September, for the North Atlantic. Tornadoes: Varies from state to state. Generally, April – August.

48. *Answers will vary to first question.* Watch: Be alert for possible tornado formation. Warning: Follow tornado safety procedures given in the chapter.

50. c
51. b
52. b
53. a
54. b
55. c
56. b
57. a
58. b

59. Any atypical contribution to the atmosphere resulting from human activities.

60. No. England had air pollution in the late 1200s.

61. Radiation temperature inversions and subsidence temperature inversions. Temperature inversions hold gases and smoke near the ground, causing the air to become polluted.

62. Complete—CO_2 and H_2O; incomplete—CO, hydrocarbons, soot (carbon).

63. The high temperatures of complete combustion cause a reaction between the nitrogen and oxygen of the air. They combine with water vapor to form haze and smog.

64. Classical smog is smoke-fog. Photochemical smog results from photochemical reactions of hydrocarbons and other pollutants with oxygen in the presence of sunlight. Ozone is the prime indicator of photochemical smog.

65. Sulfur.

66. Sulfur dioxide (and nitrogen oxides) combine with water to form acids, which fall as rain (or other types of precipitation). The acid raises the pH of bodies of water. The problem is most acute in the northeastern United States because of major industrial areas to the west, but acid precipitation may now be found almost everywhere.

67. (a) Transportation
    (b) Stationary sources (for example, electrical generating plants)
    (c) Industry
    (d) Transportation
    (e) Photochemical smog

68. d
69. c

70. Climate is the name for the long-term average weather conditions of a region.

71. Increased concentrations of CO_2 in the atmosphere could alter the amount of radiation absorbed and give rise to an increase in Earth's temperature. Particulate pollution could contribute to changes in the Earth's thermal balance. Supersonic transport aircraft emit particulate matter and gaseous pollutants that can cause climate-changing reactions.

72. Increased CO_2, increased particulate matter, and ozone reduction.

73. The interaction of CFCs with the ozone layer could deplete the ozone and allow more UV rays to reach Earth, thereby increasing Earth's temperature. In the extreme, an increase in the average temperature could affect the environment (e.g., lengthen the growing season) and melt the polar ice caps.

74. There are no natural mechanisms in the stratosphere to remove pollutants, and the pollutants could give rise to changes in climate.

75. *Answers will vary.*
76. *Answers will vary.*
77. *Answers will vary.*

A People and a Nation (American history):
"Transforming Fire: The Civil War, 1861–1865"

1. *Answers will vary.*
2. c
3. Chapter outline, visual aids, and chapter summary should be checked.
4. b
5. a
6. c
7. a
8. d
9. b
10. b
11. a
12. c
13. a
14. d
15. c
16. *Answers will vary.*
17. *Answers will vary.*
18. *Answers will vary.*
19. *Answers will vary.*
20. *Answers will vary.*
21. *Answers will vary.*
22. d
23. c
24. b
25. d
26. a
27. c
28. c
29. a
30. b
31. a
32. *Answers will vary.*
33. *Answers will vary.*
34. *Answers will vary.*
35. *Answers will vary.*
36. *Answers will vary.*
37. *Answers will vary.*
38. *Answers will vary.*
39. b
40. a
41. b
42. c
43. c
44. a
45. b
46. *Answers will vary.*
47. *Answers will vary.*
48. *Answers will vary.*
49. *Answers will vary.*
50. *Answers will vary.*
51. *Answers will vary.*
52. *Answers will vary.*
53. *Answers will vary.*

Photo Credits

Part 1
Page 9, Bonnie Kamin/PhotoEdit; page 13, Mark C. Burnett/Stock Boston; page 15, © 2002 PhotoDisc, Inc.

Part 2
Page 41, The Granger Collection, New York; page 46, Mark Wilson/Newsmakers/Liaison Agency; page 54, Dana Fineman/SYGMA; page 59, Fraser Hale/St. Petersburg Times; page 60, U.S. Department of the Interior, National Park Service, Edison National Historic Site; page 67, Joe Raedle/Newsmakers/Getty News Images.

Part 3
Page 75, Lori Adamski Peek/Getty Images; page 77, © 2002 PhotoDisc, Inc.; page 82, David Young-Wolff/Tony Stone Images; page 87 (top), Corbis/Bettmann; page 91, The Metropolitan Museum of Art, HO Havemeyer Collection, Bequest of Mrs. HO Havemeyer 1929 [29.100.129] Photo © 1985 The Metropolitan Museum of Art.

Part 4
Page 96, David R. Frazier/Photolibrary; page 98, John Chapple/Online USA; page 100, AP Photo/Nati Harnik; page 103, Robert McClaran/SABA; page 107, Jeff Greenberg/Photoedit; page 108, Rhoda Sidney/Stock Boston; page 116, © AFP/Corbis; page 125, Mark Richards/Photoedit; page 135, © Kent Wood/Science Source/Photo Researchers; page 138, Howard Bluestein/Photo Researchers; page 141, Tom Ives/Corbis/The Stock Market; page 149 (top), Merilee Thomas/Tom Stack & Associates; page 149 (bottom), Jim Wark/Peter Arnold, Inc.; page 151 (top), NOAA; page 151 (bottom), NOAA/Roger Weldon; page 152, Odyssey/Woodfin Camp & Associates; page 159, Standard Oil Co./Carnegie Library, Pittsburgh; page 160 (left), Kristen Brochman/Fundamental Photographs, New York; page 160 (right), NYC Photo Archive/Fundamental Photographs, New York; page 161, Brett Fromer/The Image Bank; page 163, Stephanie Maze/Woodfin Camp & Associates; page 164, © Tim Parker; page 165, Wide World Photos; page 166, Gordon Langsbury/Bruce Coleman, Inc.; page 167, NASA; page 179, Museum of Fine Arts, Boston; M. & M. Karolik Collection; page 182, Library of Congress; page 184, Library of Congress; page 185, Collection of Larry Williford; page 190, © Collection of The New-York Historical Society; page 193, National Portrait Gallery, Smithsonian Institution, Washington, DC; page 196, Library of Congress; page 200, National Archives; page 201, Chicago Historical Society; page 207 (both), The C. Craig Caba Gettysburg Collection, from Gettysburg. Larry Sherer © 1991 Time-Life Books, Inc.; page 208, Chicago Historical Society; page 210, Chicago Historical Society; page 212 (both), National Archives; page 215, National Archives; page 216, Anne S. K. Brown Military Collection, John Hay Library, Brown University.